DATABASE
TECHNOLOGY
AND MANAGEMENT

ROBERT C. GOLDSTEIN

Associate Professor
Management Information Systems

Faculty of Commerce and Business Administration
University of British Columbia
Vancouver, Canada

JOHN WILEY & SONS
New York   Chichester   Brisbane   Toronto   Singapore

Library of Congress Cataloging in Publication Data:

Goldstein, Robert C.
  Database: technology and management.

  (Computers and information processing systems for
business)
  Includes index.
  1. Business—Data processing.   2. Business—Data
processing—Management.   3. Data base management.
I. Title.   II. Series.

HF5548.2.G5955   1985   658'.054   84-19697

Printed in the Republic of Singapore

10 9 8 7 6 5 4

Cover Photo   (c) Joel Gordon, 1983

To the memory of my mother

PREFACE

The database concept has been with us for about two decades. It has achieved wide acceptance, despite the considerable complexity of the underlying technology and the fact that measurable benefits have been disturbingly elusive. At first, the dearth of database success stories was usually attributed to technical difficulties—insufficient memory or processing power, or excessively inefficient software. However, in recent years, the technological limitations have been largely overcome and we are forced to look for other explanations for the continuing shortage of real observable benefits. One might be inclined to wonder if this technology is really as significant as its proponents suggest or if it is just another case of the emperor's-new-clothes syndrome. This book will try to demonstrate that the potential impact of the database concept is great indeed, but that realizing the benefits depends at least as much on effective planning and administration as it does on technical excellence.

Most existing database textbooks concentrate on the technological aspects of the subject and, thus, seem especially appropriate for use by students of computer science. This book is intended specifically for business students. It is motivated by the belief that successful application of database technology depends at least as much on skilled planning and management as on technical sophistication. Understanding this book requires little in the way of computer expertise. However, for maximum effectiveness, the reader should be familiar with the basics of computer technology and its use in organizations. The level of knowledge developed through an introductory course in data processing or management information systems should be sufficient.

ORGANIZATION OF THE TEXT

The general approach taken in this book is to present database technology first and then cover topics associated with applying the technology in organizations.

However, to provide a preliminary glimpse of the ultimate objective, Chapter 1 introduces the major concepts and objectives of database management and offers a brief historical overview of the field. This is followed by a seven-chapter sequence (Part I) that covers theoretical and technical topics. This part is not intended to develop database technicians but to provide the basic understanding that is essential to the effective use and management of a complex technology. Throughout this part, pragmatic considerations are emphasized over conceptual rigor.

The first and last chapters of Part I are both devoted to the database design problem. Chapter 2 deals with this issue in a basic way, independent of any particular technical approach. This chapter also introduces a simplified example database that is designed to meet the needs of a regional library system. A significant integrating feature of the book is the use of this database for examples throughout the text.

A major portion of the technology section of the book is devoted to describing and evaluating the hierarchical, network, and relational database models. The three approaches receive equal emphasis and an attempt is made to illustrate the strengths and shortcomings of each. The likely direction of future developments in the data model area is also discussed. Chapter 8 returns to the database design topic with a deeper and more detailed treatment that takes advantage of the knowledge of data models presented earlier.

Part II of the book is devoted to specifically managerial issues associated with implementing database concepts in organizations and getting the maximum benefit from the technology. Chapter 9 examines the relatively new organizational function of Information Resources Management (IRM). Topics covered include the duties and responsibilities of IRM, its internal organization, and its interaction with user groups and the traditional data processing organization. The relationship between IRM and such other managerial roles as Data Administration and Database Administration are also discussed here. The following chapter deals comprehensively with the generalized data dictionary as a tool for information resource management. Other chapters in this part deal with the evaluation and selection of database management systems; the nature of the user/DBMS interface, including examples of a number of database languages; and the problem of protecting a database and controlling access to it.

The book concludes with two chapters on topics that are still in the process of moving from the research laboratory to the commercial world. The first of these, distributed database management, is an appealing solution to a number of problems with current systems. The other is the use of hardware designed specifically for database manipulation. This promises to make a major impact on the cost and performance of database systems.

An appendix discusses a number of currently used approaches to the physical organization and manipulation of data in computer systems. Detailed understanding of this material is not essential to the main objectives of the book, but it is often covered as part of a course in database management.

ACKNOWLEDGMENTS

A number of students at the University of British Columbia have been exposed to portions of this book in manuscript form and offered useful comments and suggestions. Special thanks go to Veda Storey for her extensive contribution to the end-of-chapter questions. The book also benefited substantially from the following reviewers' comments: Jerry Goldman, De Paul University; James Hunter, Western Carolina University; William Rasdorf, North Carolina State University; Ronald Teichman, Pennsylvania State University; and Hugh J. Watson, University of Georgia–Athens. Of course, responsibility for any errors that remain must rest with the author.

Finally, it is quite possible that this book might not have been written were it not for Nina R. Lewis of John Wiley & Sons. It was she who ultimately convinced me to go ahead with the project and who provided just the right combination of carrot and stick to keep it moving more or less on schedule.

Robert C. Goldstein

CONTENTS

CHAPTER 1

INTRODUCTION

THE TRADITIONAL APPROACH

Prior to the development of database concepts, organizations viewed their information processing as shown in Figure 1–1.[1] That is, the center of attention was on processing functions, whereas data played a peripheral role.[2] In particular, when an information processing system was designed for some task, the function would be specified first, then the data requirements would be derived. One result of this approach was that each data processing application had its own input and output files designed to meet its own particular needs.

As an organization's portfolio of computer applications grew, two things inevitably happened. First, certain items of information would be relevant to several applications and, thus, would appear in the files associated with each. Second, because each application was developed independently, different representations would often be used for the same information.

The duplication of data would, of course, increase the total requirement for data storage and, hence, storage costs. However, computer storage comes in large packages with extremely low unit cost, so, duplication per se is not necessarily a cause for excessive concern. The more serious danger is that when a piece of information is stored more than once, it becomes difficult to maintain consistency among all the versions.

As an example, several years ago a large university undertook an extensive study of its information systems[3] and discovered that at least seven different administrative entities maintained computer-based files of student addresses. Some waste of storage space was obviously taking place. More important, because students changed their addresses frequently and because the systems were quite independent of each other, there was no way automatically to propagate changes from one file to another. As time passed, the discrepancies between these files became greater and greater, despite the efforts of each of the individual groups involved to keep its own files current.

The same study also uncovered a good example of the inconsistent-representation problem. Most of the university's information systems used four-letter codes to represent the various administrative and academic units, for example, ENGL for the English Department. However, because systems were developed independently of one another, the code used for a particular entity was

---

[1] Gordon Everest, *Database Management*, McGraw-Hill, 1984.

[2] Authors in the field of Management Information Systems are usually careful to distinguish between data and information. The term "data," is used to mean raw data, whereas information is data that has been processed into a form suitable for some use. Both raw and processed data can be found in a database, and the same management considerations apply to both. Thus, the two terms will be used interchangeably in this book for stylistic reasons.

[3] Report of the Information Systems Task Force, University of British Columbia, Vancouver, February 1980.

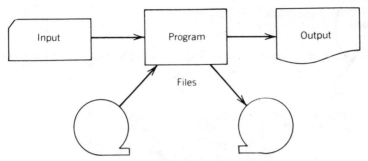

FIGURE 1-1 Traditional view of information processing.

not always the same. Computer science was CPSC in some systems, CSCI in others. Some units had as many as 10 distinct encodings.

There are a number of obvious disadvantages to this situation. First, employees who are transferred from one administrative department to another have to learn a new set of codes—a task that is made particularly difficult because the new coding system is likely to be only slightly different from the one they were using previously. In addition to the tangible costs of retraining and the intangible psychological cost, it must be assumed that the probability of error is greatly increased by these slight variations in coding systems. Second, and more important, these variations make it quite difficult to relate information automatically from different systems for analysis and planning.

The relating of data from different applications was often further hampered by incompatibility among data files, which was caused by the hardware and software techniques used to manage them. Inadequate documentation also played a role here. Because files tended to be viewed as the property of individual programs or users, it was often the case that the knowledge required to access them was not systematically available.

Many anecdotes have been told about executives who requested a report that required combining information from two separate information systems only to be told by their data processing department either that it could not be done or that a special program would have to be developed entailing much cost and delay. It is not hard to understand management's frustration at receiving such a response after years of investing large amounts of resources in the development of computerized information systems, especially when management knew perfectly well that the information it sought was already in the computer.

THE DATABASE APPROACH

The fundamental notion of what has come to be called the database approach is deceptively simple. In this approach, the traditional view of information process-

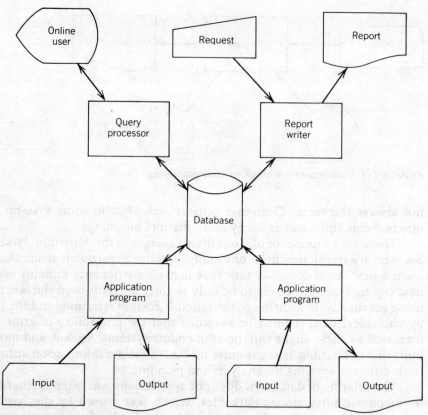

FIGURE 1–2 Database view of information processing.

ing is replaced by the one shown in Figure 1–2. Data now occupy the central position; processing functions exist on the periphery, referencing data in the central pool as needed and depositing results there. Because there is only one pool of data for use by all, duplication and, hence, inconsistency, ought never to occur. Similarly, there is only one representation for each piece of information and one mechanism for manipulating it. Therefore, it should not be difficult to establish any desired relationships among the data.

Collecting all of an organization's data together in a central pool tends to demonstrate quite dramatically the importance of information to organizational functioning and the extent of the investment required for its collection and maintenance. This has led to the suggestion that data should be viewed as one of the basic organizational resources—along with money, people, and capital—and that management structures should explicitly include a high-level position with responsibility for overall management and control of the data resource. We will have more to say about this in the second part of this book, but the basic intent is obviously to manage information coherently in order to maximize its value to the organization.

DATABASE MANAGEMENT SYSTEMS (DBMS's)

In addition to moving data to the center of the diagram, the database approach also involves placing a specialized piece of software, a Database Management System (DBMS), between the data and the users. This is illustrated in Figure 1–3. The two primary functions of a DBMS are to assist users in manipulating the database and to protect the database from the users. In addition, a DBMS assists the personnel responsible for administering the database in the performance of their duties.

User Assistance

Assistance to users is provided mainly in the form of program modules for performing standard functions, such as retrieval or modification of information. This reduces the amount of work that must be done to implement a new application, thereby increasing the productivity of a traditionally scarce resource—computer programmers. Also, the reliability of applications is enhanced by the use of standard, pretested modules for what is usually one of the trickier parts of a program.

A good DBMS also has the ability to construct different "views" of the database for different users. Portions of the database that are irrelevant to an application can be hidden from it, and the structure of what remains can be adjusted to fit the application's specific requirements.

Additional user assistance is provided through modules that allow certain functions to be performed on the database without the need for any programs to be written at all: two examples are query processors and report generators. A query processor accepts requests for information couched in a reasonably Englishlike language and provides an immediate response. Report generators can generate elaborate reports on the basis of content and format specifications supplied by the user. Again, no programming knowledge is required, and the time from entering a request to receiving the result is usually quite short.

Data Protection

Database protection is implemented primarily through what might be called a gate-keeping function for the DBMS. Any user request to insert, retrieve, or modify information in a database must be made via requests to the DBMS. There

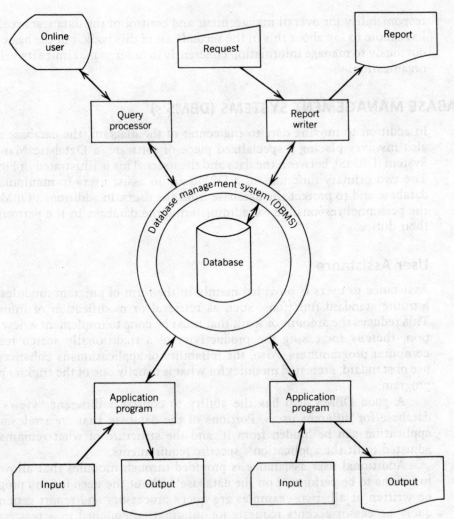

FIGURE 1–3 The role of the Database Management System (DBMS).

is no direct contact between an application program and the database. This allows the DBMS to evaluate each request and decide whether or not it should proceed. The decision can be based on both authorization criteria—Is the user *allowed* to perform this operation?—and on integrity criteria—Will the operation damage the database?

The view capability mentioned above also has a protection aspect. Because a user cannot access any data that is not in his or her view, a coarse type of access control can be achieved simply by defining the view to include or exclude particular portions of the database.

DATA INDEPENDENCE

Another important feature of a DBMS is its support of the notion of data independence—a concept that is probably best introduced through some examples. In the traditional data processing environment, files are used only by a single program or perhaps a collection of related programs. If one of these programs is changed in a way that affects a file, the file may have to be restructured. However, the need for this should be obvious at the time because of the intimate relationship between a program and its files. By the same token, changes made by *other* groups in the organization to *their* files or programs ought not to have any impact.

On the other hand, in a database environment with much sharing of information among applications, it is possible that a change made in one place for some good reason will affect many other applications, like ripples spreading out from a stone dropped into a quiet pond. Potentially, a small change made to a file to satisfy one legitimate need could require many other unrelated programs to be modified—a costly and even dangerous business.

Similarly, advancing technology and/or changes in the way information is used will sometimes make it desirable to reorganize a file or to move it from a storage device with a particular set of characteristics to another with different properties. In a traditional environment, this entails corresponding changes in the programs that use this data, but the circumstances would be such that it should be quite clear what programs would have to be changed and how. When data are being shared among many users, the potential impact of such a change in hardware or data storage strategy could be enormous.

As a final example, the traditional environment allows files to be tailored precisely to an application's needs. With all users sharing a common database, it would seem that they would have to adjust their requirements to a single structure.

The concept of data independence proposes to alleviate these problems by allowing any user or group of users to have a view of the database that is different from the views used by others—even different from the way the data are actually stored. Thus, a change made to accommodate one user can be kept invisible to others; a change made to the structure of a file or to the storage device characteristics can be hidden from all users; and each user can be given a view of the database that includes only the relevant contents in a form well suited to his or her needs.

Data independence is not an automatic benefit of using a database. On the contrary, adopting the database approach, with its emphasis on sharing of data, *causes* the problem that data independence is intended to alleviate. Solving this problem is one of the most important responsibilities of database management software.

ADVANTAGES OF THE DATABASE APPROACH

In summary, advantages claimed for the database approach include:

- Controlling data duplication and inconsistency
- Facilitating the sharing of data among applications
- Assisting the coherent management of data as a basic organization resource
- Increased programmer productivity
- Increased applications' reliability
- Enabling quick, economical response to ad hoc requests for information
- Protecting data from damage or unauthorized access
- Providing data independence

It is too much to expect that these benefits will come at no cost. Adopting database technology requires significant additional financial outlays for hardware, software, and specialized expertise. In addition, there are nonfinancial costs associated with disrupting the established organizational routines.

COSTS OF THE DATABASE APPROACH

The most visible tangible cost of the database approach is associated with the need to acquire a DBMS. These large, complex software packages can cost up to hundreds of thousands of dollars for large systems. The generality implicit in the database approach and particularly the need to provide data independence require a considerable amount of overhead processing on each access to the database. If throughput rates comparable to those of traditional, file-based systems are to be maintained, additional resources are usually required in the form of a faster processor and additional memory. Specialized (possibly scarce) expertise is also required, both for the technical task of supporting and maintaining the DBMS and for designing and managing the database.

In addition to these primarily financial disadvantages, there are others that are less easily quantified. For example, the overall reliability of the data processing operation may be reduced by the installation of a complex piece of software (the DBMS) that affects virtually every processing function. Also, the database concept includes an emphasis on *global* optimization of information usage that implies much greater coordination and centralized planning than has usually characterized the development of information systems. Users have to be persuaded to relinquish their power to make information systems decisions on a strictly local basis. Mechanisms also have to be found for compensating organizational units whose processing becomes less efficient or who are required to perform extra data collection or maintenance tasks as a result of the emphasis on global optimization.

Another oft-cited problem with the database approach is its violation of the proverb about not putting all your eggs in one basket. It is certainly true that the older approach, using many independent and often redundant files, was less exposed to certain risks. It was unlikely, for example, that an error would propagate beyond its immediate vicinity. With an integrated database, there would seem to be a much greater risk of an error spreading further and perhaps in unanticipated directions. This is a valid concern and must be taken carefully into account in the design of database management software. Chapter 13 will deal with this topic at greater length.

It is an article of faith on the part of supporters of the database approach that the advantages outweigh the disadvantages. However, this is a hypothesis that would probably be difficult to confirm in today's world. To date, many companies have made the investment in adopting database technology, but few have achieved significant, demonstrable benefits. The second part of this book is primarily concerned with the problem of making database an economic success as well as a technical one.

EVOLUTION

When a new technology comes along, and especially when early adopters seem to have a hard time making it pay, there is a tendency to suspect that it has been foisted on the world by researchers interested in technical sophistication for its own sake. This has not exactly been unknown in the computer field, but it is definitely not the case with respect to database technology. Whatever the current state of this field may be, it has reached that position primarily through being pushed by users with problems rather than through being pulled by researchers enamored with complex technology.

To provide perspective on what is to come, we present here a brief summary of some key developments in the evolution of the database concept. This view is far from complete, and those interested in a more detailed treatment are referred to an excellent article by Fry and Sibley.[4] Two major factors leading to the initial development of database technology can be identified—one, general and one, quite specific. The general influence has already been noted briefly. It was the gradual acquisition, in many organizations, of substantial portfolios of applications programs—all developed independently of one another. As these portfolios

---

[4]James P. Fry & Edgar H. Sibley. "Evolution of Data-Base Management Systems," *Computing Surveys*, Vol. 8, No. 1 (March 1976), pp. 7–42.

grew, two major problems appeared. The first concerned the difficulty in using data for purposes beyond those for which it was originally collected. The second was the growing cost of program maintenance in the face of a continuing demand for minor changes. One response to these problems was the development of a standard set of routines for accessing data that could be incorporated into application programs. A number of such packages were developed in the late 1950s and early 1960s, and all of these can be considered primitive ancestors of the database systems to come.

A specific influence that played a major role in shaping the early development of database technology was, in fact, one member of this class of packages that was developed in response to a rather unique problem—the commitment by the United States to land astronauts on the moon before 1970. This commitment led to the establishment of the APOLLO project, surely one of the largest and most complex undertakings ever contemplated by humankind. The prime contractor for APOLLO, North American Rockwell, realized quite early that success would hinge critically on carefully coordinating the work of thousands of individual subcontractors. Not only was there a large and complex collection of research and production groups to be managed, but also it was necessary to ensure on a technical level that each of millions of individual components would correctly fit into the entire assembly and work properly with all of the other parts supplied by all of the other firms.

Rockwell management recognized that satisfactory administrative and technical coordination would depend on an effective information system. Because no available systems had the capability of dealing with such a large and complex collection of data, Rockwell asked IBM if it could develop one. IBM accepted the challenge, and working together with Rockwell personnel, developed the Generalized Update Access Method (GUAM), which became available for use in 1964. It is interesting to recall that this was the year in which IBM's System/360 was also introduced, marking the start of the third generation of computing hardware. At the time, there was a widespread feeling that computing had come of age— that the early period of experimentation was over. For example, although many higher level programming languages—including FORTRAN and COBOL—had been successfully developed by then, the introduction of System/360 hardware was accompanied by a new language called Programming Language/1 (PL/1). The name suggested the belief of its developers that it somehow represented a new start.

The administrative data required for the APOLLO project was basically a large organization chart; as such, it had a hierarchical structure. Similarly, the technical data could be viewed as a parts explosion on a large scale, which is also inherently hierarchical. Thus, GUAM was designed to deal with data whose logical structure was hierarchical. However, because it was originally developed for second-generation hardware, it envisioned that such a large collection of data might have to be stored on magnetic tape, which permits only sequential processing of data, rather than on direct access storage devices. The possibility of having a physical data structure for storage management purposes different from the logical structure seen by the users is one of the most important features of a modern database management system.

By the time GUAM was operational at North American Rockwell, IBM felt it had something that might be of more general value. It did some further development, and in 1966 announced the availability of Data Language/1 (DL/1). Again, there seems to be a suggestion in the choice of name that DL/1 was viewed as superceding all that had gone before and providing a fresh start. Eventually, DL/1 became the basis for IBM's Information Management System (IMS), undoubtedly the most influential of early database management systems.

Another major milestone in database technology occurred as an outgrowth of the development of the COBOL programming language. When the committee that designed COBOL began work, one of the things it knew was that a language intended for business computing would need elaborate data structuring facilities. The language specifications, including both nested structures and repeating groups, were approved as an international standard in 1961.

Shortly thereafter, some COBOL users began to be concerned that there was another important data structuring concept that should have been included in the language—the ability to refer to one record from another one. This is generally accomplished by having a "pointer" data type that can be used to hold the address of a record or a block of data. Pointers are useful, for example, in constructing lists of items without requiring that successive elements be physically adjacent. The insertion and deletion of items in lists implemented using pointers are much cheaper and easier to accomplish than when the items are stored in physical sequence. In the latter case, many elements may have to be physically moved to make room for an insertion or to close up the space left by a deletion. PL/1, which was specified after COBOL, included the pointer data type.

In 1968 a List Processing Task Group was established by the committee responsible for managing COBOL development to make a recommendation concerning how list processing capabilities should be introduced into the language. This committee quickly came to the conclusion that what was needed was not simply the ability to manipulate lists, but a generalized facility for defining and managing complex data structures. The task group also felt that such a facility should not be a part of COBOL, but should have a separate, independent existence so that it could be used by application programs written in any programming language. The group proceeded to rename itself the Data Base Task Group[5] (usu-

---

[5]One of many debates of greater or lesser profundity that have marked the development of this technology is whether it is to be called "data base" or "database." Most early works seem to use the two-word version, whereas recent practice favors the one-word approach. The latter convention wil' be followed here, except where historical accuracy requires use of the two-word name.

ally abbreviated as DBTG) and altered its mandate to encompass this wider view. By the time all this was taking place in 1968, experience with IBM's DL/1 had revealed some serious limitations of the hierarchical approach, which will be described in Chapter 3. Thus, the DBTG opted for a more general structure, called a network, as the basis for its approach to managing databases.

There were two important factors influencing the DBTG's work. First, even though the task group was no longer looking specifically at COBOL enhancements, it retained a strong COBOL orientation that is apparent in many of its decisions. Second, the group was composed primarily of representatives from computer vendors and large users. Thus, it may fairly be described as being strongly concerned with issues of practicality and efficiency, and perhaps less with theoretical elegance. In Chapter 4, where the network model is examined in detail, a number of examples of this will become evident.

One result of the DBTG's COBOL connection was that it was quite interested in the idea of getting a standard defined for database systems and having it accepted by the appropriate national and international bodies. (The early acceptance of a standard definition for COBOL is widely credited for its swift movement to a predominant position in the business programming field.) Standards are attractive to users because they reduce uncertainty. For example, a company could invest resources in developing COBOL programs secure in the knowledge that it was not committing itself forever to a particular computer or even vendor and that there would always be a pool of programmers available who were familiar with that language. The commitment to a database system is probably every bit as significant as the choice of a programming language. Many organizations were reluctant to undertake the massive effort required to implement a database unless they could be reasonably assured that their investment would be protected. Thus, users tended to be strong proponents of standardization efforts, as did those who (for other reasons) wanted to encourage the rapid adoption of database concepts.

Opposition to standardization was based on two grounds. First, the existence of a standard tends to create a certain amount of inertia. Many people felt that the database field was in need of a great deal more experience and research before the standardization decision could be made intelligently. Others were simply dissatisfied with the DBTG proposal, which was the only active candidate for standardization. The entire subject of database standardization will be discussed more fully later. For the purposes of this historical overview, it is sufficient to note that a strong push was made to have the DBTG proposal accepted as a standard but that there was enough opposition to prevent these efforts from succeeding. Nevertheless, a number of vendors went on to develop database management software based on the DBTG design. Thus, the main objective of standardization was achieved to a limited extent without the stifling effect on future research that might have accompanied formal adoption.

All of the activity described so far took place within the real-world data processing community. Needs appeared, and results-oriented development projects by users and/or vendors were initiated to meet them. By the end of the 1960s, however, researchers were beginning to discover that the database area contained many interesting and significant questions that needed examination. Historical surveys of any field inevitably run into difficulty as they approach the present because it becomes increasingly difficult without the benefit of perspective to judge what are the really significant events. However, the entry of the research community into the database arena can probably be conveniently dated from a paper published in 1970 by E. F. Codd of IBM Research.[6]

Codd proposed an approach to managing databases based on the mathematical theory of sets and relations that was quite elegant. Its simplicity had strong appeal for potential users who had found previous systems excessively complicated and confusing. The elegance and theoretical foundation of Codd's approach also attracted the interest of other researchers. Previously, most database research consisted of building a large software system and learning about its properties by actually using it. This is not without value, but it is a slow, expensive way to acquire knowledge, and there is often great difficulty in generalizing from the experience with a single system. For the first time, it appeared possible to study database issues theoretically by using powerful mathematical tools that could produce general results.

The simplicity of Codd's relational approach made it appear that one could build database management systems with much less effort than was required for the hierarchical or network varieties. Many systems based on this model were actually built throughout the 1970s with quite modest investments. However, this simplicity was misleading in a sense because when relational DBMS's were implemented in simple, straightforward ways, they tended to have extremely poor performance. As a result, the relational model was labeled in many people's minds as an approach that might be of theoretical interest but that was incapable of dealing with problems of realistic size.

As time went on, computer technology continuously improved, making it possible partially to substitute brute force computing power for the lack of sophistication in design of the DBMS. However, this was clearly not going to solve the entire problem, and a variety of researchers began working on the problem of making a practical relational database system. One of the most significant of these efforts was the System R project at the IBM San Jose Research Center. In addition to studying a number of important issues, such as backup, recovery, and concurrent access—issues that had often been ignored by earlier relational system developers—the System R team investigated the use of highly

[6]E. F. Codd, "A Relational Model for Large Shared Data Banks," *Communications of the ACM*, Vol. 13, No. 6 (June 1970), pp. 377–387.

sophisticated, complex techniques for storing and manipulating the data. In this way, the team was able to achieve performance on large databases roughly comparable to performance of DBMS's based on other, less congenial approaches. Several practical relational DBMS's are now available in the marketplace. Although these contemporary relational systems employ a variety of complex techniques to improve performance, it is important to recognize that this is all hidden from the users of the system who still see a simple, logically coherent view of the database.

The inherent simplicity and theoretical basis for the relational model mean that it is the vehicle for most database research. However, knowledge gained by studying relational systems can be, and has been, applied to other types of database systems. Also, there has been some work in recent years on developing more advanced database models that are designed to deal with certain shortcomings of the relational model. These newer proposals generally represent minor enhancements of the basic relational approach.

As academic and industrial researchers continued to enhance our basic understanding of database processing, users have been adopting the approach in ever-increasing numbers. According to the *Datamation* annual surveys, more than 40% of IBM mainframe sites had some type of database software in use by 1982, and a further 10% were planning to install database softwear during 1983. Database software was in use in 1982 at 74% of sites using large-scale IBM (or compatible) hardware. By 1983, this number had grown to 77%.[7] With such widespread acceptance of the database approach, efficiency and cost/effectiveness have become major issues. Database systems could probably be much more efficient than they are if they operated in a more suitable computing environment. Two major impediments to DBMS performance are the architecture of current hardware and the relationship between the DBMS and the operating system (OS). This latter problem can be clarified by looking at the database management process in more detail (Figure 1–4). Users and their application programs make requests to the DBMS. If the request is valid, the DBMS takes responsibility for performing the necessary database manipulations. However, it is not able to do this directly. In nearly all modern computer systems, only the OS, through the use of instructions that run in a privileged mode, can directly perform input and output operations. Thus, the DBMS must invoke the file-handling capabilities of the OS to read or write data, which introduces additional overhead.

It might seem logical to solve this problem by collapsing the DBMS and OS into a single entity. After all, the DBMS performs a role that is, in many ways, an evolutionary replacement for the traditional file-handling task of an OS. However, such an approach is not often found in current practice. Most current OS's

[7] IBM Mainframe User Survey, 1982/83 and 1983, *Datamation*.

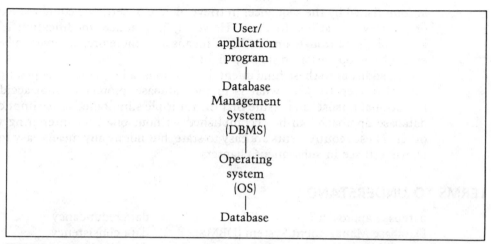

FIGURE 1–4 Relationship between the Database Management System (DBMS) and the operating system (OS).

were designed before the era of database management, therefore, they did not incorporate the needed facilities. DBMS's, which were developed later, had to appear to the OS as just another user program. It seems likely that any newly developed OS will either incorporate DBMS functions directly or, at least, provide a way for a DBMS add-on to bypass the traditional file-system functions, most of which are irrelevant in a database environment.

There has also been work at the level of the computer hardware itself, which is aimed at making database operations more efficient. Most current computer systems employ the basic hardware architecture proposed by John von Neumann in the 1940s, a time when almost all computer applications involved massive computation and little data handling. These machines are far from optimal for database applications. The tremendous investment that has been made in conventional computers makes it unlikely that they will soon be scrapped. However, it is possible that computers specialized for database processing will be used in tandem with more conventional systems. We will discuss this work further in the final chapter of this book.

FUNDAMENTAL CAPABILITIES

Although database management is a rather complicated topic, the basic functions are surprisingly few and simple. There are only four primary operations that must be performed. We need to be able to *insert* information into the database, to *retrieve* it, and to *delete* it when it is no longer required. We also must be able to *modify* the contents of the database. If we recognize that modification can be

accomplished by the sequence, {retrieve, delete, insert}, we could reduce our list of primary operations to three. However, in practice, modification is usually accomplished through a more direct means and, therefore, deserves to be considered a basic operation in its own right.

In addition to these fundamental operations, a DBMS to be of practical value mut also keep track of what is in the database, protect it from accidental or intentional misuse, and assure that the multiple simultaneous use implicit in the database approach can be accomplished without one user interfering with another. These requirements are easy to state, but not by any means easy to meet—as we will see in subsequent chapters.

TERMS TO UNDERSTAND

database approach
Database Management System (DBMS)
data independence

data redundancy
data consistency
data sharing

REVIEW QUESTIONS

1. Describe at least five costs associated with adopting the database approach.

2. Describe at least seven claimed advantages of the database approach.

3. What are the four basic data manipulation operations? Which one is not quite as basic as the others? Why?

4. What are the primary functions of a Database Management System (DBMS)? What additional facilities are needed for a commercially useful DBMS?

5. Outline the major milestones in the evolution of database technology.

PART I

DATABASE DESIGN

CHAPTER 2

DATABASE DESIGN—I

THE REAL WORLD AND ITS REPRESENTATION

Databases exist because of a need to be able to store and retrieve information about things in the real world. Thus, it seems appropriate before starting to look at the technical aspects of Database Management Systems (DBMS's) and their use to have a clear idea of the relationship between reality and its representation in a database.

Figure 2–1 illustrates a model with four levels of abstraction or generality. The first level consists of *entity-types*. An entity-type is a class of things, such as "employee," "company," or "course." The entity-type, employee, for example, does not refer to any specific employee, but rather to the general *idea* of one. Each entity-type has a set of attributes associated with it. These are characteristics of the entity-type that serve to identify or describe particular entities of that type. Name, employee number, sex, years of service, and job title, among others, might be attributes of the employee entity-type. Needless to say, entity-types, which are just concepts, do not actually appear in any database. However, they represent the level of abstraction relevant to the database design task. That is, the designer will think in terms of entity-types when deciding what is to be represented in the database.

A particular employee would be an instance of the entity-type, employee. Such instances are called *entity-occurrences*, and they exist at the next more concrete level of the model. Entity-occurrences do not actually appear in databases either because they are real, existing physical things; but it is entity-occurrences that are the subjects of the information in a database.

An entity-occurrence is represented by the set of values of certain attributes associated with its entity-type. This third level of our model is called the *logical representation* level. Note that the logical representation of an entity-occurrence does not express everything about it, that is, it need not contain values for *all* of the attributes of its entity-type. Rather, specific attributes will be selected on the basis of their relevance to the organization compiling the data, and the values of that set of attributes will comprise the logical representation of the entity-occurrence.

The fourth and most concrete level of the model is the *physical representation* level. This is simply some physical encoding of the logical representation. One encoding might consist of Arabic digits and upper case Roman letters printed on paper. Thus, `"DAN PRICE, 4064, M, 7, PROGRAMMER, . . ."` is a physical representation of an employee. (The values given correspond to the attributes mentioned earlier for this entity-type.) An alternative physical representation might employ both upper and lower case letters. Another might represent each character by its hexadecimal equivalent according to the ASCII coding system, and so on. It is interesting to note that the physical representation level is the only one for which an actual example can be given in Figure 2–1. The entity-

Level	Example
Entity type	The "idea" of an employee
Entity occurrence	An actual employee
Logical representation	The set of attribute values used to describe that employee
Physical representation	An encoding of the attribute values, such as: `[DAN PRICE, 4064, M, 7 PROGRAMMER, . . .]`

FIGURE 2–1 Levels of representation abstraction.

type is just a concept, having no concrete representation; the entity-occurrence is a live human being; and the logical representation is a set of values, but not restricted to any particular way of representing them. There will normally be a considerable variety of alternative physical representations for any logical representation, so, this distinction is not trivial.

One might well wonder what the relevance of this rather abstract model is to the study of database management. Subsequent sections of this book will refer to all four of these levels, and it will be helpful to have a clear understanding of how they relate to each other as well as a systematic set of terms. In fact, some of the disputes and confusion that have occurred in the database field in the past can be attributed to the fact that the participants were referring to different levels.

DATA TYPES AND VALUE SETS

Anyone who has ever programmed a computer is accustomed to the fact that you usually have to tell the computer whether the information stored in a particular location is an integer, a real number, a character string, a Boolean value, or whatever. Most computers have one electronic circuit for adding two integers and another for adding two real numbers, and, of course, addition does not make any sense at all, in general, for character strings. Because the pattern of bits in a storage location can usually be interpreted as any of these, the computer must be told what is intended. This specification is known as the "type" of the data. Identifying a data object as being of a particular type has the effect of defining an internal representation for the object. It also specifies which operations may be performed on that object and their effects. For example, the internal representation of an integer in most modern mainframe computers is a string of 32 bits in 2's complement format. The external representation is a character string in which only the digits 0 to 9 and the minus sign may appear. Suitable interpretations of all the standard arithmetic and logical operations are also implied when a data object is declared to be of type integer.

It is also true (but perhaps less obvious) that declaring a data object to be an integer defines a collating system for occurrences of that object. That is, it specifies how the relatively complex operation, sort, should operate. Specific algorithms for converting between internal and external representations are also implied.

Stating the data type for each attribute is one requirement for defining the physical representation of an entity. Other characteristics that have to be specified include size of the storage area allocated to each attribute and its location in the computer's memory relative to other attributes of that entity. These properties all have to do with what might be called the syntax of an attribute.

However, every value that satisfies these specifications may not be valid for that attribute. For example, the syntactic specification of an attribute, Color, may state that it is a character string of length 8 at a certain location in storage. If that location happens to have "Saturday" stored in it, the syntactic specification is satisfied, but that is unlikely to be a valid value for an attribute whose name is Color. It should be possible greatly to increase the integrity of a database and, hence, its usefulness if it could be guaranteed that the values recorded in it were valid for each attribute. One way of accomplishing this would be to specify the permissible values as part of the definition of each attribute. In some cases, this specification could take the form of a list (e.g., female or male for Sex). In the case of a numerical attribute, a range might be more appropriate (e.g., 200 to 800 for College Board test scores). Such a specification of the legal values for an attribute is its value-set.[1]

The ideal way to describe the representation of an attribute would be to state that it is an instance of some type that has exactly the right syntax, operations, and value-set. This would imply, of course, a much wider range of data types than is customarily available. Such a situation can be achieved by employing the concept of abstract data types (ADTs). ADTs have been discussed in the context of programming languages since the early 1970s.[2] For example, the Pascal language includes features for defining additional data types in terms of the tradi-

---

[1] Some other authors and, indeed, some DBMS's use the word "domain" for essentially the same concept. Although this has the advantage of some current usage, it is not really the correct term. In mathematics, the domain of a function is the set of values over which the function is defined, and the set of values that the function can assume is referred to as its "range." For example, the domain of the sine function is the real numbers and its range is from -1 to $+1$. Consistency with this terminology would suggest using "range" to describe the set of legal values for an attribute. However, there does not seem to be any support for this in the literature.

[2] B. Liskov and S. Zilles, "Programming with Abstract Data Types," *ACM SIGPLAN Notices*, Vol. 9, No. 4 (April 1974), pp. 50–59.

tional basic ones and then employing the new ones to define the actual data objects used in a Pascal program. Each programmer can define types to meet his or her particular needs. Thus, one person might define a type WORKDAYS to be a character string whose value must be one of "Monday," "Tuesday," "Wednesday," "Thursday," or "Friday." In another context, another programmer might include the string "Saturday" in this definition. WORKDAYS is an example of an ADT. It is defined as a subset of the basic data type, character string, and this determines most of its properties. The ability to define a new data type in terms of already existing ones and to inherit properties greatly simplifies the use of ADTs.

Thus, in a personnel system, the attributes Employee's Name, Spouse's Name, and Supervisor's Name would all be described as instances of the ADT, Person's Name. The detailed specification of exactly how names are to be represented internally and externally would be provided only once—as part of the ADT definition—and would automatically be applied to all relevant attributes. This simplifies database design by eliminating the need to define the detailed structure of a common attribute, such as name or telephone number each time it appears. At the same time, it guarantees that all such appearances will have the same behavior. The inclusion of standardized procedures for converting between the internal and external representations as part of the definition of an ADT reduces the application programmer's work and also ensures attributes that refer to the same kind of thing will be represented in the same way.

Specifying that two attributes are instances of the same ADT implies that it is semantically legitimate to compare them. Furthermore, because the same representation definition applies to both, a given value will always have precisely the same internal representation. The importance of this becomes apparent when one considers a query such as:

Find the names of all employees who work for their spouse.

Assume that Supervisor's Name and Spouse's Name are both attributes of an employee. Processing the query then requires searching employee records for matching values of these two attributes. In a traditional system, many entities that should be selected by this query might be missed because the representations of the two attribute values are not identical, even though referring to the same individual. It is not easy to program a computer to recognize that "John Bradley," "John S. Bradley," and "John Stewart Bradley" probably all refer to the same person. Such discrepancies arise because the two attributes have slightly different definitions and/or because the actual values were entered at different times using different procedures.

This problem would be avoided if the definition of the two attributes specified that they were both instances of the "person's name" ADT. Although this would not absolutely prevent someone from entering a name that was different from that already in the system for the same individual, it should greatly reduce the likelihood. In addition, it informs the system that Supervisor's Name and Spouse's Name are instances of the same kind of thing and that it is, therefore, meaningful to compare them.

Similarly, if Employment Date and Degree Date are both identified as instances of the ADT "date," then the system knows that it is meaningful to look for employees who received their degree after joining the company. On the other hand, such a mechanism would allow a system to reject, or at least question, a query asking for a list of all those whose Zip Code is greater than their shoe size. Both of these are probably stored as integers, so, on a syntactic basis alone, it is a feasible query. However, these attributes should be instances of different ADTs so that a database system using this facility would be able to recognize this as a nonsensical query. The use of ADTs can help to reduce the incidence of invalid values in a database. Also, specifying that two attributes are, or are not, instances of the same ADT tells us much more about what operations may be meaningfully performed on them than merely knowing their types in the traditional sense.

KEYS

All attributes describe some aspect of an entity. Some attributes perform the additional role of *distinguishing* one particular entity occurrence from all others of the same type. For example, if care is taken not to assign any employee number to more than one person, then knowing an individual's employee number should be sufficient to locate all of the other attribute values for that individual. An attribute that can be guaranteed to have a unique value for each entity is called a *key*.

Sometimes there may be more than one attribute of an entity that uniquely identifies each occurrence. For example, if the personnel records include Social Security Numbers (and if it is felt that the controls on issuing duplicate Social Security Numbers are adequate), then either Employee Number or Social Security Number could be used as the key for identifying employees. Keys are fundamental to virtually all methods of physically managing data in computer systems. (See Appendix 1 for descriptions of the most common data structuring techniques.) When there is more than one possible key, the alternatives are referred to as candidate keys. Normally, one of these will be selected as the primary key and used to determine where the record will be stored. Other candidate keys that may be used to facilitate retrieval are called secondary keys.

DATABASE DESIGN

The model introduced at the beginning of this chapter provides a starting point for understanding what is involved in designing a database. Based on this model, a three-step procedure might be deduced:

1. Identify the relevant entity-types.
2. Choose a logical representation for each. This involves deciding which attributes of each entity-type are to be included in the database.
3. Determine a physical representation for each attribute.

Except for being considerably oversimplified, this is not a bad description of the database design process. However, it omits one critical task. In the real world, entities do not exist in isolation from each other. Many different types of associations between entities can be found, and these must also be represented in the database.

At some point, a database design must take into account the particular capabilities and limitations of the database management system that will be used. For example, some DBMS's can only represent certain types of associations. However, it is generally agreed that the designer should begin by modeling the real-world application in a DBMS-independent way and then convert that design to fit the special characteristics of the chosen DBMS. A useful tool for the first part of this process is the entity-relationship (E-R) model developed by Peter Chen.[3] This is briefly introduced in the following section and then applied to an example that will be used throughout the text.

THE ENTITY-RELATIONSHIP (E-R) MODEL

The E-R model employs two basic constructs. An *entity* is a "thing" that can be distinctly identified. Examples of entities include individual students, books, automobiles, and so on. A *relationship* is an association among entities. Ownership is an example of a relationship between a student and a book. Note that each entity in a relationship plays a particular and distinct *role*. Students own books; books do not own students. Specification of roles in relationships is one way that the E-R model expresses something about the meaning of data.

A relationship can involve more than two entities. For example, a firm supplying a certain part for use in a specific product is a relationship among three entities: a supplier, a part, and a product. Relationships are also characterized in terms of the number of each entity type that can participate. It is usual to distinguish three classes of relationships. Marriage, for example, can be represented as a *one-to-one* (1:1) relationship between two person entities. Assuming that a department has many employees but each employee works for only one department, the relationship between department and employee would be of the *one-to-many* (1:N) variety. A good example of a *many-to-many* (M:N) relationship is the one between students and courses. A student can be taking a number of courses, and each course usually has many students.

[3] Peter Chen, "The Entity-Relationship Model—Toward a Unified View of Data," *ACM Transactions on Database Systems*, Vol. 1, No. 1 (March 1976), pp. 9–36.

The E-R model also includes the concepts of *entity-sets* and *relationship-sets*. Each such set has associated with it a condition that can be used to determine if a given entity or relationship belongs to it. For example, DATABASE-STUDENTS might be an entity-set defined by the condition that its members are all entities of type STUDENT enrolled in a database course. Because every member of a set must satisfy the condition associated with the set, membership in a set is another mechanism for attaching meaning to data objects.

Both entities and relationships can have *attributes*. However, attributes are not viewed as fundamental components of the model. Rather, an attribute is viewed as simply a relationship between an entity-set or a relationship-set and a value-set. For example, Date-of-Birth is a likely attribute to associate with a STUDENT entity-type. In the E-R model, this would be expressed by defining DATE-OF-BIRTH as a relationship between the STUDENT entity-type and the value-set of all dates. Any number of attributes may be defined on the same value-set.

The E-R approach includes a special notation (called an E-R diagram) for expressing models. Rectangles are used to represent entity-sets, diamonds for relationship-sets, and circles for value-sets. The lines linking relationship sets to entity-sets are labeled to identify roles and to indicate the number of entities of the specified type that may participate in the relationship. E-R diagrams for the relationships mentioned above are shown in Figure 2–2. For simplicity, it is usual to depict only the entities and relationships on a basic E-R diagram. Subsidiary diagrams, such as the one in Figure 2–3, can be used to show the attributes of each entity- and relationship-type.

On first exposure, the E-R model seems quite simple and straightforward. A closer look, though, reveals some unexpected subtleties. For example, the E-R treatment of relationships is considerably more general than that permitted by most database management systems. Some of the latter have difficulty with $1:1$ and/or $M:N$ relationships for example. Some DBMS's always assume that a relationship involves precisely two entity-types, whereas as has been seen, an E-R model relationship can be defined on a single entity-type as well as on three or more types. The complete E-R model also includes some capabilities that will not be discussed further here, such as the ability to make the existence of an entity *dependent on* the existence of some other entity.

Another (perhaps surprising) subtlety in the E-R model is associated with the fact that although the distinction between an entity and a relationship seems quite clear, there are many things in the real world that can be treated either way. Is a marriage, for example, an entity or is it a relationship between two persons? In fact, it could be considered as either and still produce a valid E-R model. However, as shown in Figure 2–4, the models produced by these two alternatives would not be the same. The database designer must use his or her judgment to decide which of these is more appropriate in a particular case.

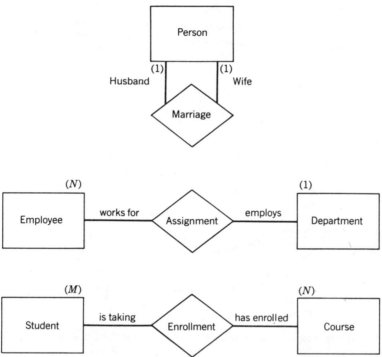

FIGURE 2–2 Entity-relationship (E-R) diagrams.

EXAMPLE DATABASE

Throughout this book, examples will be used to illustrate important ideas. To integrate the discussion and facilitate comparison among different approaches, nearly all of the examples will be based on a single application whose basic characteristics should be familiar to everyone—a rudimentary database for library administration. Much of the complexity that would be required for a real library will be omitted. However, one complication that is explicitly included is a requirement that the database serve a collection of libraries rather than just a single one. For many of the possible uses of such a system, it would be useful to have the database include information about all of the libraries in a geographic area.

A library consists of a number of branches, each of which has its own book collection. Although a new borrower probably applies for a library card at one of the branches, the card may be used at any branch, so, it is best to think of the borrowers as being registered with the library as a whole rather than with a particular branch.

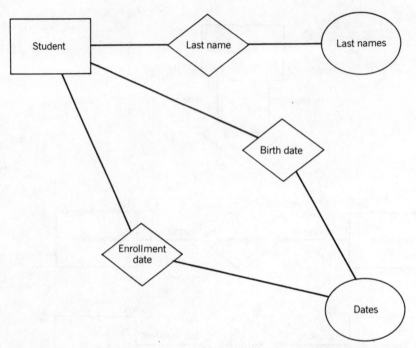

FIGURE 2–3 Attribute representation in an entity-relationship (E-R) model.

The major entity-types in this application are libraries, branches, books, and borrowers. A number of relationships among the entities can also be identified. Each branch belongs to precisely one library—an example of a $1:N$ relationship. A borrower can be related to any number of libraries through having valid library cards—obviously a many-to-many $(M:N)$ relationship.

The relationships involving books are somewhat more complicated. There may be copies of a book at several branches, and several different borrowers may have copies of a book on loan at the same time. Distinguishing among the various copies of a work can be facilitated by creating a new entity-type—VOLUME.[4] A volume is a particular copy of a book. The distinction between BOOK and VOLUME entity-types is an interesting one. VOLUME entities are concrete physical things that can be picked up and held in the hand. A BOOK, on the other hand, is an abstract entity without distinct physical existence. If there is only one copy of some book in the library, then there is a $1:1$ relationship between BOOK and VOLUME. In the more usual case, where multiple copies exist, the relationship is of the $1:N$ variety. Each VOLUME is the property of some BRANCH.

---

[4] It is quite common in database design to find that one's initial list of entity-types is incomplete. The process of working out the relationships often results in discovering important new entity-types.

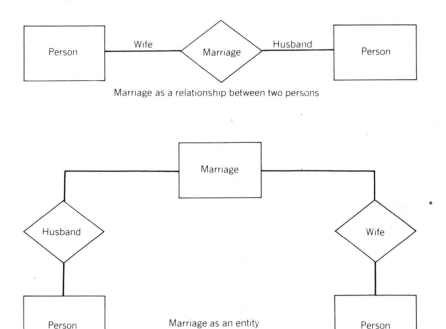

Marriage as a relationship between two persons

Marriage as an entity

FIGURE 2–4 Two entity-relationship (E-R) views of marriage.

When a VOLUME is borrowed, a relationship is created between the BOOK and BORROWER that lasts until the VOLUME has been returned. These are clearly both 1:N relationships. An E-R diagram for this database is shown in Figure 2–5.

This design assumes that the library database maintains LOAN relationships only for *current* loans. It would be possible, of course, to keep a historical record that would make it possible to determine all the people who have ever borrowed a certain book or all of the books that someone has ever borrowed. Such applications would not present any particular technical difficulty, but they might be viewed as morally inappropriate.

DATA STRUCTURE DIAGRAMS

Another pictorial technique for expressing database designs is the Data Structure Diagram, sometimes called a Bachman Diagram after its originator, C. W. Bachman.[5] Rectangles are used to represent entity-types, and connecting arrows for relationship-types. Only entities can have attributes, and these are not actually

[5]C. W. Bachman, "Data Structure Diagrams," *Data Base*, Vol. 1, No. 2 (Summer 1969), pp. 4–10.

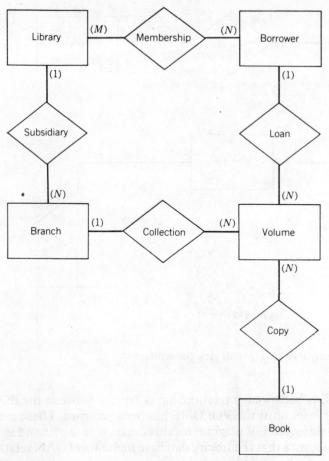

FIGURE 2–5 Entity-relationship (E-R) diagram for library database.

shown in the diagram. One-to-many relationships are the only ones that can be directly represented. The direction of the relationship is shown by drawing the arrows so that they point from the "one" to the "many."

Attributes are usually used to represent one-to-one relationships. Marriage, for example, would probably be handled by simply adding a Spouse's Name attribute to each person entity-occurrence. The value of this attribute could be used to locate the record corresponding to the spouse. The main drawback to this approach is that the relationship is not explicitly shown in the Data Structure Diagram.

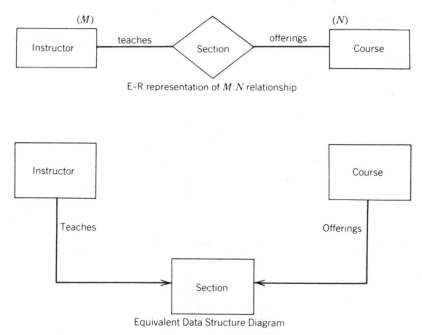

FIGURE 2–6 Transforming a many-to-many relationship.

Many-to-many relationships can not be represented at all. Fortunately, there is a simple general technique for converting an $M{:}N$ relationship into two $1{:}N$ relationships. This is done by creating a new entity-type to serve as a link between corresponding occurrences of the original pair. This is illustrated in Figure 2–6. Figure 2–7 presents a Data Structure Diagram for each of the E-R diagrams in Figure 2–2.

One may wonder why one would ever use a Data Structure Diagram as they seem to have significantly less powerful representation capability than E-R diagrams. In fact, this is precisely their value! The more limited constructs of the Data Structure Diagram are quite close to what can actually be represented in most existing database management systems. Thus, translating an E-R diagram into this more restricted form is a useful step toward the final database design.

There are no $1{:}1$ relationships in the library database as it was originally developed. However, there is a many-to-many relationship between libraries and borrowers. Figure 2–8 shows the E-R diagram of Figure 2–5 transformed into a Data Structure Diagram.

Because the Data Structure Diagram does not explicitly show the attributes for each entity-type, these are listed in Figure 2–9. Most of these attributes have intuitive interpretations that will suffice for present purposes. A few require

1:1 Relationship—Marriage

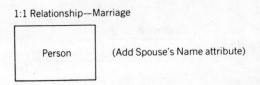

(Add Spouse's Name attribute)

1:N Relationship—Employment

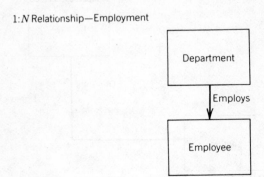

M:N Relationship—Course registration

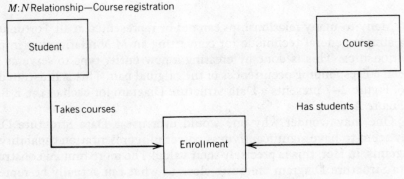

FIGURE 2–7 Data Structure Diagram samples.

some clarification. It is assumed that each library is free to assign branch names and card numbers without regard to what other libraries are doing. Thus, these do not uniquely identify a particular branch or borrower except within the context of the library that assigned them.

It would be nice to have a system for identifying books that associated the same number with a given book across all libraries. There are at least two candi-

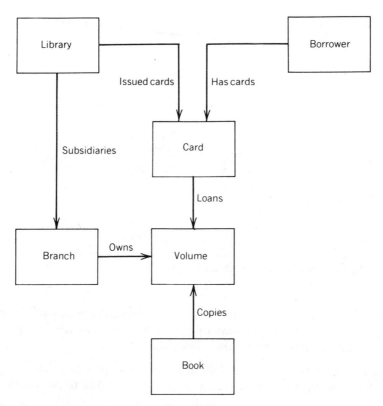

FIGURE 2–8 Data Structure Diagram for library example.

dates available: the Library of Congress Catalog Card Number and the International Standard Book Number. It is assumed that one of these is chosen. Note, though, that Catalog-No is not sufficient to identify a specific *volume.* When this is required, library and branch identifiers as well as a Copy-No will also have to be supplied.

SAMPLE QUERIES

Some problems with a proposed database design may only appear when one attempts to process queries against it. Although one of the virtues of the database approach is supposed to be its ability to deal with unanticipated queries, there can be no doubt that it helps in producing an effective database design to know something about the use that will be made of it. In the next chapter, the three most common approaches to database management will be briefly introduced,

LIBRARY:	Name
	Director
BRANCH:	Name
	Address
BOOK:	Catalog-No
	Title
	Author
	Publisher
BORROWER:	Borrower No
	Name
	Address
VOLUME:	Copy-No
	Date-Due

FIGURE 2–9 Entities and attributes for library database.

using the library database as an example. To illustrate how each of these approaches works, three queries that might be expected to arise frequently in a library application will be examined. They are:

Q1 Determine the current status of a particular volume, that is, is it available for loan or, if not, who has it and when is it due to be returned.

Q2 Find the branches (of any library) that own a copy of a particular book.

This is a sort-of global library catalog application. An individual wishing to find a book could enter this query to determine all the locations where that book could be borrowed. As a side benefit, it ought also be possible to determine whether or not the book is currently on loan.

Q3 What are all the books currently held by a particular borrower

This query might be initiated via a library administration function. Because an individual holding cards from several library systems would certainly have different borrower nos. for each, it really only makes sense to ask this question with respect to a single library.

TERMS TO UNDERSTAND

entity-type	syntax of an attribute
entity-occurrence	semantics of an attribute
logical representation	key

physical representation   candidate keys
relationship-type   primary key
data-type   secondary keys
abstract data-type (ADT)   entity-relationship (E-R) diagram
value-set   Data Structure Diagram

REVIEW QUESTIONS

1. Explain the difference between a *type* of entity or relationship and an *occurrence.*

2. Identify five abstract data-types (ADTs) that would be useful in business data processing. Specify an internal and external representation for each.

3. What advantages are associated with the concept of abstract data-types (ADTs) in database systems? Are there any disadvantages?

4. In a sense, entities, relationships, and attributes can all be considered fundamental concepts. The entity-relationship (E-R) model dispenses with the attribute as a fundamental concept by treating it as a particular type of relationship. Presumably, it would also be possible to consider a relationship as a particular type of entity. What would a model based on this premise look like?

5. The Last National Bank (LNB) has several branches and offers three types of accounts: savings, checking, and loan. A customer can have any number of accounts and there may be several customers associated with a single account. Drawn an entity-relationship (E-R) diagram to represent this situation. Identify the attributes for each entity and relationship-type and specify its value-set.

6. Draw a Data Structure Diagram for the Last National Bank (LNB) database described in question 5.

7. Suppose you were interested in constructing your family tree and wanted to set up a database to do so. The main entry in the database would be people. For each person, you want to be able to retrieve their date and place of birth, date and place of death, and the names and birth dates of each of their children. It should also be possible to locate all of someone's ancestors or descendants, including those related through marriage.

   Draw an entity-relationship (E-R) diagram and a Data Structure Diagram for this database. Indicate the important attributes of each entity-type and show the mapping ratio of each relationship, that is: $1:1$, $1:N$, or $M:N$.

8. Construct an entity-relationship (E-R) model for a department store. Make provision for: (a) various departments, (b) employees, (c) inventory, and (d) suppliers.

C H A P T E R 3

DATA MODELS

WHAT IS A DATA MODEL?

Understanding a complex system can often be made easier through the use of an abstraction that preserves its critical properties but suppresses much specific detail. In the case of a Database Management System (DBMS), such an abstraction is called a data model. A data model consists of three main components—structures, operations, and constraints. The structure portion specifies how elementary items of data are grouped into larger units. Mechanisms for the insertion, deletion, retrieval, and modification of data are provided by the operations component. The constraints are used to control the conditions under which a particular data object may exist, be altered, and so forth. In keeping with the relatively high level of abstraction at which data models exist, the three components are described in terms of the capabilities seen by a user of the system. Details of *how* to provide particular capabilities are left for the designers of actual DBMS's.

Of necessity, every DBMS that has ever been constructed has an underlying data model. In the case of many DBMS's developed when the field was new, the data model is unique to the particular system. However, as experience and formal knowledge accumulated in the field, three data models emerged as being of particular importance. One, the hierarchical model, is important because it is the basis for one of the most widely used commercial DBMS, the Information Management System (IMS) of IBM. IMS illustrates the case in which the DBMS was developed first and the data model abstracted afterward. The other two data models that will be discussed in detail, the network model and the relational model, were both consciously developed as abstractions of how a DBMS ought to work *prior* to any attempt to implement real systems based on them. Numerous actual DBMS's have subsequently been built based on each of these models.

Most of this chapter will be devoted to a brief, intuitive overview of these three data models. Understanding them will be of major assistance in trying to understand the capabilities and limitations of actual DBMS's.

EVALUATING DATA MODELS

All data models are not equivalent. Each emphasizes certain features or capabilities at the expense of others. In general, the strengths and weaknesses of the various models reflect different philosophies of database management. How important is efficiency compared to user-friendliness for example? Can it be assumed that most database manipulation can be planned far in advance or is the ability to deal with unanticipated queries important? Do users interact with the database directly or through the intermediation of applications programmers? The three data models to be introduced in this chapter differ significantly on these and other dimensions.

A useful framework for evaluating data models has been proposed by McGee.[1] He suggests two sets of criteria: those dealing with *usability* of the model and those dealing with *implementability and performance*. Usability is important when the model has to be learned, when it is used to design a database for a real application, and when its constructs are used in a computer program to define and manipulate data structures. McGee's second set of criteria deal with the ease of implementing a database system that uses a given data model and the potential for achieving acceptable performance.

Some of the specific criteria proposed by McGree are:

- Simplicity. A model should have the smallest possible number of structure types, composition rules, and attributes.
- Modeling directness. A model should have as many direct counterparts to real-world concepts as possible.
- Elegance. A model should be as simple as possible for a given direct modeling capability.
- Picturability. Model structures should be displayable in pictorial form.
- Modeling uniqueness. A model should not provide alternative equivalent direct modeling techniques.
- Implementation independence. A model should be free of implementation-specific considerations.
- Nonconflicting terminology. A model should use terminology that does not conflict with other established terminology.
- Proximity to implementation base. The constructs used in a model should be close to those provided by the underlying hardware/software base on which the model will be implemented.
- Applicability of safe implementation techniques. A model should permit the use of proven, well-understood implementation techniques.

The reader is invited to keep these criteria in mind during the presentation of the three major data models. The remainder of this chapter will give an informal introduction to the database structuring and manipulation capabilities of each data model, using the library example described in Chapter 2. Chapters 4 through 6 contain more detailed discussions of the three models.

THE HIERARCHICAL MODEL

The hierarchical model was the basis for some of the earliest work on database systems. The most widely known system of this type is IBM's Information Man-

---

[1] William C. McGee, "On User Criteria for Data Model Evaluation," *ACM Transactions on Database Systems*, Vol. 1, No. 4 (December 1976), pp. 370–387.

agement System (IMS). IMS terminology is usually used for describing the hierarchical model and that practice will be followed here.

Structure

An initial "hierarchical definition tree" for the library database is shown in Figure 3–1. This has been derived from the information in Figures 2–8 and 2–9. The smallest units of information, that is, Author or Date-Due, are called *fields*, and the collection of fields referring to a single entity is known as a *segment*. Note that the relationships among segments are strictly hierarchical. The segment at the very top of a hierarchy (LIBRARY in this example) is referred to as the root. *Each* segment other than the root has a parent segment that is the one immediately above it in the hierarchy. Any segment may also have child segments below it, and the children may be of different types. In Figure 3–1, LIBRARY segments have children of type BRANCH and also of type BORROWER. The segment for a particular library along with all of its descendant segments is called a *database record*. There would, in general, be many database records in a complete database. In our example, there would be one for each library.

The fields defined for each segment in Figure 3–1 are basically what one would expect. That is, the attributes of a library are fields in a LIBRARY segment,

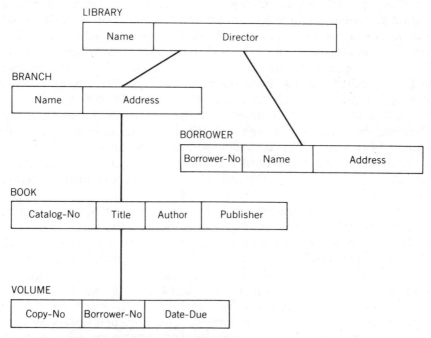

FIGURE 3–1 Hierarchical library database.

those of a borrower are fields in a BORROWER segment, and so forth. Relationships among these entity-types are represented by the hierarchical connections between the segment-types. For a volume not currently on loan, the Borrower-No and Date-Due fields would be null.

One implication of this database design should be noted that may not be apparent from Figure 3–1. Each BOOK segment located underneath a BRANCH refers specifically to a work in the collection of that branch. Thus, if some book is owned by 20 different branches, there will be 20 distinct BOOK segments for it, each containing the identical information. Such duplication is unavoidable in this case, as is the consistency problem resulting from it. Furthermore, there is no simple way to keep track of all the duplicates. If it were found that the wrong publisher had been initially entered for a book, it would be necessary to scan the entire database to find all of the segments that needed to be corrected.

Another property of the hierarchical model that can cause difficulty is that a nonroot segment-occurrence can only exist in the database if it is attached to a parent. Thus, there is no place to store information about a book that is being considered for purchase or one that has already been purchased but not yet assigned to a branch.

Data Manipulation

Hierarchical databases are manipulated in a hierarchical manner. That is, to reach a particular segment, one must first find the root of the database record containing that segment. This would usually be accomplished using the value of one of the root segment's fields. It is then possible to move down, from parent to child, selecting segments on the basis of type and possibly on the values of fields until the desired one has been reached. There are three basic commands for locating a segment, GET UNIQUE, GET NEXT, and GET NEXT WITHIN PARENT.

With a GET UNIQUE command, the user specifies the segment type to be retrieved, and values for enough of its fields to determine uniquely a particular segment of that type. This command searches a database, starting from the root of the first database record until it has located a segment meeting the specified criteria. If, in fact, the criteria specified do not uniquely identify a single segment, the first one encountered will be retrieved.

The GET NEXT command is similar, except that it begins searching at the "current" position in the database rather than at the beginning. The current position is that of the segment retrieved by the most recent GET UNIQUE or GET NEXT command. The GET NEXT WITHIN PARENT command works the same way, except that its scope is confined to those segments that are descendants of the record retrieved by the most recent GET UNIQUE or GET NEXT.

For example, using the database of Figure 3–1, a GET UNIQUE command might be used to locate the root segment for a particular library by specifying a value for the Name field. Then a sequence of GET NEXT BOOK commands specifying

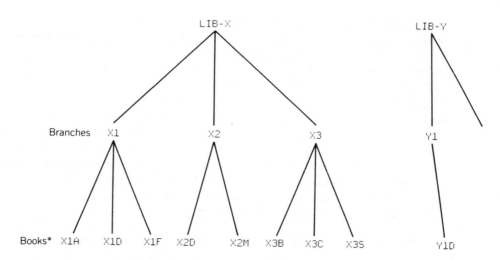

* "D" indicates a book by Dickens.
If LIBRARY segment for LIB-X has been selected, then:
A sequence of GET NEXT commands will retrieve X1D, X2D, Y1D, and so on.
A sequence of GET NEXT WITHIN PARENT commands will retrieve X1D, X2D, and then terminate.
FIGURE 3–2 GET NEXT versus GET NEXT WITHIN PARENT command.

that the value of Author is to be "Dickens" would retrieve all of the books by that author held by any branch of that library. Executing the command again after retrieving the last Dickens book held by this library will produce the first Dickens book held by the next library, and so on until all of the libraries have been examined. If it is desired to confine the search to only the one library, the GET NEXT WITHIN PARENT command should be used. This distinction is illustrated in Figure 3–2.

The links from parent to child are the only ones that exist in a true hierarchical database system. In particular, there could be no direct link from a BORROWER to a VOLUME in this example. This is a severe disadvantage of the hierarchical model, causing duplication of information and/or extensive additional processing for some queries. Some commercial systems avoid these difficulties by adding nonhierarchical linking capabilities.

Queries

Consider the three typical queries described in Chapter 2:

Q1 Determine the current status of a particular volume, that is, is it available for loan or, if not, who has it and when is it due to be returned.

It is assumed that all of the information needed to identify the volume is known. This query is dealt with rather easily. The first step uses a GET UNIQUE operation to find the root segment for the particular library system. Next, the appropriate BRANCH segment underneath this LIBRARY must be found. (Either a GET NEXT or GET NEXT WITHIN PARENT operation could be used. (Discussion of the detailed implications of the choice is left to Chapter 4). In a similar manner, a BOOK child of that BRANCH is located, then a VOLUME child of that BOOK. The VOLUME segment contains precisely the desired information. If further information about the borrower is required, the borrower identification from the VOLUME segment could be used to reenter the hierarchy at the root and get the name and address from the corresponding BORROWER segment. The hierarchical model works well for this query because, at each step, it is possible to eliminate from further consideration a large fraction of the remaining segments.

Q2 Find the branches (of any library) that own a copy of a particular book.

Assume that the catalog-no of the desired book is known. There will be a distinct occurrence of the BOOK segment under each BRANCH that owns this book. These BOOK segments would be located using a series of GET NEXT operations. For each BOOK segment that is located, its parent BRANCH segment can be retrieved.[2] Note that virtually every BOOK segment will have to be examined and that this may be expected to be a large fraction of all the segments of the database. This particular hierarchical design does not offer any shortcuts to getting this answer.

Q3 What are all the books currently held by a particular borrower?

First, the root segment for the relevant library must be located. Then, the correct BORROWER child could be located as described for query Q1. Unfortunately, though, BORROWER segments do not contain any information about what books that individual currently has from the library. Thus, the only way this query could be handled would require a comprehensive scan of all the VOLUME segments under that LIBRARY looking for the specified Borrower-No. This is actually a simple query to construct using the GET NEXT WITHIN PARENT operation. If VOLUME is specified as the segment-type of interest, the intervening BRANCH and BOOK segments will be ignored. When a qualifying VOLUME segment is found, any information about the book in question can be found by moving up the hierarchy to the parent BOOK segment. Although this query may be easy to construct, it promises to be expensive and time consuming to execute because of the large number of segments that must be examined.

---

[2] The details of moving from a segment to its parent will be discussed in Chapter 4. However, because each (nonroot) segment has only one parent, it is reasonable to assume that this is a feasible and relatively efficient operation.

Both queries Q2 and Q3 are awkward and/or expensive to process using the given hierarchical database definition. Alternative designs that use the hierarchical model and that alleviate these particular problems are possible. However, it is a basic property of the hierarchical model that queries where the natural order of processing is downward from the root work well, whereas those that must be processed beginning at a lower level do not. Thus, no single hierarchy can be efficient for all of the sample queries. In processing Q1, retrieval goes from library to branch to book to volume—always moving away from the root. A minimal number of segments are examined. Q2 and Q3, on the other hand, logically begin several levels down in the hierarchy and require sequential scanning of large amounts of data. If the intended usage of a database is known, the design can be optimized for the most frequently occurring query types. However, if this information is not available or if there are important query types that demand different hierarchical structures, this model is not going to work particularly well.

THE NETWORK MODEL

Although some early database systems employed network techniques, the term is usually used to refer specifically to the proposal of the Conference on Data Systems Languages (CODASYL) Data Base Task Group (DBTG).[3] The basic concepts of this model are not too complicated, but implementations can become exceedingly complex.

Structure

Entities are normally represented by *records*. The attributes of an entity are stored in the *data-items* that comprise a record. It is usual to distinguish between record-*types* and record-*occurrences*. Record-types are generic, whereas occurrences are specific. The library database, for example, will have a record-*type*, BOOK, and a record-*occurrence* for Crime and Punishment.

Relationships in the network model are represented by a construct called a *set*,[4] and again, it is necessary to distinguish between set-types and set-occurrences. A set-type consists of one record-type called the *owner* and another record-type called the *member*. A set-occurrence automatically exists for every record-occurrence of the owner record-type and may have any number of members, including zero. A record-type may be the owner of some set-types and the member of others; in general, it may participate in any number of sets. The only restrictions are that the owner and member record-types of a set must be differ-

---

[3] CODASYL, *Data Base Task Group Report*, Association for Computing Machinery, April 1971.

[4] A set in the DBTG proposal is quite different from a set in mathematics. A bit more will be said about this in Chapter 5.

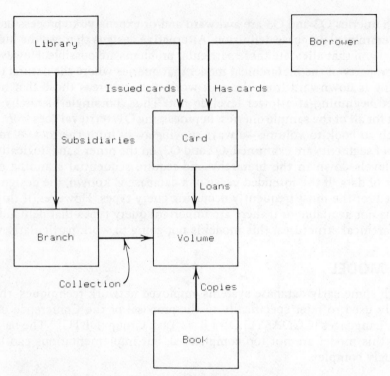

FIGURE 3–3 Network design for library database.

ent, and no record-occurrence may be a member of more than one set-occurrence of a given type.

The first of these restrictions means, among other things, that a set can not be used directly to represent relationships such as the fact that one employee supervises certain others. The "obvious" way to do this would be to construct a set owned by the supervisor's record with the records for his or her subordinates as members. However, because both the supervisor and subordinates are represented by EMPLOYEE records, this set definition would not be permitted. The second restriction implies that $N:N$ relationships can not be directly expressed. Fortunately, the library database has already been purged of $M:N$ relationships in the process of constructing the Data Structure Diagram in the last chapter.

Figure 3–3 repeats the Data Structure Diagram of Figure 2–8. It requires no further alteration to be implemented using the network model. Each rectangle in the diagram becomes a record-type and each arrow becomes a set-type. The arrow points from the owner record-type of the set to the member record-type.

There are a couple of important differences between the network implementation of this database and the previously discussed hierarchical one. First, there need be no duplication of records. Only one BOOK record-occurrence is required for a work, no matter how many branches have copies of it. In this case, a set construct is used to associate all of the VOLUME record-occurrences with a single occurrence of the BOOK record. In addition, because nonhierarchical relationships are permitted, a VOLUME record-occurrence can be simultaneously linked (through set membership, of course) to a BOOK, a BRANCH, and a BORROWER. Thus, lengthy searches are no longer required to make any of these connections.

Data Manipulation

The network model includes a repertoire of functions for locating record-occurrences based on both data-item values and set associations. There is a generalized GET command, similar to the GET UNIQUE of the hierarchical model, that can locate any occurrence of a record-type based on values of its data-items. Record-occurrences can also be located through their participation in a set relationship. The network facilities for processing sets are far more powerful than the GET NEXT WITHIN PARENT, which is the only operation in the hierarchical model that locates segments based on their relationship to another segment.

GET NEXT and GET PRIOR commands can be used to go from one member to another within a set. The owner of a set can be reached from any member via a GET OWNER command, and one can begin searching the members when the owner is known, using either a GET FIRST MEMBER or GET LAST MEMBER operation. All of these set manipulation commands can specify search conditions based on data-item values as well. Figure 3–4 illustrates a set occurrence. The arrows show the direct references between record-occurrences. There is no implication, however, that all of these pointers are actually stored in any specific implementation.

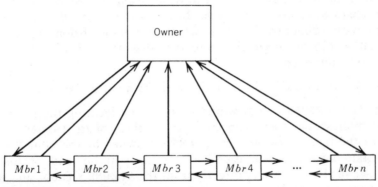

FIGURE 3–4 Logical representation of a set.

Queries

Q1 Determine the current status of a particular volume, that is, is it available for loan or, if not, who has it and when is it due to be returned.

The answer to this query is clearly to be found in a VOLUME record. The specific record-occurrence needed is identified by the fact that it is a member of two sets: one owned by the BOOK record of interest and one by the relevant BRANCH record.

There are two obvious ways to find this VOLUME record. The first begins by locating the relevant LIBRARY record and then scanning its SUBSIDIARIES set, looking for the member with the appropriate name. The COLLECTION set for that branch is then scanned sequentially. As each VOLUME record is located, the ownership of the COPIES set to which it belongs is checked. When the relevant BOOK record appears as owner, the correct COPIES set, and hence the correct VOLUME record, have been found. This example illustrates quite well why the term "navigation" is often used to describe the processing of a query in a network database.

The second approach to processing this query is the inverse of the first. The correct BOOK record is located and then each member of its COPIES set is examined, checking for one that belongs to the proper BRANCH. Although these are logically equivalent, there will be an enormous difference in performance between them. In the first case, a COLLECTION set that could easily have 1 million members or more must be searched sequentially, whereas in the second case, it is a COPIES set that gets scanned, and this is unlikely to have more than a few dozen members. In the network model, responsibility for selecting the access path lies with the user or with the programmer who writes a retrieval program.

Q2 Find the branches (of any library) that own a copy of a particular book.

This query begins by using the value of Catalog-No to go directly to the BOOK record of interest. This record will own a COPIES set with a member for each VOLUME of that book. The members of this set would be retrieved one at a time, and the owner of the COLLECTION set to which each VOLUME belonged would be retrieved. That owner would, of course, be a BRANCH record. If it were necessary to get information about the library to which that branch belonged, the owner of the SUBSIDIARIES set to which the particular BRANCH record belonged would also have to be retrieved.

Q3 What are all the books currently held by a particular borrower.

The relevant BORROWER record would be found by locating the record for the library of interest and then scanning the members of its ISSUED-CARDS set looking for the right Card-No. The LOANS set owned by the BORROWER record would contain one member for each book currently in the hands of this individual. The Due-Dates are found directly from the VOLUME records, and the book identification data can be found by going to the BOOK record that owns the COPIES set to which each VOLUME belongs.

Although query processing for the network model may seem more complicated than for the hierarchical one, there has been no need to duplicate record-occurrences, and it has never been necessary to resort to a sequential scan of large numbers of records to process a query. Because there is not a single starting point to a network (analagous to the root of a hierarchy), queries based on branch, book, or borrower can all be handled with equal ease. It is important to note, as in example Q1, that the choice of access path can have an enormous impact on the time and cost of processing a query. The developers of the network model were primarily concerned with efficiency. They chose to give the user (or programmer) this degreee of control over DBMS operations because they believed that the DBMS could not make these decisions as well as a person. However, it should be clear that a significant responsibility goes along with this control.

THE RELATIONAL MODEL

Structure

The relational model is the simplest in appearance of the three discussed alternatives. There is only one basic construct, the relation, which is used to represent both entities and relationships. A relation can be thought of as a two-dimensional table. A column in the table corresponds to each attribute of the entity or relationship-type, and there is a row (called a "tuple"—rhymes with "couple") for each occurrence of it. Duplicate tuples are not allowed. An important feature of the relational model is that it has a sound theoretical basis that makes it possible to apply formal, analytical methods to both the study of database management and the design and manipulation of actual databases. An initial set of relations for the library example (Figure 3–5) was produced simply by defining one for each entity-type in Figure 2–9. To decide whether this is a good, or even adequate, design, let us examine it more closely. Because there are no structural links in the relational model corresponding to the parent-child relationships or sets of the hierarchical and network models, any such connections that are needed must be expressed explicitly. For example, the design of Figure 3–5 offers no way of determining the library to which a particular branch belongs or the one that has

```
        LIBRARY   {Name, Director}
        BRANCH    {Name, Address}
        BOOK      {Catalog-No, Title, Author, Publisher}
        BORROWER  {Borrower-No, Name, Address}
        VOLUME    {Copy-No, Borrower-No, Date-Due}
```

FIGURE 3–5 Relational library database—I.

assigned a given card-no to someone. To correct this, an attribute identifying the library must be added to the BRANCH and BORROWER relations.

Extra attributes such as these take the place of the structural links in the other two models. It might seem that this is a wasteful and inelegant approach. Questions of elegance will be deferred for the time being, but as regards waste, it is important to realize that the lines used to show structural connections in the hierarchical and network models are not implemented without cost. One way or another, storage is required to represent them, and some studies of network database design suggest that more storage is needed to implement the "invisible" links between records than for the explicit data-items!

Similarly, there is no information in this database about where a particular book may be found. There are at least two possibilities for dealing with this. The first would add library and branch attributes to the BOOK relation. The difficulty with this approach is that if five branches all had copies of a particular book, five tuples would be needed in the BOOK relation, and they would all contain the same descriptive information. In earlier discussions of the hierarchical and network models, an intuitive argument was put forth against such duplication. Because the relational model has an underlying theory, it is actually possible to prove that bad consequences result from such a course. Informally, this design is poor because it combines in one relation two different kinds of information—descriptions of books and data about where they can be found. This argument will be formalized in Chapter 6, but for the present, let it suffice to observe that a good rule of relational database design is to segregate different kinds of information into separate relations. Thus, the BOOK relation will be left unchanged as a general source of information about books themselves.

In fact, the "things" that are actually found in libraries according to this database design are not books but volumes. Thus, the VOLUME relation appears to be the most appropriate place to include information on location. If a branch has four copies of a book, the location information will be repeated in each of the four VOLUME tuples for that book. However, not only is this apparent duplication not harmful, but it is actually useful! It all depends on correctly interpreting the meaning of the VOLUME relation. It is not stating four times that a particular book is owned by that branch. Rather, it is stating that four *copies* of that book are owned. Furthermore, combined with other attributes of the VOLUME relation, it is actually possible to tell whether any of those copies are currently available for loan. With these changes, the database appears as in Figure 3–6.

The relational database design seems to be acceptable now. However, a check is still needed to ensure that there will be no duplicate tuples. This is done by examining each relation to see if there is an attribute or group of attributes that can be guaranteed to identify uniquely each tuple in the relation. Such an attribute or group of attributes is called a key. If there are several possible keys for a relation, they are referred to as candidate keys and one must be chosen to serve

```
LIBRARY     {Name, Director}
BRANCH      {Lib-name, Br-name, Br-address}
BOOK        {Catalog-no, Title, Author, Publisher}
BORROWER    {Lib-name, Borrower-no, Bor-name, Bor-address}
VOLUME      {Lib-name, Br-name, Catalog-no, Copy-no,
               Borrower-no, Date-due}
```

FIGURE 3–6 Relational library database—II.

as the primary key. Primary keys are used by the DBMS to determine how tuples will be stored and retrieved. They are also used in certain tests that can be applied to a relational database design. This will be discussed further in Chapter 6. Figure 3–7 repeats the final version of the sample relational database design with the key attribute(s) for each relation underlined. The reader is invited to verify that the key attribute(s) will be unique and that no other choice of key would lead to a simpler acceptable design.

Data Manipulation

Relational databases are processed quite differently from hierarchies or networks. Both of those models use data manipulation commands suitable for following the structural connections from one record or segment to another. Retrieval of records (or segments) occurs one at a time. A relation, on the other hand, can be viewed as a collection of records (tuples) and the standard relational operations apply to entire relations.

At the most elementary level, there are only three operations that need to be discussed: projection, selection, and join. *Projection*, when applied to a relation, produces a new relation containing only the columns (attributes) from the original relation specified in the projection request. For example, for a mailing list application, one might use projection to produce a new relation that contained

```
LIBRARY     {Name, Director}
BRANCH      {Lib-name, Br-name, Br-address}
BOOK        {Catalog-no, Title, Author, Publisher}
BORROWER    {Lib-name, Borrower-no, Bor-name, Bor-address}
VOLUME      {Lib-name, Br-name, Catalog-no, Copy-no,
               Borrower-no, Date-due}
```

FIGURE 3–7 Relational library database with keys.

only the Name and Address columns from the BORROWER. If an individual held library cards from several libraries in the system, the relation resulting from this projection operation might be expected to include several tuples with his or her name and address. However, because one of the basic properties of a relation is that there must not be any duplicate tuples, the projection operation will automatically eliminate any that might naturally occur.

The second basic relational operation is *selection*. Just as projection can be used to obtain only certain columns, selection produces a result containing only the rows (tuples) from the original relation that meet some condition. A VOLUME relation that only listed the books in a certain library could be constructed using a selection operation to retrieve only those tuples with a certain value for the Library-Name attribute. Because the results of projection and selection operations are, themselves, relations, it must be obvious that these functions can be applied sequentially to produce a result that is any desired subset of an original relation.

The third basic relational operation, called *join*, is used to combine data from two relations into one. The join operation produces a result relation containing all of the columns from both of its input relations. Tuples from the two input relations are combined by looking for matching values in a specified common attribute of each.

As an example of how join works, suppose that a branch library wanted to print out a catalog for patrons. The VOLUME relation specifies which books are available at each location, but it refers to books only by number. To be useful, a catalog would also have to include the descriptive information from the BOOK relation. The first step would be to use a selection operation to extract from VOLUME only those tuples whose Library-Name and Branch-Name attributes match the branch for which the catalog is to be produced. Because all of the tuples in the result will have the same Library-Name and Branch-Name values, it seems unnecessary to retain these columns. A projection operation can be used to extract just the Catalog-No, Borrower-No, and Date-Due attributes. Call this relation BRANCH—VOLUMES.

If a join operation is now performed on BRANCH-VOLUMES and BOOK, tuples from the two relations will be matched on their common attribute, Catalog-No. The result will contain a tuple for each match that is found. The attributes of the result relation will be all of those from BRANCH-VOLUMES *and* all of those from BOOK, except that Catalog-No, which is found in both relations, will only appear once in the result. This process is illustrated in Figure 3–8.

Most relational database systems actually present users with a data manipulation language quite different from what has just been described. These languages are usually relatively Englishlike and tend to hide the actual structure of the database from the user. They have not been used in this discussion because they are not too useful for understanding the behavior of the relational data model itself. Some of these user-level languages will be discussed in Chapter 12.

BRANCH-VOLUMES

Cat-No	Borrower-No	Date-Due
2124		
2725	122	85-10-04
3750	465	85-10-02
4361		
7094		
7095	122	85-10-04

BOOK

Cat-No	Title	Author	Publisher
1021	Cinderella	Feltham	ABC Books
2124	Estate Tax	Richardson	State Pub
2725	Income Tax	Dexter	State Pub
3101	Three Pigs	Wood	ABC Books
3278	Springtime	Hayes	Stewart
3750	Mod Astrology	Gardner	Univ Press
4361	Dick & Jane	Jansen	Modern
7090	Sys Analysis	Davies	EDP Press
7094	Three Bears	Blaine	ABC Books
7095	Intl Finance	Mitchell	Univ Press
8086	Basic WP	Meredith	EDP Press

Result of JOIN operation

Cat-No	Borrower-No	Date-Due	Title	Author	Publisher
2124			Estate Tax	Richardson	State Pub
2725	122	85-10-04	Income tax	Dexter	State Pub
3750	465	85-10-02	Mod Astrology	Gardner	Univ Press
4361			Dick & Jane	Jansen	Modern
7094			Three Bears	Blaine	ABC Books
7095	122	85-10-04	Intl Finance	Mitchell	Univ Press

FIGURE 3–8 The JOIN operation.

Queries

Q1 Determine the current status of a particular volume, that is, is it available for loan or, if not, who has it and when is it due to be returned.

Again, it is assumed that all the information needed to identify the volume—library-name, branch-name, catalog-no, and copy-no—are known. These values are used by a selection operation on the VOLUME relation to locate the tuple that describes the current status of the specific volume. If it is currently on loan, the only information that will be directly provided about the borrower is his or her Borrower-No. If other attributes are needed, the selection result can be joined to the BORROWER relation.

Q2 Find the branches (of any library) that own a copy of a particular book.

Again, assume that the catalog-no of the book is known. If that were not the case, it would be necessary to perform a selection on the BOOK relation, supplying whatever identifying information was available to obtain the Catalog-No. A selection operation on the VOLUME relation with the Catalog-No supplied will immediately identify all libraries and branches that own copies of that book.

Q3 What are all the books currently held by a particular borrower.

Borrowers are identified by library-name and card-no. If this information is not known, it can be obtained through an appropriate selection on the BORROWER relation. Then, that result could be joined to the VOLUME relation producing a result with a tuple for each volume borrowed by that individual. The books would be identified only by Catalog-No. If more detail was required, this result could be joined to BOOK.

Our discussion of each of the relational queries stopped at the point where a result relation had been produced containing the required information. In most cases, the result also contained columns that were not needed. These can be eliminated by doing a projection on the result.

Two things to note in looking at the handling of these queries in the relational model are the power of the basic operations and the fact that, generally speaking, the user is neither required, nor even permitted, to specify how the query will actually be processed. The only control available to the user lies in the ability to specify the order in which the operations will be performed. Projection and selection operations reduce the amount of data that is being manipulated, whereas joins usually increase it. Because the cost and time required to perform an operation is roughly proportional to the amount of data that must be processed, naive users can follow the simple rule of doing projections and selections before joins whenever possible. As mentioned previously, most commercial relational DBMS's present the user with a somewhat higher level, more Englishlike language than the one described here. In these systems, the sequencing of the basic operations is handled automatically.

INTEGRATING THE DATA MODELS

For a long time, experts in the database field engaged in debate over the comparative merits of the three data models in an attempt to determine which one was "best." That debate produced no clear overall winner. It is obvious that the hierarchical model suffers from some significant inherent shortcomings. However, these have been circumvented in the most popular commercial offerings by adding additional capabilities with the result that these systems no longer adhere strictly to the hierarchical model.

The network and relational models are both free of the difficulties noted for hierarchies. A choice between these two depends largely on one's point of view. The network model may be thought of as a rational extension of the hierarchical one, and it is similar in its focus on individual entity-occurrences which are manipulated one at a time. This model gives the user (or programmer) considerable control over the details of storage allocation and structure and over the specific paths that are used to get from record to record. The relational model, on the other hand, is concerned more with what capabilities the system will provide to users and really has little to say about the underlying mechanisms that will be used to provide them. Many early relational systems were built without paying much attention to these implementation issues; not surprisingly, they tended to be quite inefficient. This led to a widely held view that the relational model was much easier for users to understand but that only the network model could provide the kind of performance required for large applications.

It now seems clear that there is no basic conflict between these two data models. Modern database systems appear to be moving in the direction of using the relational model at the user level while employing complex, networklike techniques internally to achieve good performance. Thus, it might be said that the primary difference between these two data models lies not in the techniques used, but in the extent to which these techniques are visible to the user.

It is a basic tenet of the relational model that the user should be isolated from all of the complex mechanisms used inside the database system. This is partly a philosophical position and partly a belief that the system can make better decisions about access paths and storage structures than the user. Network advocates, on the other hand, tend to believe that a user who understands the environment can guide the system to greater efficiency than could be achieved otherwise. They contend that, for really large applications, maximizing efficiency must be the overriding consideration and that only a clever, experienced human being can determine how to accomplish this. Advocates of the relational approach feel that users will rarely be able to achieve this level of efficiency and that often they will do worse than the database system on its own.

In many respects, this debate is reminiscent of another one between advocates of assembly languages and high-level procedural languages for computer programming. Most of the alleged inefficiencies of high-level language use have now been overcome and the more machine-oriented assembly languages have virtually disappeared from common use. It seems likely that the same type of evolution will take place for data models.

"MODERN" DATA MODELS

The three models just discussed have been around for a long time and have attained something of the stature of classics. Most discussions of data models consider only these three. However, there are other models of more recent vintage that may become important in the future. Most of these are extensions of the basic principles embodied in the relational model. Probably the most common characteristic of the "modern" data models is that they include semantic information—that is, information about what the data actually means—rather than just information about its structure.

The entity-relationship (E-R) model is an example of one that includes some semantic content. The role descriptions associated with relationships and the criterion for including occurrences in an entity- or relationship-set are both ways that the E-R model represents meaning. Such semantic information is necessary to determine whether or not certain database operations are sensible. It also makes it possible to evaluate database designs more effectively than can be done with only structural information.

TERMS TO UNDERSTAND

data model   network model
hierarchical model   relational model

REVIEW QUESTIONS

1. Describe how each of the three primary data models represents each of the following: (a) entity-type, (b) entity-occurrence, (c) relationship-type, (d) relationship-occurrence, (e) attribute.

2. Design a hierarchical database for the library example that is optimized for sample Q2. How well does this database perform on Q1?

3. Design a hierarchical database for the library example that is optimized for sample Q3. How well does this database perform on Q1?

4. Consider a new query for the library database: list the names of all borrowers who currently hold overdue books. Describe algorithms for processing this query using each of the three database designs shown in the chapter. Are there any special difficulties or inefficiencies associated with handling this query?

CHAPTER 4

THE HIERARCHICAL MODEL

BASIC PROPERTIES

The crucial defining characteristic of the hierarchical data model is, of course, that only hierarchical relationships can be directly represented. This is not as much of a limitation as it may appear. In the first place, hierarchical structures are common in the real world. Most organized groups of people, be they families, businesses, clubs, or governments, employ a hierarchical structure. Hierarchies are also used in engineering to describe how a complex system is built up from simpler components (Figure 4–1). In addition, hierarchies can be used to represent structures that are not naturally hierarchical. This usually requires either accepting considerable duplication of information or splitting the structure into several separate pieces. Because the library example used in this book is certainly not a natural hierarchy, it provides an opportunity to see how such transformations are done.

The terminology usually used in connection with the hierarchical model is that of IBM's Information Management System (IMS), a database system that has received wide acceptance since its introduction in the late 1960s. This terminology is occasionally at variance with traditional data processing usage. For example, the collection of fields describing an entity-occurrence, which would normally be called a record, is referred to as a *segment* in IMS. Relationships between entities are represented by the hierarchical connections between segments.

The segment at the very top of a hierarchy is called the *root*. Every segment other than the root must be connected to exactly one at the next higher level, which is its *parent*. Any segment *may* also be connected to others at the next lower level, its *children*. Thus, the relationships that can be directly represented are all one-to-many. If these relationships are thought of as being represented by arrows from the "one" to the "many," then all of the arrows must point away from the root. Every nonroot segment in a hierarchical database *must* have a parent—there can be no "free-floating" segments.

In the preceding chapter, a distinction was made between entity-*types* and entity-*occurrences*. Segment-types and segment-occurrences are distinguished in exactly the same way. The general term "segment" may be used to refer to either a type or occurrence when the precise meaning is clear from the context. For example, a library database would have a segment-type, BOOK, with various attributes, such as title and author. There would be an *occurrence* of the book segment-type for each actual book in the library. Each occurrence would contain the values of the attributes corresponding to that book. Data Structure Diagrams, discussed in Chapter 2, are always drawn in terms of entity-types rather than occurrences.

A Data Structure Diagram that meets all of the constraints of the hierarchical data model is called a *hierarchical definition tree*. An occurrence of the root segment together with all of its descendants is a *database record* and has, of

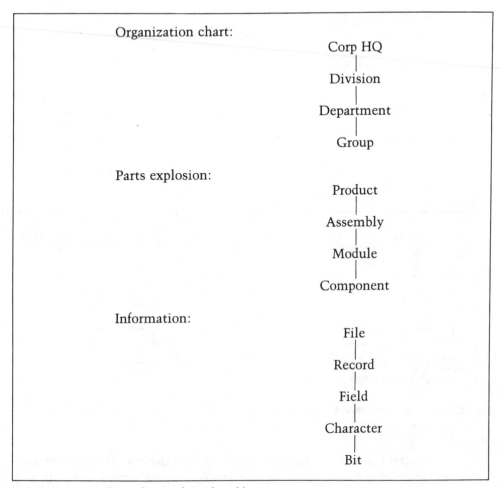

FIGURE 4–1 Some hierarchies in the real world.

course, a hierarchical structure.[1] In any actual application, there would normally be many database records. The complete collection of database records corresponding to a given hierarchical definition tree is called a *logical database* (LDB), and is actually a collection of hierarchies. Transforming a nonhierarchical Data Structure Diagram to fit the hierarchical model may result in splitting it into

---

[1] The use of the term, record, for a complete hierarchy is related to the way hierarchical databases were stored as sequential tape files in the original version of IMS. Once this definition of "record" is accepted, it becomes obvious why "segments" are called that.

Hierarchical definition trees:

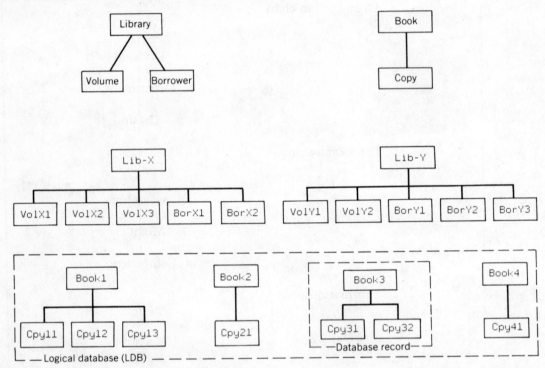

FIGURE 4–2 Hierarchical model terminology.

several hierarchical definition trees. Each of these will have a corresponding LDB. These terms and their interrelationships are illustrated in Figure 4–2.

DATABASE DEFINITION

The process of designing a database must always begin with a study of the users' information requirements. Through a complex process of analysis, the entities, attributes, and relationships that must be represented in the database are determined. Chapter 2 began to discuss this process, and it will be considered further in Chapter 8. Because this chapter and the two following ones are concerned with the relatively technical issues associated with particular data models, it will be assumed that this analysis has been completed and has resulted in the Data Structure Diagram of Figure 2–8, which is reproduced in Figure 4–3.

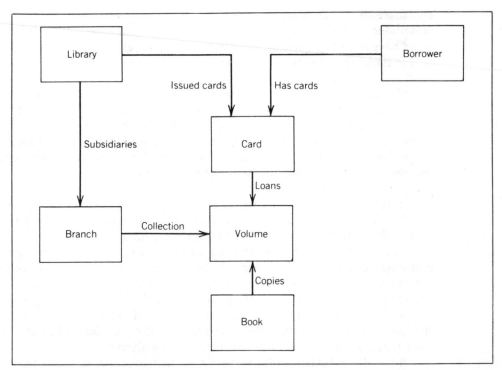

FIGURE 4–3 Data Structure Diagram for library database.

It is immediately apparent that the structure of Figure 4–3 does not meet the requirements of the hierarchical model. In particular, it would seem that the VOLUME segment-type has to have three parents, and the CARD segment-type, two. There are two general techniques that can be used to transform this data structure into an acceptable hierarchical one. The first is duplication. If the data from each BORROWER segment-occurrence are added to all of its CARD children, then the need for the BORROWER segment-type disappears.

Because any individual may be expected to hold only a small number of library cards, the amount of "wasted" space is small. As has been pointed out repeatedly, the management of updates is a more serious concern in such a situation. In this particular case, there is also another difficulty. If information about borrowers appear only under LIBRARY segments, there is no direct way to find out about *all* of the book-borrowing activities of an individual. The portion of the database for each library would have to be examined separately. However, because nearly all of the imaginable uses of such a database do not require linking an individual's activities across libraries, this appears to be a reasonable way to eliminate this nonhierarchical element in the Data Structure Diagram. For the remainder of this chapter, it is assumed that the BORROWER and CARD segment-types have been collapsed into one, which will be called BORROWER, even though it appears in the hierarchy in the spot formerly occupied by the CARD segment-type.

Similarly, the number of parents of a VOLUME can be reduced to two by eliminating the BOOK segment-type entirely and appending its fields to the VOLUME segments. This means that all of the information that specifically describes a book—title, author, publisher, and so on—will be repeated for each *copy* of the book that exists anywhere in the entire library system. This, obviously, increases the storage requirements of the database. Less obvious, but perhaps even more important, it means that updating any of these fields will require changing it in every VOLUME segment-occurrence for that book. This could not only be expensive, but could lead to consistency problems if some update operations fail to catch all of the affected VOLUME segments.

The significance of these problems can only be assessed in the context of a particular situation. For example, if the number of copies of most books in the system is small or if a BOOK segment consists of only a few small fields, the storage penalty for this duplication will not be great. Similarly, the update problem will not be serious if the fields that are to be duplicated are rarely altered. In the library system, for example, it would seem that the fields of a BOOK segment, once entered correctly, would never have to be altered.

It is still necessary to eliminate one of the two remaining parent connections for the VOLUME segment-type. The purpose of these two connections is to associate each volume with the branch that owns it and the individual who has borrowed it. The link to BRANCH essentially represents the catalog for that library. It is a static link, that is created when a book is acquired and destroyed when the book is disposed of. It may be expected to be heavily used. One of these links always exists for every volume in the entire library system. By contrast, the link to BORROWER is dynamic and is utilized much less frequently. It is created when a book is borrowed and destroyed when it is returned. The link exists only for books that are actually out of the library at the moment—usually a relatively small proportion. Thus, it would seem that the inconvenience of losing the BOR-ROWER—BOOK link would be substantially less than that associated with dropping the one connecting BRANCHes to BOOKs.

If the BORROWER—BOOK link is cut, this relationship will have to be represented some other way. One solution would involve adding an additional field, Borrower-No, to each VOLUME segment. This diagram (Figure 4–4) now conforms to the requirements of the hierarchical model. Placing the Borrower-No field in each VOLUME segment actually facilitates queries of the form: "Who currently has a particular volume?" On the other hand, there is no longer an efficient way to find out what volumes are in the hands of a specified borrower.

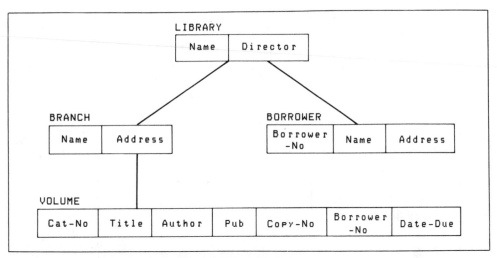

FIGURE 4–4 Library system hierarchical definition tree—I.

Queries of this type would require scanning all VOLUME segments and examining the Borrower-No field of each.

The alternative of retaining the BORROWER—VOLUME connection and eliminating the one between VOLUMEs and BRANCHes could also be considered. This would also produce a logically correct design, but one that would be far clumsier and less efficient in use. Another potential solution would store VOLUME segments under both BRANCH and BORROWER. This, of course, implies considerable duplication, and because loan information is quite dynamic, the problem of maintaining consistency would become severe.

An alternative design that virtually eliminates data duplication is shown in Figure 4–5. In this approach, two hierarchies are created, one with LIBRARYs as the roots and the other with BOOKs. The LIBRARY segment type has BRANCHes and BORROWERs for children as in the previous version. However, no information about books is present in this hierarchy. The VOLUMES-HELD segment-type under BRANCH would consist of the three fields: Catalog-No, Borrower-No, and Date-Due. This segment would perform part of the catalog function, in that it would show directly which books were held by a given branch and what their loan status was. The VOLUMES-BORROWED segment-type under BORROWER would be made up of the fields: Catalog-No, Branch-Name, and Date-Due. It would give a complete statement of each borrower's current dealings.

There is some duplication of information here, but its storage impact is small. The consistency problem is minimized by the simple relationship between the two new segment types. The VOLUMES-HELD segment-occurrences would be

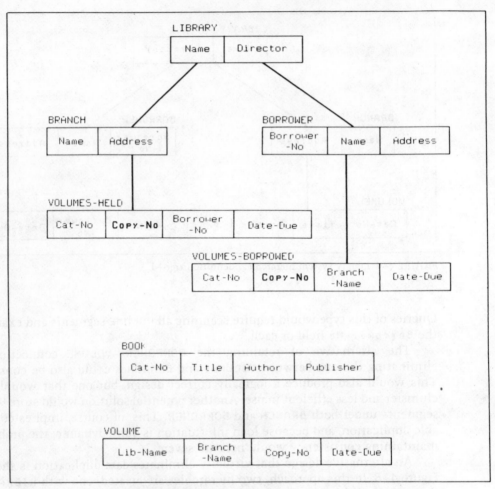

FIGURE 4–5 Library system hierarchical definition tree—II.

created when a branch acquired a volume and would not be deleted until the volume was disposed of. The `Date-Due` and `Borrower-No` fields would be updated each time the book was borrowed or returned. On the other hand, occurrences of the `VOLUMES-BORROWED` record-type would be created when a book was borrowed and destroyed when it was returned.

    All information about books would be contained in a second hierarchy with the `BOOK` segment-type as its root. This segment-type would be identical to the `BOOK` segment-type in the original design. Just below the `BOOK` segment, there would be a new segment-type called `VOLUME` would consist of the fields: `Library-Name`, `Branch-Name`, `Copy-No` and (possibly) `Date-Due`.

This database could be used in the following ways: first, queries concerning the holdings of a particular library or branch or the books currently in the possession of a given borrower would begin in the LDB headed by the relevant LIBRARY segment. The response would be in terms of Catalog-No's because that is the only information about books contained in that LDB. If further information about the books was desired, the Catalog-No's would be used to retrieve appropriate BOOK segments from the second LDB.

Queries concerning the availability of a particular book would begin in the second LDB. The VOLUME children of the selected BOOK segment would show immediately where that book was normally available and (perhaps) what its current loan status was. Whether or not to include the Date-Due field in this LDB and, thus, have an easy way to determine the current status of each volume is not a simple question. The convenience of having it there is obvious. However, the cost of keeping it up to date is probably significant. If the Date-Due field is omitted, the second LDB is almost static. It would have to be updated only to reflect additions and deletions to a library's holdings. On the other hand, if the Date-Due field is included, this LDB would have to be updated each time a book was borrowed or returned.

These are just a few of the many alternatives for this database design that might be considered, depending on the needs of the users and the limitations on the available resources. Throughout the rest of this chapter, the design of Figure 4–5 will be used because it offers somewhat greater scope for exploring the capabilities and limitations of the hierarchical approach.

The actual mechanics of defining a database depend on the particular Database Management System (DBMS) being used. However, the basic information that must be provided will be the same for any hierarchical system. This would include the name of each segment-type and its constituent fields. For each field, it is also necessary to provide some specification of type and format. The hierarchical relationships between segments may be declared either explicitly or implicitly. An example of the explicit approach would be a specification of the form "PARENT = . . ." for each nonroot segment-type. The implicit alternative would involve simply nesting the definition of a segment-type within that of its parent. Figures 4–6 and 4–7 depict definitions of part of the library database using these two approaches.

The order in which segment-types are defined is significant. As will be seen in the following section, there is a comprehensive ordering of all the segment-occurrences in a hierarchical database. Among the occurrences of a single segment-type, this ordering is determined by the value of the key field. The ordering of segment-types, themselves, is on the basis of hierarchical level of course. For segment-types at the same level, the ordering will be the same as the order in which the segment-types were defined. Thus, in the examples shown, Branch segments will precede those for Borrowers, even though they are at the same level.

```
DATA BASE LIBSYS HIERARCHICAL
  SEGMENT LIBRARY
    FIELD LIBNAME, STRING (20):KEY
    FIELD LIBDIR, STRING (30)
    SEGMENT BRANCH
      FIELD BRNAME, STRING (16):KEY
      FIELD BRLOC, STRING (60)
      SEGMENT VOLHELD
      FIELD BKNO, NUMERIC (8,0):KEY
      FIELD BORNO, NUMERIC (6,0)
      FIELD DATEDUE, DATE
    END VOLHELD
  END BRANCH
          ⋮
END LIBRARY
```

FIGURE 4–6 Partial explicit definition of hierarchical library database.

DATABASE MANIPULATION

Hierarchical databases are manipulated by locating the appropriate database record and then following the hierarchical paths to reach a particular segment. Some important characteristics of this process will be illustrated using the example database of Figure 4–8. Suppose that the BORROWER segment-occurrence labeled 37 in Figure 4–8 has been reached—via a GET UNIQUE or GET NEXT operation for

```
DBD    NAME=LIBSYS
SEGM   NAME=LIBRARY, BYTES=50
FIELD  NAME=(LIBNAME, SEQ), BYTES=20, START=1
FIELD  NAME=LIBDIR, BYTES=30, START=21
SEGM   NAME=BRANCH, PARENT=LIBRARY, BYTES=78
FIELD  NAME=(BRNAME, SEQ), BYTES=16, START=1
FIELD  NAME=BRLOC, BYTES=60, START=17
SEGM   NAME=VOLHELD, PARENT=BRANCH, BYTES=20
FIELD  NAME=(BKNO, SEQ), BYTES=8, START=1
FIELD  NAME=BORNO, BYTES=6, START=9
FIELD  NAME=DATEDUE, BYTES=6, START=15
          ⋮
```

FIGURE 4–7 Partial implicit definition of hierarchical library database.

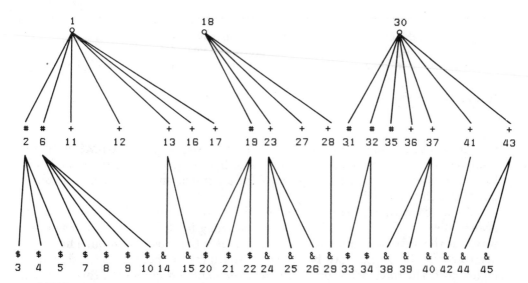

o = LIBRARY segments
# = BRANCH segments
+ = BORROWER segments
$ = VOLUMES-HELD segments
& = VOLUMES-BORROWED segments

FIGURE 4–8 Skeleton of library database.

example. That segment is said to be "selected" and any of its fields may be retrieved or altered.

Selecting one segment also confers special status on a number of others. For example, suppose that a user wanted to get some information about the library where this borrower was registered. There is no possible ambiguity about which LIBRARY segment is the appropriate one—it is clearly determined by the hierarchical relationship. In general, it may be noted that selecting any segment also unambiguously identifies a specific occurrence of each segment-type between the selected one and the root of the logical database. This process is called *qualification*, and the ancestors of a selected segment are said to be *upward qualified*.

Selecting a BORROWER occurrence also uniquely identifies a particular group of VOLUMES-BORROWED segments—those that are children of the selected BOR-ROWER. In general, all segment-occurrences that are descendants of a selected one are described as being *downward qualified*. Upward qualification is a particularly useful concept because it always results in identifying exactly one segment of each type above the selected one and, thus, can unambiguously be used as the basis for retrieval. Downward qualification normally identifies a number of segments of a given type. If a BORROWER segment is selected and the user then asks

1. Visit the current segment if it has not already been visited.
2. Else, visit the leftmost child not previously visited.
3. Else, if no descendants remain to be visited, back to the parent segment. ·

FIGURE 4–9 Preorder traversal algorithm.

for the Catalog-No of the VOLUME-BORROWED segment, the DBMS will not know which one to retrieve if the individual has borrowed more than one book. However, downward qualification is useful for restricting the scope of a subsequent search operation.

As noted earlier, there is an implied ordering among all of the segment occurrences in a hierarchical database. This may be defined in more than one way, but the approach called *preorder traversal* is the most common. The preorder traversal algorithm may be stated in the form of three rules as shown in Figure 4–9. The traversal begins at the root segment and applies the three rules in sequence to *each* segment that is reached. If the roots of each database record are assumed to be children of an imaginary superroot, then all of the segments in a logical database can be ordered using this algorithm. The numbers next to each segment in Figure 4–8 show the ordering implied for them by preorder traversal. It will be noted that the movement is generally in a top-to-bottom, left-to-right direction. An intuitive interpretation of the algorithm can be given by imagining that the hierarchical paths are actually walls. Preorder traversal is the order in which the nodes would be visited by someone beginning at the root and walking with his or her left hand always in contact with the wall.

There are some interesting implications to this ordering. First, it shows how a hierarchical database can be mapped onto a sequential storage medium, such as magnetic tape. As will be seen shortly, the hierarchical retrieval operations make use of this sequencing. So, it is not impossible to imagine processing a hierarchical database on tape, a result that probably seems surprising. Second, every segment-occurrence (except, of course, the very last) has a well-defined next-segment occurrence, and hierarchical DBMS's usually have a retrieval command that allows movement from the currently selected occurrence to the next one. If the BORROWER segment marked 27 in Figure 4–8 is currently selected, then the next segment is the BORROWER segment marked 28. However, its next segment is a VOLUME-BORROWED segment, and its next segment is the LIBRARY segment that is the root of the next database record.

It is convenient to divide all of the various data manipulation commands into two categories, those used to retrieve something from the database and those used to modify it. This latter category includes insertion and deletion of segment occurrences as well as changing the values of fields. Retrieval commands will be discussed first because one usually has to do a retrieval before a modification can be performed—if only to identify the segment that is to be changed. Hierarchical databases typically offer three approaches to locating a particular segment. The first, GET UNIQUE, has the general form:

```
GET UNIQUE segment-type qualification-expression
```

where segment-type identifies the type of segment to be retrieved and the qualification-expression specifies a condition used to determine which segment-occurrence of that type to retrieve. This command is used either to retrieve directly a single segment or to establish an initial position from which to begin sequential processing. Conceptually, it may be thought of as starting at the beginning of the logical database and checking each segment in order until it finds one of the correct type that satisfies the specified condition. For example, if today is January 24, 1985, then

```
GET UNIQUE VOLUME-HELD WHERE DATE-DUE < JANUARY 24, 1985
```

could be used to directly select a VOLUME-HELD segment for an overdue book. It may be observed that although this command is called GET UNIQUE, it is not necessarily the case that there will only be a single segment meeting the specified condition. In this case, the *first* segment, as defined by the preorder traversal algorithm, will always be selected. If no segment in the database meets the condition specified, the DBMS should return a status indication to that effect.

As an aside, it may be noted that the correct functioning of this operation also depends on the DBMS understanding how to interpret the "<" operator in the case of dates. This would likely be specified as part of the definition of the Date value-set if that concept is supported by the DBMS.

The second type of retrieval command in the hierarchical model is GET NEXT. It has three possible forms:

```
GET NEXT segment-type qualification-expression
GET NEXT segment-type
GET NEXT
```

All three of these begin their preorder traversal of the database at the currently selected segment occurrence rather than at the beginning of the physical database. Except for this, the first form performs identically to the GET UNIQUE operation.

The second form simply selects the next segment in the sequence that is of the specified type. The third form selects the next segment in sequence, regardless of its type. One might wonder about the value of this form because a user could not even be sure what type of segment was going to be selected. However, it is precisely this property that is needed to examine a database to find out what is there. Of course, for this command to be generally useful, the DBMS should have a facility that enables the user to determine the type of the currently selected segment so that it can be properly processed.

The use of this general GET NEXT operation can be illustrated by the following outline of a program to dump the entire contents of a hierarchical database:

```
GET UNIQUE . . . */ locate root of first database record
WHILE NOT END OF DATABASE
    GET NEXT */ retrieve subsequent segments
```

It should be pointed out that dumping a database, no matter how trivial the program, is practical only for rather small databases!

The third general type of retrieval command, GET NEXT WITHIN PARENT, is the only one that explictly refers to the hierarchical structure. It has precisely the same three forms as the GET NEXT operation and differs from it in only two ways. First, the scope of GET NEXT WITHIN PARENT is restricted to those segment-occurrences that have been downward qualified by the currently selected segment. Second, the GET NEXT WITHIN PARENT does not change the *selected* segment. Thus, if two GET NEXT WITHIN PARENT operations are executed sequentially, the second will have exactly the same scope as the first. This is in contrast to what would probably be expected, which is that the segment retrieved by the first operation would determine the scope of the second one.

Beginners do not always appreciate that the entire subtree below a selected segment is included in a GET NEXT WITHIN PARENT search, not just the segments one hierarchical level below the selected one. For example, a sequence of GET NEXT VOLUME-HELD WITHIN PARENT operations after a BRANCH has been selected would retrieve all of the books held by that branch. The same sequence after selection of a LIBRARY would retrieve all of the books held by all of the branches of that library. The intervening BRANCH segments would be ignored.

Any operation that is going to modify the database must obviously begin by finding the segment that is to be changed. The various forms of the GET operation can all be used for this purpose. However, one normally has to advise the DBMS at the time the GET is issued that one intends to alter the retrieved segment. The reason for this is that it will probably be necessary to restrict the availability of the segment and its descendants to other users until the modification operation has been completed in order to maintain the integrity of the database. This topic is discussed in considerable detail in Chapter 13. However, it should be clear that any modification activity has the potential to interfere with concurrent processing by other users. This is most easily seen in the context of an application like airline reservations. At a given moment, several agents may be dealing with customers desiring seats on a particular flight. Suppose that each issues a GET for the status of that flight and finds that there is exactly one seat left. If each now proceeds to subtract 1 from the Seats-Remaining field, the same seat will have been sold several times!

The usual solution to this is to require that a retrieval operation that *may* result in a modification indicate that fact so that potentially conflicting usage by others can be prevented. The intention to update is usually indicated through use of a variation of one of the normal GET commands, often specified as GET HOLD. In the hierarchical model, it is necessary to lock all of the descendant segments as well because, if the update operation results in deletion of the held segment, all of its descendants will also disappear. The cancellation of an entire flight would be an example of this in the airline example.

Insertion of a new segment-occurrence requires a slightly different procedure. In this case, it is necessary to specify *where* the new segment is to go. This is done by selecting the parent of the new segment. In addition, precautions must be taken to make sure that the parent is not deleted by another user in between the time it is selected and the insertion performed. Thus, this is another case where the GET HOLD form must be used.

EVALUATION

There are two primary advantages to the hierarchical database model—its relative simplicity and the fact that it provides a natural representation for the many real-world systems that are inherently hierarchical.

The main disadvantage of this model lies in the awkwardness of representing any real-world system that is *not* truly hierarchical. It is usually necessary in such a case either to resort to extensive duplication or to accept that certain types of queries will be time-consuming and expensive to process. Furthermore, many applications that *appear* to be hierarchical turn out, on closer examination, to be somewhat more complex.

For example, a university registration system seems to be a natural hierarchy, consisting (in a simple case) of departments, courses, and students. A hierarchical database with department segments as roots will be quite efficient for producing lists of all the students enroled in a certain course. However, preparation of a transcript listing all the courses taken by a specified student will be quite inefficient. If the hierarchy is turned upside down so that student segments are roots, transcript production becomes simple, but printing class lists is costly.

This illustrates the inherent asymmetry of the hierarchical model. Queries that proceed from the root toward the leaves are efficient to process, whereas those that must be handled in the opposite direction tend to be extremely inefficient. To make matters worse, this distinction is often not apparent to users, who, therefore, may have great difficulty in determining which queries formulations should be avoided.

TERMS TO UNDERSTAND

segment

root

parent

segment-type

segment-occurrence

hierarchical definition tree

database record

logical database (LDB)

upward qualification

downward qualification

preorder traversal

REVIEW QUESTIONS

1. Employees work for managers who, in turn, work for other managers. How would you represent this relationship in a hierarchical model?

2. Employees work on several projects, and a project is worked on by several employees. Represent this situation as a hierarchical structure.

3. Design a hierarchical database for the family tree database of Chapter 2, Question 7. Show the hierarchical structure and list the fields for each segment-type.

4. Design a hierarchical database for the Last National Bank (LNB) (Chapter 2, Question 5). Explain how you have resolved the problem of representing this situation as a hierarchy and why you have selected that particular approach.

5. Design a hierarchical database for university administration that can be used to prepare the following reports:

   • Student timetables

   • Class lists

   • Faculty teaching schedules

   Assume that the university consists of departments that offer courses. Several sections of a course may be offered. A student is registered in a particular department but may take courses in other departments. Faculty members may teach courses in departments other than their primary one.

CHAPTER 5

THE NETWORK MODEL

BASIC PROPERTIES

The network data model may be thought of as a generalization of the hierarchical model formed by removing the restriction that each segment must have exactly one parent. There have been many implementations of database systems based on network concepts. However, the term is most commonly used to refer to the specification developed by the Data Base Task Group (DBTG) of the Conference on Data Systems Languages (CODASYL). CODASYL is a cooperative undertaking of a group of computer manufacturers and large users and is best known for its sponsorship of the project that developed COBOL. In fact, CODASYL's DBTG was originally established to investigate adding list-handling facilities to COBOL.

This chapter will employ the terminology of the DBTG model and generally follow its specifications. However, because of the overwhelming complexity of the DBTG proposal and the mass of low-level detail it contains, only its most important features will be covered. It is worth mentioning that, despite the DBTG proposal's great complexity, it does not include a number of capabilities that might reasonably be part of a network database model. The DBTG was strongly influenced by organizations with practical concerns for the efficient processing of large databases. This bias led to the intentional omission of a number of useful features because they did not appear to have efficient implementations. In addition, conceptually desirable properties, such as data independence, were generally given a lower priority than efficiency of processing. This preoccupation with efficiency has also resulted in the dropping of certain original proposals from later versions of the DBTG specification. Some of these will, nevertheless, be discussed in this chapter because of their inherent interest and relevance to the network approach to databases.

Records

In DBTG terminology, the collection of fields describing an entity, which would be called a segment in the hierarchical model, is called a record. This is, of course, the conventional nondatabase term as well. The fields themselves, which hold attribute values, are referred to as data-items.

A network database record can have a rather complex structure. The traditional data processing concept of the repeating group, for example, is permitted. In the library database, this could be used to store information about all the books an individual currently has on loan directly in the BORROWER record. A repeating group could be defined consisting of the data-items Catalog-No and Date-Due. One such group would be created in an individual's BORROWER record each time a book was borrowed and would be deleted when the book was returned.

This would probably be an appropriate solution in a conventional, nondata-base environment. However, it does not seem to be the best way to deal with this situation if a database system is available. It requires that the application program deal with a level of complexity in the record structure that can better be left to the Database Management System (DBMS). Even more serious, important information about *books*—who has them and when they are due to be returned—is now hidden in BORROWER records. There would be no simple way to find out the current status of a particular book. This is an example of an anomaly that can be discussed more naturally in the context of the relational database model, but it is just as troublesome in either of the other models. Because of such difficulties, repeating groups will not be used in any of our network model examples.

The DBTG specifications also provided for another level of complexity in the design of records through the ability to specify that the value of a data-item is to be derived from other data-items in the same or related records. An arbitrary procedure may be used to express the way in which the derivation is to be performed.

If a derived data-item is actually stored, the derivation specification becomes a kind of integrity constraint, assuring that a specified relationship will be maintained between the given data-items. However, it is also possible to specify that the derived data-item should not be actually stored, but rather computed from the underlying data each time it is accessed. This saves storage and data duplication, but at the cost of additional computation. The choice between these two approaches depends on such issues as the relative frequency of updating and retrieving and the relative cost of storage and computation. Because almost all of the derivation techniques depend on set relationships, a more detailed discussion of this topic will be deferred until after the properties of sets have been explored.

Sets

The most distinctive aspect of the network model is the construct called a *set*, which is used for representing relationships. *Set* is, of course, a term with a specific meaning in mathematics. The DBTG notion of a set is something quite different, and it is perhaps unfortunate that this term was chosen. Some authors have suggested alternative names, such as *data structure sets* or *owner-coupled sets*. However, none of these more elaborate terms seems to have attracted much of a following.

The network set is a direct representation of a $1:N$ relationship. It consists of one record, called the *owner* and zero or more records, called *members*. It is similar to the relationship in the hierarchical model between a segment and its immediate children. The important differences are the following: first, it is permissible in the network model for a record to exist without being a member of any set. This is analagous to a hierarchical segment not being attached to any parent, which, of course, is not permitted. Second, a network record can be a member of several different sets at the same time. This is equivalent to having multiple parents. The only restrictions are that a record may not belong to more than one set of a given type at any one time and that the owner and members of a set may not be of the same type.

In a hierarchical database, it is possible (indeed, likely) that a segment will have children of different types. For example, in the library example, LIBRARY segments have children of type BRANCH *and* children of type BORROWER. Because a network set has been described as equivalent to the relationship between a segment and its immediate children, it must seem that a set can have members that are not all of the same type. This was, in fact, true of the original DBTG specification, but it does not appear to be a particularly useful feature and has been dropped in later versions.

The set construct is normally used to group together all the records (members) that have some particular relationship to another record (the owner). BRANCHes and BORROWERs are both related to LIBRARYs, but the nature of the relationship is different. Thus, two distinct sets would be established. Both would be owned by LIBRARY records. BRANCH records would be members of one of the sets and BORROWER records of the other one. Sets are given names that can (and should) be used to indicate the relationship that the set represents.

It is always important in discussing databases to distinguish between *types* of things and specific *occurrences* of them. This is especially critical for the network model. Although record- and set-occurrences are the things that physically exist in a database, certain control information is maintained at the level of record and set *types*. For example, the Library database contains a record-type, BRANCH, and another one, BOOK, and a set-type, COLLECTION, which relates the two. Record-occurrences are instances of the corresponding types containing actual data. Thus, there would be a BOOK occurrence for *Oliver Twist*. A set-occurrence automatically exists for each occurrence of the owner record-type. This means that each BRANCH will have a corresponding COLLECTION set, even if, at some particular moment, that branch does not have any books. Record-occurrences are the units that are transferred between the database and applications programs. Thus, the network model, like the hierarchical one, is characterized by a one-record-at-a-time mode of processing.

Currency

In the hierarchical model, only one segment can be "selected" at a time. The network model, on the other hand, is able to keep track of a number of distinct positions simultaneously. It is possible to select a BORROWER record-occurrence, for example, then select a BOOK occurrence without giving up the previously selected BORROWER, and then perform some operation that simultaneously involves the two occurrences. Because many record-occurrences can be selected and available for processing at the same time, it is necessary to have some method for keeping track of all of them. This is accomplished through the use of *currency indicators*, which identify particular records.

There is a currency indicator associated with each record-*type* and with each set-*type*. There is also a currency indicator for each realm and one for the run-unit.[1] Currency indicators may be thought of as pointers to particular record-occurrences. For example, the currency indicator for the record-type, BOOK, will always point to some actual BOOK record. The currency indicator for a *set-type* also points to some particular *record-occurrence*. The record-occurrence must be an instance of either the owner or member record-type for that set-type. Thus, a set-type currency indicator serves two functions. It identifies a particular instance of the set-type as well as some particular record-occurrence associated with that set-occurrence. The record pointed to by a currency indicator is referred to as the "current" of that particular record- or set-type.

Currency indicators are changed as a byproduct of most database manipulation operations. For example, when a record-occurrence is accessed, it normally becomes the "current" of the run-unit, of its realm, of its record-type, and of any set-types in which it participates as either owner or member.[2] The currency indicators provide a convenient way to refer implicitly to particular record-occurrences so that they do not have to be identified in detail in each database manipulation operation. The rules governing updating of currencies are intended to ensure that the records most likely to be referred to at a given moment are "current." However, because the effect of most operations depends critically on the values of the currency indicators, it can be difficult to determine what a database manipulation program will do just by reading it.

DATABASE DEFINITION

The DBTG proposal includes a special language called a Data Definition Language (DDL) for expressing database definitions. The overall definition of a network database is called a *schema* and consists of four major sections:

- An introductory section
- A REALM section

---

[1] A realm is a logical subdivision of a database, which will be explained further in the section on database definition. "Run-unit" is a term used in the DBTG model to refer to the overall execution of a program. It is roughly comparable to a "job" in many systems.

[2] There are circumstances in which it is desirable to access a record without changing all of the currency indicators. The DBTG specification includes a provision for inhibiting the updating of currency indicators. This is discussed in the section on database manipulation.

- A RECORD section
- A SET section

The introductory section names the schema and specifies global controls over access to, and modification of, the schema. For example, a user or program may have to know a certain password to invoke the schema and another password to be able to modify it. Permission to invoke a schema is needed to be able to do anything to the database described by that schema.

The REALM section specifies the realms that are defined for this database. A realm is a logical subset of the entire database; it consists of all the occurrences of one or more specified record-types. As many realms as desired may be defined, and they may overlap in the sense that a single record-type may be specified as belonging to more than one realm. The realm concept is significant for access control and for processing efficiency. Specific access authorization procedures can be associated with a realm in addition to those specified for the schema as a whole. Thus, highly sensitive information can be placed in a separate realm and subjected to special controls. Realms can also be assigned to specific physical storage devices. This capability could be used to ensure that frequently accessed data is stored on a high-performance device, whereas information that is less frequently used could be stored on a less expensive one.[3] The realm concept is one example of DBTG facilities for tuning system performance at the physical hardware level. In most other database models, the designer does not have facilities for specifying the physical location of data.

Record Definition

The RECORD section of the schema contains a statement defining each record-type and describing the data-items that comprise it. The data-items are described by specifying their names, types, and sizes in a manner similar to COBOL Data Division specifications. A straightforward version of the Record Section of the library database schema is shown in Figure 5–1.

If a key is defined for a given record-type, that information is also included in the record section. Keys are not required in the network model, but if they are being used to facilitate retrieval, certain information must be provided. For example, the DBMS must be told what to do about attempts to store a record-occurrence whose key value is already present in the database. If duplicates are disallowed, the system will reject an attempt to store a record with a nonunique key; hence, the key can be used as the basis for storing and locating record-

---

[3] As with most things in life, there is a definite relationship between the cost and performance of data storage devices: the higher the performance, the higher the cost. For an organization with a large database and a variety of available storage technologies, there could be significant benefits associated with controlling which data is stored where.

```
RECORD NAME IS LIBRARY
   KEY LIBKEY IS LIB-NAME ASCENDING
      DUPLICATES ARE NOT ALLOWED.
   02 LIB-NAME                          .              PIC X(25).
   02 LIB-DIRECTOR                                     PIC X(20).
RECORD NAME IS BRANCH
   KEY BRKEY IS BR-NAME ASCENDING
      DUPLICATES ARE NOT ALLOWED.
   02 BR-NAME                                          PIC X(12).
   02 BR-LOC                                           PIC X(30).
RECORD NAME IS BOOK
   KEY BRKEY IS BK-NO ASCENDING
      DUPLICATES ARE NOT ALLOWED
      FREQUENCY OF DIRECT RETRIEVAL IS HIGH.
   02 BK-NO                                            PIC 9( 7).
   02 BK-TITLE                                         PIC X(40).
   02 BK-AUTHOR                                        PIC X(20).
   02 BK-PUBLISHER                                     PIC X(12).
RECORD NAME IS BORROWER
   KEY BORKEY IS BOR-NO ASCENDING
      DUPLICATES ARE NOT ALLOWED
      FREQUENCY OF DIRECT RETRIEVAL IS HIGH.
   02 BOR-NO                                           PIC 9( 6).
   02 BOR-NAME                                         PIC X(20).
   02 BOR-ADDRESS
      03 STREET                                        PIC X(20).
      03 CITY                                          PIC X(20).
RECORD NAME IS VOLUME
   02 COPY-NO                                          PIC 9( 2).
   02 DATE-DUE                                         PIC 9( 6).
```

FIGURE 5–1 Record section of library schema.

occurrences. If duplicates *are* allowed, the user must specify whether new record-occurrences are to be stored in front or in back of existing ones with the same key.

It is possible to specify that a key is a composite of two or more data-items. The uniqueness property, then, refers to the composite, not to the individual, data-items that comprise it. More than one data-item or composite may be specified as unique keys. In that case, one of the keys will be used as the basis for storing record-occurrences, and the others will be used to construct inverted lists (See Appendix 1) for accessing.

The record section of a schema may also include statements indicating that a particular record-type is subject to an unusually high frequency of retrieval, either sequentially, directly, or both. This information will be used by the DBMS in deciding how and where to store these record-occurrences.

Set Definition

Sets are defined by specifying the names of the owner and member record-types. Information must also be provided to guide the DBMS in determining how actually to implement each type of set. This additional information includes:

- The logical ordering of member records within the set
- Rules governing the insertion and removal of members
- Rules for determining which occurrence of a set into which to place a member (needed if the DBMS is to handle insertions automatically).

Part of the set section of the library schema is shown in Figure 5–2.

The logical ordering specified for a set does not necessarily have anything to do with how the member record-occurrences are actually stored. It merely specifies the order in which they will be retrieved by a sequence of GET NEXT WITHIN SET operations.

```
SET NAME IS BRANCHES
   OWNER IS LIBRARY
     ORDER IS SORTED BY DEFINED KEYS.
   MEMBER IS BRANCH
     INSERTION IS AUTOMATIC
     RETENTION IS FIXED.
   KEY IS ACENDING BR-NAME
     DUPLICATES ARE NOT ALLOWED.
   SET SELECTION IS BY LIB-NAME IN LIBRARY.
                                           ⋮

SET NAME IS LOANS
   OWNER IS BORROWER
     ORDER IS SORTED BY DEFINED KEYS.
   MEMBER IS VOLUME
     INSERTION IS MANUAL
     RETENTION IS OPTIONAL.
   KEY IS ASCENDING DATE-DUE IN VOLUME
     DUPLICATES ARE LAST.
   SET SELECTION IS BY BOR-NO IN BORROWER.
```

FIGURE 5–2 Sample set definitions for library database.

There are two basic alternatives for ordering members within a set. The first is in sorted order according to a specified key, which may be composite. Either ascending or descending sequence may be specified; in the case of a composite key, the order may be ascending on some data-items and descending on others. The second possibility is in chronological order, where the position of a record in a set is determined at the time the record is initially inserted. There are four options for this type of ordering. INSERTION IS FIRST places the newly inserted record at the beginning of the set. INSERTION IS LAST places it after the last previous member. The other two possibilities, PRIOR and NEXT, insert the new member, respectively, in front of, or behind, the "current" member.

The second piece of information that must be provided for the member record-type is its so-called membership class, which consists of two parts—an insertion class and a retention class. The insertion class specifies how a record-occurrence gets to be included in a set for the first time while the retention class is concerned with what happens to it after its initial insertion.

If the insertion class is MANUAL, then records of this type do not become members of sets unless they are explicitly inserted using the CONNECT verb. (Data manipulation commands are discussed in the following section.) If, on the other hand, AUTOMATIC insertion is specified, then the record will automatically be placed in a set when it is first stored in the database. The specific occurrence of the relevant set-type that will receive the new member is determined by the SET SELECTION clause discussed below.

The retention class may be FIXED, MANDATORY, or OPTIONAL. FIXED means simply that once a record has been placed in a set it cannot be removed, except by deleting the record from the database entirely. MANDATORY retention means that this record once entered into a set must always belong to *some* occurrence of that set-type, but not necessarily the same occurrence forever. That is, it cannot be the object of a DISCONNECT operation, but it may be moved from one occurrence of the set-type to another using RECONNECT. The third choice, OPTIONAL, allows a record to be removed from a set-occurrence at will.

In the library database, for example, a VOLUME record must always be associated with the BOOK record of which it is an instance. This implies a membership class of AUTOMATIC, FIXED for the COPIES set. It is probably also true that a volume, once acquired, must always belong to some branch of a library. However, because it is certainly possible to imagine transferring volumes from one branch to another, AUTOMATIC, MANDATORY would seem to be the appropriate membership class for the COLLECTION set. On the other hand, a volume is associated with a borrower only when it has been taken out. Thus, a MANUAL, OPTIONAL membership class for the LOANS set allows a volume to be inserted in a set-occurrence when someone takes it out and removed from the set when it is returned. A VOLUME that is not currently on loan would not be a member of any LOANS set.

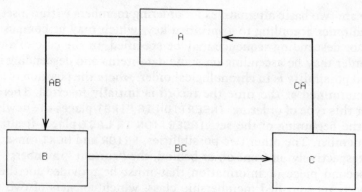

FIGURE 5–3 Example of cyclic sets.

An important use of the MANUAL insertion class is to break cycles. It is quite possible to define a network database, like the one in Figure 5–3, where record-type A is the owner of set-type AB with member record, B; Record-type B, in turn, owns set BC with member C; and C owns set CA with member A. If all three of these sets are assigned AUTOMATIC insertion class, it will be impossible to ever get any data into the database. The reader is invited to verify that this is, indeed, the case. The impasse can be broken by assigning one of the sets MANUAL membership. This will allow the first record to be inserted, and everything can proceed smoothly after that. It does not make any difference, in principle, which set in a cycle is given MANUAL membership, but in most actual cases, one candidate will suggest itself as being most suitable.

When a newly stored record is to be placed in a set by virtue of an AUTOMATIC insertion class, the DBMS must be able to determine which occurrence of the specified set-type to use. There are also a number of other situations, some of which will arise in the following section, where the system needs to be able to select a set-occurrence automatically.

The rules for accomplishing this are specified in the SET SELECTION clause associated with each set definition. There are three possibilities: if nothing else is specified, the system will simply use the "current" of the specified set-type. The user is responsible for ensuring that the appropriate set-occurrence is made current before it is needed. The second alternative is to identify the owner of the desired set-occurrence. The SET SELECTION clause, in this case, specifies a location in the User Work Area (UWA)[4] where the key of the owner record can be found. This is sufficient to identify an owner occurrence and there is a 1:1 correspondence between owner records and set-occurrences.

---

[4] The user work area (UWA) is an area in each user program that is used for communication between the program and the DBMS. It is discussed further later.

The third approach to selecting a set is to have a data-item in the member record, itself, that identifies the owner record. For example, if the L i b r a r y - N a m e data-item appeared in BRANCH records, it could be used to determine the appropriate SUBSIDIARIES set for each BRANCH record. This appears to be the simplest method of all. However, it has certain drawbacks that must be considered. First, it is clearly redundant to have this data-item in the BRANCH records because it duplicates information represented by the set linkage. Such duplication may sometimes be used for the sake of efficiency, but it is not without risk. Consider, for example, the implications of altering the value of L i b r a r y - N a m e in a BRANCH record after it has been inserted in a SUBSIDIARIES set on the basis of this value.

Derived Data-Items

The advantage of having L i b r a r y - N a m e available in a BRANCH record, even though it is clearly redundant, suggests the value of being able to include in record definitions data-items that are required to relate to certain other data-items in a specified way. The DBTG proposal accomplishes this through the device of *derived data-items*. This capability will be discussed in some detail because it is a powerful general capability that could also be employed in other data models. When a derived data-item is included as part of some record definition, the description specifies how its value is to be determined.

Two examples will be given to illustrate the use of derived data-items. The first considers the addition of a data-item, F i r s t - D u e , to the BORROWER record-type to contain the earliest date on which a borrower must return something to the library. Obviously, the value of this data-item would have to match the D a t e - D u e in one of the VOLUME records in the borrower's LOANS set—in particular, it would have to be the earliest D a t e - D u e of all those in the set. To accomplish this, a program would have to be written that searches the LOANS set to find the earliest D a t e - D u e. This program would then be made available to the DBMS and identified in the schema. The DBMS automatically invokes the program whenever necessary to maintain the correct value of the derived data-item. This could occur either when any data that could effect the derived item changes or simply whenever the derived item is to be retrieved. Such procedures, called *database procedures*, can be written in any standard programming language supported by the DBMS implementation and can refer to data-items in the record where the derived data-item appears or in any records that are members of sets owned by that one. In the library example, the F i r s t - D u e data-item could be defined in the schema by the statement:

```
FIRST-DUE IS ACTUAL RESULT OF FIND-FIRST-DATE ON MEMBERS OF
LOANS.
```

It is assumed that FIND-FIRST-DATE is the name of a user-supplied program that can traverse the members of the LOANS set and return as its value the earliest Date-Due encountered.[5]

The appearance of the specification ACTUAL in this definition indicates that the First-Due data-item should actually appear in each BORROWER record and that each time there is any change to the LOANS set owned by a BORROWER, its First-Due data-item will be updated. In this case, the definition of First-Due may be thought of as an integrity constraint specifying how the value of this real data-item is to relate to the values of the real Date-Due data-items in the member records of the LOANS set.

Alternatively, the First-Due data-item could be defined to be VIRTUAL. In this case, no storage would be allocated to it in the BORROWER records and no additional computation would be required when the LOANS set was updated. Instead, whenever the First-Due data-item was retrieved, the defining database procedure would be executed to determine its value based on the current contents of the LOANS set.

It is obvious that the ACTUAL alternative would be preferred if this information were retrieved frequently and updated rarely. If the opposite behavior was expected, then it would make more sense to define the derived data-item as VIRTUAL.

A slightly different approach is available for the case where the derived data-item is in a *member* record of a set whose *owner* contains the desired information. For example, a situation might frequently arise in the library database where a VOLUME record has been located by virtue of its association with a BORROWER and it is necessary to determine the identity of the branch from which the volume was borrowed.

This can obviously be accomplished by simply requesting the owner record of the COLLECTION set to which the VOLUME record belongs. However, this would imply another database operation that will not be without cost, will complicate the application program somewhat, and will have the almost certainly undesired side effect of altering certain currency indicators.

These difficulties could be avoided by adding a Branch-ID data-item to the VOLUME record-type and storing the required information in each VOLUME record. Because a library database will include a large number of VOLUME records, a significant amount of additional storage would be used that would not provide any information that is not already available.

The DBTG proposal offers a way around both of these problems. The Branch-ID data-item could be defined as:

---

[5] The word "user" in this discussion probably does not refer to the end user of the application. Most database procedures would be constructed as part of the database definition process.

```
BRANCH-ID IS VIRTUAL AND SOURCE IS BR-NAME OF OWNER OF
COLLECTION.
```

No storage will be allocated, but the necessary information will be retrieved on demand and without altering any currency indicators.

A specification of this type may also be taken as a warning to the DBMS that this particular member-owner path will be traversed relatively frequently, and the system should use this information in selecting an implementation strategy for the set. This is another example of the capabilities provided in the network model for the database designer to influence the physical behavior of the system.

Schemas and Subschemas

One aspect of the DBTG proposal that was not commonly found in previous database systems was the idea of separating the overall definition of the database, the schema, from the definition of a particular user's view of the database (called a subschema). There are advantages to this approach for both the users and the system administrators. For example, a user with a particular task can be given a view of the database tailored specifically to his or her needs. He or she is spared having to even know about anything in the database that is not relevant to the task at hand. In addition, a subschema can present a data structure differing in significant ways from that of the underlying schema. Thus, although the data will actually be stored in the manner deemed most efficient overall, it can be made to appear to individual users to be structured appropriately for their particular applications.

The subschema idea also provides an effective (although not very subtle) way of dealing with some aspects of database security. This arises from the fact that all of a user's database operations are specified in terms of his or her subschema. There is no way to even construct a query for something that is not in the subschema. There is not even any way to determine if something is in the database if it is not described in the user's subschema.

Figure 5–4 shows a subschema of the library database that might be appropriate for users in the cataloging department of a single library. Only the BRANCH, BOOK, and VOLUME record-types are included, along with the sets that relate them. In general, a subschema can omit set-types and/or record-types that are present in the underlying schema as long as consistency is maintained. That is, if a record-type is omitted, then any set-types in which that record appears must also be omitted.

It is also possible to leave selected data-items out of a record-type, again as long as they are not needed to maintain subschema consistency. This feature is often used to support database security objectives. For example, the subschema for most users of a personnel database might exclude the salary data-item. The

```
RECORD NAME IS BRANCH
  KEY BRKEY IS BR-NAME ASCENDING
    DUPLICATES ARE NOT ALLOWED.
  02 BR-NAME                                      PIC X(12).
  02 BR-LOC                                       PIC X(30).
RECORD NAME IS BOOK
  KEY BKKEY IS BK-NO ASCENDING
    DUPLICATES ARE NOT ALLOWED
  FREQUENCY OF DIRECT RETRIEVAL IS HIGH.
  02 BK-NO                                        PIC 9( 7).
  02 BK-TITLE                                     PIC X(40).
  02 BK-AUTHOR                                    PIC X(20).
  02 BK-PUBLISHER                                 PIC X(12).
RECORD NAME IS VOLUME
  02 COPY-NO                                      PIC 9( 2).
  02 DATE-DUE                                     PIC 9( 6).
SET NAME IS VOL-HELD
  OWNER IS BRANCH
    ORDER IS SORTED BY DEFINED KEYS.
  MEMBER IS VOLUME
    INSERTION IS MANUAL
    RETENTION IS OPTIONAL.
  KEY IS ASCENDING DATE-DUE IN VOLUME
    DUPLICATES ARE LAST.
    SET SELECTION IS BY BR-NAME IN BRANCH.

SET NAME IS CATALOG
  OWNER IS BOOK
    ORDER IS SORTED BY DEFINED KEYS.
  MEMBER IS VOLUME
    INSERTION IS MANUAL
    RETENTION IS OPTIONAL.
  KEY IS ASCENDING COPY-NO IN VOLUME
    DUPLICATES ARE LAST.
    SET SELECTION IS BY BOOK-NO IN BOOK.
```

FIGURE 5-4 Subschema for library cataloging function.

main difficulty with this approach to access control is its all-or-nothing character. It makes no provision, for example, for giving a manager access to the salaries of members of his or her own department without also granting access to those of other employees. Access control at this level of selectivity is possible using the network model, but not through the subschema mechanism. Access control is discussed in detail in Chapter 13.

The structure of a subschema is quite similar to that of a schema. Of course, because a subschema will be referenced by users of the database, it must have a syntax that is compatible with some programming language. As mentioned previously, the network database model was specified by a group with strong connections to COBOL. Thus, it used COBOL as the host environment for designing the first subschema facility. Subschema DDL's suitable for use with FORTRAN and PL/1 have also been proposed.

A COBOL subschema consists of three divisions. The Title Division names the subschema and specifies the schema on which it is based. The Mapping Division defines any changes of name that may be either desired or necessary. Because a subschema refers to only a portion of the whole database, different names for record, sets, and/or data-items may sometimes be more appropriate. More significant, naming restrictions in programming languages may force the use of names different from those in the underlying schema. The most obvious example of this would be the limitation of six characters on the size of FORTRAN variable names.

The final division of a subschema, the Structure Division, looks very much like a schema, containing a Realm Section, a Record Section, and a Set Section. Data-items may have different types than in the underlying schema, and they may appear in a record in a different order. It is also possible to specify a SET SELECTION clause for a set that will override the one in the schema.

User Work Area (UWA)

The DBTG proposal includes the notion of setting up an area in each user's memory for communication between the user's application program and the DBMS. This area is called the User Work Area (UWA) and is capable of holding one occurrence of each record-type defined in that user's subschema. This part of the UWA essentially acts as a buffer between the DBMS and the user program. Results of DBMS retrieval operations are placed here and it is also where the DBMS will expect to find information to be inserted into the database. Other portions of the UWA are used for communication between the DBMS and the user program, including the passing of status information and parameter values.

DATABASE MANIPULATION

The DBTG proposal also envisioned a special language for specifying the operations to be performed on a database. This Data Manipulation Language (DML), like the subschema DDL, must be compatible with the host programming language with which it will be used. The DBTG specification includes a DML for use with COBOL. It consists of less than 10 basic functions, but some of these have many optional forms. Because the DML is intended to be embedded within a standard programming language, any proposals for specific DMLs would have to be approved by the international standards organizations that control the development of the various programming languages.

Because DML facilities have not yet been included in any official language standards, two options are available to implementors of DBTG database systems. The first is to construct the DML as a set of subroutines that can be invoked using the standard calling facilities of the host language. The other is to embed the DML statements directly in the host language and require that programs be processed by a special precompiler that eliminates the nonstandard statements and replaces them by subroutine calls.

Retrieval Functions

If one DML statement can be singled out as being the most important, it would have to be FIND. The general form of this statement is:

```
FIND record-selection-expression
```

The function of FIND is to locate a record-occurrence in the database and make it the "current" of the run-unit. That is, the currency indicator for the run-unit will be set to point to this record-occurrence. Other currency indicators will also be changed by a FIND command, but because most DML statements refer implicitly to the current of run-unit, that currency is the most important one. The record-selection-expression (r-s-e) designates which record is to be located. Seven different r-s-e forms were originally specified by the DBTG, but one has since been abandoned. Examples of the remaining six forms are presented below. The intention is to illustrate typical query forms rather than to be formally precise. The first form of the FIND command is illustrated by the following program fragment:

```
MOVE 'WAR AND PEACE' TO TITLE IN UWA-BOOK.
FIND ANY BOOK USING TITLE IN UWA-BOOK.
```

The first statement is standard COBOL and stores the desired title in the appropriate place in the UWA. The FIND then locates a BOOK record using the value in the UWA. If there happened to be more than one BOOK record with this title, the particular one to be located would depend on the approach taken by the DBMS implementor. It is important to note that no data is actually retrieved as a result of executing a FIND statement. Its sole function is to alter currency indicators. The second form of FIND is closely related to the first:

```
FIND DUPLICATE BOOK USING TITLE IN UWA-BOOK.
```

Assuming that one BOOK record has already been found using the first form, this statement will find another record-occurrence having the same title. Repeatedly executing this statement (e.g., in a program loop) will eventually locate all of the records satisfying the r-s-e without retrieving any of them more than once. However, the exact order in which the records will be retrieved is left to the implementors of the DBMS.

Execution of this statement when no more BOOK records qualify for retrieval will store a nonzero value into the UWA location, DB-STATUS. Every data manipulation language statement sets the value of DB-STATUS as a means of reporting to the user conditions that may require attention. A DB-STATUS value of zero means that the operation completed normally. Any other value indicates an exceptional condition of some sort. The application programmer is expected to provide special procedures to deal with all of the nonzero status values that might occur, and the appropriate one of these procedures will automatically be invoked by the DBMS when needed. Lest this appear to be an overwhelming requirement, it should be pointed out that these exception procedures are usually quite short and that a single one can be specified as applying to more than one condition.

It is also possible to locate a record based on its membership in a set. A FIND statement of the first form makes current the COPIES set owned by that BOOK record. An individual VOLUME of *War and Peace* could then be located with a type-3 FIND statement:

```
        ┌ FIRST ┐
        │ LAST  │
 FIND  ┤        ├ VOLUME WITHIN COPIES.
        │ NEXT  │
        └ PRIOR ┘
```

This type of retrieval can be extended to select only record-occurrences meeting a given criterion. For example, suppose a user wanted to find a volume of *War and Peace* that is not currently out on loan. (Assume that this is reflected by a Date-Due value of zero.) This could be accomplished by moving zero to the Date-Due location in the UWA and then executing the type-4 DML command.

```
FIND VOLUME WITHIN COPIES USING DATE-DUE IN UWA-VOLUME.
```

A sequence of similar FIND DUPLICATE statements with the USING clause (fifth form) could be used to locate all of the VOLUME satisfying this condition.

The sixth form of the FIND statement locates a record on the basis of a specified database address. It might be hard to see the value of this form because, if the record-occurrence has not already been found, its database address is unknown. This form of the FIND command is usually used to get *back* to a record-occurrence that has already been retrieved once without having to again undertake a full database search. Suppose that a record has been retrieved using any of the possibilities just discussed. The user wishes to do something to this record, but only after having done other database manipulations that will result in this record no longer being current. All that is needed is to store the value of the currency indicator, that is, the database address, in a local program variable and then use this form of FIND to reestablish it as current when it is needed again.

A generalization of this capability is also available in the most recent revision of the DBTG specification. The application programmer can define a local storage area called a keep list, which will be used to store a list of database addresses. If such an area has been assigned the name KEYLIST, then the statement

```
KEEP USING KEYLIST
```

will add the database address of the current of run-unit to the designated list. The maximum number of addresses that can be held in a keep list is declared when the list is defined.

At some later time, the program could use a loop containing the statement:

$$FIND \begin{Bmatrix} FIRST \\ LAST \end{Bmatrix} WITHIN KEYLIST$$

This retrieves the designated record *and removes it from the keep list.* A nonzero DB-STATUS value will be returned when the list is empty.

The value of the keep list construction is that it makes it possible to locate a set of records meeting some condition and then process them again without having to perform the complete search a second time. This might be useful when a collection of records need to be updated but the changes that must be made cannot be determined until all of the records have been read. Giving a 10% raise to all employees with five years experience whose salary is currently below the average for that group would be an example of this.

The FIND statement using database addresses is probably the best example of a feature in the DBTG proposal that violates data independence in the interests of efficiency. It makes it possible for a program to avoid repeating a search when the same record must be referred to repeatedly. However, the fact that a user program is able to get its hands on a database address can be dangerous when the database administrator, for any of many valid reasons, decides to reorganize part of the database. If such a reorganization should take place in between the time a database address has been stored away and the time it is used, the address may no longer refer to the same record!

The last aspect of the FIND operation that needs to be discussed is the facility for suppressing updating of currency indicators. This example will also help to

1. Find BORROWER record where Bor-Name is Joan Reader.
2. Find next CARD within HAS-CARDS set; if none, stop. (This loop makes sure that all of Ms. Reader's library cards are considered.)
3. Find next VOLUME within LOANS set; if none go to 2. (The current CARD record owns a LOANS set that is also current. The selected VOLUME record and its associated COLLECTION and COPIES sets all become current.)
4. Find next VOLUME within COPIES set; if none go to 3. (This finds another VOLUME that is a copy of that BOOK and makes it current. As a result, different COLLECTION and LOANS sets become current. Thus, when statement No. 3 is eventually executed again, it will not refer to the correct LOANS set.)
5. Find owner of LOANS set.
   (This identifies the CARD used to borrow the new copy of one of Ms. Reader's books.)
6. Find owner of HAS-CARDS set.
   (This locates the BORROWER of that other copy.)
7. Go to statement No. 4.
   (See if there are any more copies of this book.)

FIGURE 5–5 Outline of algorithm for Ms. Reader's query.

illustrate the subtleties that are associated with the network model's currency concept. Consider the case of Joan Reader who wishes to find the names of everyone who currently has on loan any of the same books that she has.

The procedure for answering this query must begin by FINDing Ms. Reader's BORROWER record (Figure 5–5). This will also make her LOANS set current because the BORROWER record is the owner of the LOANS set. The procedure must then execute a loop in which each VOLUME record that is a member of her LOANS set is retrieved. For each of these VOLUMEs, the COPIES set of which it is a member is traversed, thus locating all other VOLUMEs that are copies of the same book. The owner of the LOANS set for each of these VOLUMEs is a BORROWER who meets the terms of the query. At least, that sounds like it ought to work!

Unfortunately, although the algorithm just outlined does not contain any errors that can be detected by the DBMS, it does not answer the question that was asked. The problem lies in what happens to the currency indicators. The algorithm begins by making the LOANS set belonging to Ms. Reader current, and each time it returns to the top of the outer loop, it expects to retrieve the next member of this set. However, each time that another volume is found of one of Ms. Reader's books, the process of locating the associated borrower makes some other LOANS set current. The next time that the

FIND NEXT VOLUME WITHIN LOANS SET

statement is executed, it will get the next one in the set owned by the most recently discovered duplicate borrower rather than in the one owned by Ms. Reader.

This problem can be circumvented by replacing the statement in line 4 of the algorithm with

```
FIND NEXT VOLUME WITHIN COPIES RETAINING LOANS CURRENCY.
```

This causes updating of the currency indicator associated with the set-type, LOANS, to be suppressed. In general, the suppression of currency indicator updating can be specified for a record-type, for any set-type(s), and/or for all realms involved.

Other Data Manipulation Functions

GET

The GET command retrieves actual data from the record-occurrence that is current of run-unit and stores it in the UWA. Because it always operates on the current of run-unit, it is not actually necessary to attach any parameters to a GET. However, it is usually used in the form:

```
GET record-type.
```

Specifying the record-type makes it much easier for someone reading a program to understand what it is doing. This also allows the DBMS to do some additional checking. If the current of run-unit is not of the specified record-type, the GET is aborted and an appropriate status message returned.

Finally, a GET command may specify that only certain data-items are to be transferred to the UWA:

```
GET CATALOG-NO IN BOOK, AUTHOR IN BOOK.
```

Where the record contains a large number of fields and only a few are needed, this may significantly reduce the amount of data to be transferred. Transferring data between primary and secondary memory is the most common bottleneck affecting the performance of database systems.

STORE

The STORE operation creates a new occurrence of a record-type and adds it to the database. The newly created record will also be included in any sets that have this record-type as member and AUTOMATIC insertion class. The record will become the current of run-unit, of its record type, of its realm, and of any sets in which it participates as either owner or member.

The STORE command may be illustrated by the following:

```
MOVE 1 TO COPY-NO IN UWA-VOLUME.
MOVE 0 TO DATE-DUE IN UWA-VOLUME.

MOVE 0142377 TO CATALOG-NO IN UWA-BOOK.
MOVE 12 TO BRANCH-NO IN UWA-BRANCH.

STORE VOLUME
```

The first two COBOL statements place the data for a new VOLUME record in the UWA. The next two establish the basis for automatic selection of COPIES and COLLECTION sets for this volume, and the last one performs the actual insertion. Note that nothing is done about specifying a LOANS set for the VOLUME because this set-type has manual insertion class and a VOLUME is not added to a LOANS set until someone borrows it.

ERASE

The ERASE command deletes the current of run-unit (and possibly other records as well) from the database. There are 2 forms. The first is illustrated by:

```
MOVE 7 TO BRANCH-NO IN UWA-BRANCH
FIND ANY BRANCH USING BRANCH-NO IN UWA-BRANCH
ERASE ALL BRANCH
```

This makes current the record for Branch No 7 and then deletes it as well as all VOLUME records for volumes belonging to that branch. In other words, this might be an appropriate command for a branch that had been utterly destroyed by fire along with all of its books.

The ERASE ALL version deletes the specified record and all records that are members of sets owned by the specified one. Furthermore, this rule is applied recursively so that any records owned by members of the specified one are also deleted, and so on. ERASE ALL applied to a LIBRARY record would delete all of the BRANCH and BORROWER records for that library as well as all of the VOLUME records held by any of those branches. It should be obvious that the ERASE ALL command is extremely powerful and must be used with great care. Incidentally, the ERASE ALL example for a library branch that has been destroyed by fire is almost certainly inappropriate because it would delete VOLUME records corresponding to books in the possession of borrowers at the time of the fire and, therefore, not actually lost.

The second form of ERASE is simply:

```
ERASE record-type
```

The effect of this operation will depend on the retention class of any sets owned by the specified record. If any of these sets have MANDATORY retention and those sets currently have members in them, then the ERASE will fail because completing it would leave those members without a set in which to belong in violation of the specified retention class.

If there are no sets with MANDATORY retention class *or* if they exist but have no members, then the specified record is potentially deletable. Any records belonging to sets with OPTIONAL retention class will simply be disconnected, whereas any with FIXED retention will also be deleted. However, before this can happen, it is necessary to see whether deleting *these* records will cause any nonempty MANDATORY sets to be left without owners, and so on, recursively. If all of these checks are satisfied, then the specified deletions and disconnections will take place. Otherwise, the operation fails.

The reader is probably surprised to discover how complex a simple-sounding command like ERASE can get. However, if one considers the implications of the three set retention classes, it will be seen that the algorithm for ERASE just outlined is reasonable.

MODIFY

The MODIFY command is used to alter the contents of the record that is current of run-unit. The following sequence of operations could be used to change the address of a borrower:

```
MOVE 558588 TO CARD-NO IN UWA-BORROWER.
FIND ANY BORROWER USING CARD-NO IN UWA-BORROWER.
GET BORROWER.
MOVE '3408 Elm Street' TO STREET IN UWA-BORROWER.
MODIFY BORROWER.
```

When, as in this example, the MODIFY command specifies just a record-type, the entire record is replaced. Alternatively, individual data-items could have been specified in a manner similar to that described for the GET command.

CONNECT

The CONNECT command is provided for adding record-occurrences to sets. It is applicable only to sets with MANUAL or AUTOMATIC, OPTIONAL membership classes. Why? The general form of a Connect statement is:

```
CONNECT record-type TO set-type
```

The record that is actually going to be added to a set must be the current of run-unit. Thus, as in many other DML statements, the specification of a record-type in the Connect statement is, in a sense, optional. However, its inclusion makes the statement much more readable as well as permitting the DBMS to verify that the current of run-unit is an occurrence of the expected record-type.

The set-occurrence to which the record will be added will be the current of the specified set-type. Thus, adding a record-occurrence to a set typically involves three statements: one to make the correct set-occurrence current, one to make the correct record-occurrence current, and then one to perform the actual connection. It should be clear that there must not be any statements that will alter the current of run-unit between the one establishing currency of the record and the Connect. Also, the record must not currently be a member of any occurrence of the specified set-type because one of the fundamental rules of the DBTG model is that a record may not simultaneously belong to more than one instance of a single set-type.

DISCONNECT

The DISCONNECT statement removes a record-occurrence from a set. The general form is:

```
DISCONNECT record-type FROM set-type
```

The specific record-occurrence that will be removed must be the current of run-unit. Needless to say, it must be a member of some instance of the specified set-type, and its membership class must be OPTIONAL.

RECONNECT

The RECONNECT command is needed to move records from one occurrence of a set-type to another when that operation cannot be performed by a DISCONNECT/ CONNECT sequence. The most common such situation would be when the set-type has MANDATORY membership class. Recall that this means that the member records must *always* belong to some instance of that set. The use of RECONNECT can be illustrated by a transfer of a volume from one branch of a library to another. It is assumed that volumes must always be associated with some branch, so, the COLLECTION set has MANDATORY membership class. This means that a DISCONNECT operation can not be performed, even if it were intended to follow it immediately with a CONNECT.

The specifics of a RECONNECT operation are as follows:

```
FIND . . . (the new BRANCH)
FIND VOLUME . . . (to be moved)
RECONNECT VOLUME WITHIN COLLECTION
```

The record-occurrence to be moved must be the current of run-unit. Thus, the two finds must occur in the order shown, and there must not be anything between the second FIND and the RECONNECT that will alter the "current" of run-unit.

EVALUATION

The data manipulation commands in the network model are few in number, and except for the many forms of FIND, they have simple syntax. This simplicity is misleading however. It is achieved by making many aspects of the commands implicit. To determine the effect of any DML statement, it is necessary to know precisely the values of all related currency indicators. In addition, critical aspects of some DML functions are determined by the data definition specifications. These can both affect the *way* certain DML commands will work, as in the case of a SET SELECTION clause, and even trigger other data manipulation functions that are not mentioned at all in the procedural part of the program.

This approach has both positive and negative implications. An advantage of dealing with so many procedural matters implicitly or in the database definition is that it transfers much of the complexity of the network model from the user or applications programmer to the database design staff. Presumably, this latter group is smaller and better trained in specific database technology matters. In addition, specification of operational details in the schema and subschema ensures that they will be consistent across all of the application programs that use those definitions.

The specification of currency indicator behavior is intended to allow routine functions to be performed as simply as possible. However, the other side of this coin is that the actual operation of DML statements is much more complex than appears on the surface, and if one wishes to perform a function that is not entirely routine, great care must be taken to consider the impact of currencies both on the function being performed and on those that will come after it. It is not a simple matter to read a sequence of DML commands and determine exactly what they will do because it depends so much on the contents of the database and on the previous values of the currency indicators. Also, command sequences that appear equivalent often turn out not to be so because of subtle differences in their effect on currency indicators. Recall that in the CONNECT and RECONNECT statements, for example, it is necessary to FIND the set *before* FINDing the record to be inserted.

Another noteworthy characteristic of the DBTG network model is the extent to which the database designer is allowed—sometimes even required—to control relatively low-level details. As has been mentioned previously, this degree of control is intended to aid a user in wringing the last increment of efficiency out of the database. Although that is certainly a desirable objective, it is not the only one. It must be balanced against accessibility of a system to less highly trained people. It is hard to imagine an end-user dealing with a DBTG database other than through a human or programmed intermediary.

Finally, this preoccupation with efficiency may be self-defeating. It is reminiscent of the assertion that used to be almost universally accepted: where program efficiency is a critical objective, assembly language is the only acceptable alternative. This claim is rarely heard any more, for several reasons. First, translation programs for problem-oriented languages have improved to the point where they challenge the efficiency achieved by typical assembly language programmers. Second, it has been found that assembly language programs are far harder to maintain than those written in higher level languages. As hardware costs drop and personnel costs rise, the tradeoff point between execution efficiency and ease of maintenance is constantly shifting in the direction of the latter. It has also been found that although a theoretically optimal assembly language program may outperform one produced using a high-level language, actual assembly language programs written by real programmers show much less, if any, advantage. Finally, the decision to use assembly language—especially to use it to maximize efficiency—tends to tie one quite closely to a specific hardware-operating system environment. This not only makes it hard to transport programs from one environment to another, but also raises the more subtle issue that, as the environment evolves, the quality of decisions that were optimal when a program was written may deteriorate.

The argument surrounding assembly language programming has been reviewed in so much detail because it seems to have strong parallels to the case of the DBTG database model. It is almost certainly true today that a database application optimally coded using a procedural DBTG system will outperform the same application using a system in which detailed operational decisions are left to the system. However, as has already become apparent in the programming language realm, this optimum is not easy to reach, whereas the quality of system-determined strategies may be expected to steadily improve.

In addition, it should be clear that the basic DBTG system is intended primarily for use by professional programmers, not end-users. The latter group would interact with the database through applications programs developed through the usual corporate channels. This approach, then, offers little in the way of a solution to the lengthy backlogs that plague most application programming departments today or to the user frustration that goes with long delays between request and delivery of a usable program. (The use of a database system is usually expected to have a favorable impact on the applications backlog through increasing programmer efficiency.)

A more subtle, hence more serious, danger is that the very goal of efficiency that this approach is intended to encourage will often turn out to be more illusory than real. Assume that the programmer of an application is skilled enough and understands the database and the user's requirement well enough to choose the optimal access strategy. The program will then be turned over to the user, who will continue to use it for some period of time. During this time, many things can happen to reduce the efficiency of the access strategy built into the program. Part or all of the database may be restructured by the database administrator. Changing patterns of data input and update may result in a significant increase or decrease in the sizes of sets. The specific needs of the user may change slightly. Because the program is basically a "black box" to the user, he or she will probably not be in a position to detect that the access strategy is no longer optimal, and it is quite possible that a program might continue in use for quite a long time, becoming progressively less efficient. At the very least, an organization that adopts this approach for reasons of efficiency needs to have some mechanism for periodically reviewing applications programs to detect when assumptions made when the programs were developed are no longer valid.

TERMS TO UNDERSTAND

record	database procedures
data-items	insertion class
currency indicator	retention class
realm	data definition language (DDL)
database definition	Data Manipulation Language (DML)
user work area (UWA)	

REVIEW QUESTIONS

1. What are the main differences between the hierarchical and network models?

2. People belong to various clubs, and a club has various members: represent this situation as a network.

3. Design a network database for the family tree of Chapter 2, Question 7. List the data-items for each record-type, and identify the owner and member record-types for each set.

4. Design a network database for the Last National Bank (LNB) (Chapter 2, Question 5).

5. Design a network database for the university administration problem (Chapter 4, Question 5).

6. Suppose we had the following network model:

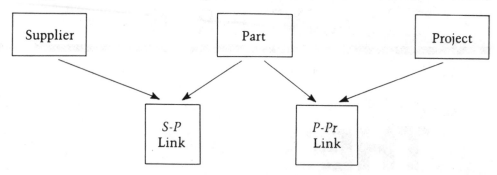

It is obviously impossible to determine from this database which suppliers provide a given part TO A PARTICULAR PROJECT. Why? Such a situation is called a connection trap. Modify the model so that this information will be retreivable.

7. Consider the various alternatives for set insertion and retention classes. For each combination that makes sense, give an example of a situation where it would be used. For each other combination, explain why it does not make sense.

8. Describe a modification of the network model that would allow direct representation of $M:N$ relationships.

9. Consider the problem of simulating a hierarchical Database Management System (DBMS) with a network one so that programs designed to use the original system would work correctly without change. How could a hierarchical database be described using network Data Definition Language (DDL)? How could the GET NEXT and GET NEXT WITHIN PARENT operations be implemented using the network model?

C H A P T E R 6

THE RELATIONAL MODEL

BASIC PROPERTIES

The hierarchical and network models discussed in the preceding chapters bear certain basic similarities. They both use blocks of storage (segments in the hierarchical model and records for the network one) to represent entities. Relationships are represented in both models by explicit links between the storage blocks. Finally, both take a relatively low-level view of their role, dealing with data one record (or segment) at a time and relying on the user to specify the actual path to be used to reach a desired data object.

The relational model adopts an entirely different approach. First of all, there is only a single construct, the relation, which is used to represent both entities and relationships. In addition, the basic relational operations operate on entire collections of entities or relationships rather than dealing with them individually. Finally, the user typically has little, if any, control over how queries will be processed. It is a fundamental tenet of the relational approach that the user should specify *what* is wanted, but leave it up to the system to decide how to do it.

One implication of this is that relational systems appear much simpler and less technical to the user. Totally untrained people exposed to all three models tend to prefer the relational one overwhelmingly. The conceptual simplicity of the relational model also makes it possible to implement a Data Base Management System (DBMS) with much less effort than for either of the others. However, the apparent ease of implementation of a relational DBMS is deceptive, in that relational systems implemented in a simple, straightforward way tend to have quite poor performance. Many such DBMS's have been produced; as a result, there is a widespread impression that relational systems are inherently poorer performers than the alternatives. A number of recently developed systems have shown, though, that it is possible for a relational DBMS to achieve the same level of efficiency as the other models if similarly complex and sophisticated internal strategies are utilized. Fortunately, the user is still spared any need to be concerned with this complexity.

Although this book employs intuitive explanations for almost all technical matters, it should be realized that the relational model is actually based on a rigorous mathematical theory. Its primary construct is the *relation*, which is formally defined as an (unordered) set of ordered n-tuples. An n-tuple is merely a set of n values; in a conventional file system it would be called a record. For convenience, the term "tuple" is often used instead of n-tuple where no confusion would arise. The values within a tuple have to be ordered because, just as with conventional records, the values do not carry identifying labels. The fact that a certain value is an employee number and another one is a telephone number is implicit in their positions within the tuple. On the other hand, although records in a conventional file are sequenced according to key values, there is no particular significance to the order of tuples in a relation. Thus, it does not make sense to refer to the "first" tuple in a relation or the "last" one, or even to the "next" or "prior" one.

Relations are often described as two-dimensional tables. In terms of the model presented in Chapter 2, the table as a whole represents an entity or relationship *type*. A column corresponds to an *attribute* and there is a row for each *occurrence*. The main shortcoming of this tabular representation of a relation is that the rows of a table inevitably appear in some order, whereas (as previously stated) there is no significance to the order of tuples in a relation.

One important way in which a relation is different from an ordinary table is that a relation may not contain any duplicate rows. It follows that there will always be at least one collection of attributes that uniquely identifies each tuple. (The collection may have to include all the attributes in a relation.) Each such collection of attributes is called a *candidate key* for the relation. One candidate key must be chosen as the *primary key*. Keys are used at the implementation level in all database models, but in this one, they are also used during the database design process to avoid designs that have undesirable properties. This will be discussed further in the following section.

The irrelevance of the sequencing of tuples in a relation is unusual in the world of data processing, which tends to place a lot of emphasis on sorting. Of course, in most real-world applications, sequence *is* important. If entries in a telephone directory were inserted at random, one would have to search sequentially to find a particular number, and the usefulness of the volume would be greatly reduced. The reason that order is not important in a relation is that the data manipulation operations provided by the relational model refer to tuples by *content* rather than *location*.

NORMALIZATION

It might appear that because relations are just tables, designing a relational database is merely a question of specifying a set of tables that contain all of the required attributes. However, early in the development of this model, it became apparent that some database designs worked much better than others for the same application. Normalization is the process of converting an arbitrary relational database design into one that will have "good" operational properties.

It is interesting to note that the same variation in quality existed and was observed in the earlier hierarchical and network models as well. However, because those models were not solidly grounded in a mathematical theory, it was not possible to investigate these problems in the systematic, rigorous way allowed by the relational model. The process of converting an arbitrary relational database design to one that avoids certain anomalies is referred to as normalization. Lessons learned studying normalization of relational databases have been applied to improving network and hierarchical designs as well.

The objective of normalization is to produce a database design that can be manipulated in a powerful way with a simple collection of operations while minimizing data anomalies and inconsistencies.

The normalization process does not use any information about the numbers (relative or absolute) of particular entities and relationships or about the types or frequencies of the queries to be processed. Thus, it is not biased toward a particular usage environment. This is in distinct contrast to the network approach where tuning the design to achieve maximum efficiency for the expected workload is a basic principle of the model. Such considerations are ignored by normalization theory, but, of course, a database designer is free to ignore the theory when it appears to result in an inappropriate design.

Proponents of database design approaches based on normalization theory would argue that the information about usage needed to optimize a design is rarely available in advance. In addition, usage patterns change over time and are even influenced by the act of introducing database technology. Thus, the belief that a design can be effectively tailored to the specific needs of an application may be an illusion. In the relatively new, but rapidly growing, area of Decision Support Systems it is normal not to know exactly how the data will be used at the time a system is being built. Thus, a design discipline that produces a result guaranteed to be free from certain anomalies and not biased toward any particular usage pattern may be exactly what is wanted. In any case, the importance of normalization lies not in following it slavishly, but in using it to make explicit trade-offs between efficiency and integrity.

To illustrate the basic principles of normalization as well as to demonstrate the pitfalls of a too simplistic approach to database design, consider a straightforward mechanization of a library's card catalog in the form of a relation. Obviously, there will be a tuple for each volume. An initial set of attributes might consist of:

Call Number

Title

Author

Publisher

City of Publication

There is, of course, other information that usually appears in a card catalog, but these items will suffice for present purposes. Also, because a *computerized* catalog is envisioned rather than a set of manually maintained cards, it is tempting to add two additional attributes:

> Borrower Number
>
> Date Due

to record important information about each volume that is out on loan. The obvious choice for a key for this relation is Call Number. Every relation must have a name. If this one is called CATALOG, then it can be expressed in the usual notation of the relational model as:

```
CATALOG
{Call-No, Title, Author, Publisher, Pub-City, Borrower-No,
Date-Due}
```

First Normal Form (1NF)

Normalization theory is traditionally expressed through a set of so-called normal forms that progressively constrain the structure and contents of a relation. First Normal Form (1NF) provides that all tuples in a relation must have the same set of attributes and that the attributes must be atomic, indivisible items. 1NF may be regarded as a definition making up part of the specification of the relational model. There is no fundamental reason why missing or complex attributes could not be dealt with. However, they would obviously complicate the model and any DBMS's based on it. Furthermore, it can be proven that no additional functionality would be obtained by allowing this extra complexity. Therefore, the model chooses to restrict itself to relations that are at least in 1NF.

Applying the definition of 1NF to the CATALOG relation requires, first of all, that the two attributes dealing with loan status must be present in every tuple—not just those that are out on loan. This does not cause any great difficulty because it can be agreed that for volumes not on loan, these two attributes will have null values. A null value is quite a different thing than a missing attribute. The relational model permits null values for nonkey attributes only.

At any given moment, most of a library's volumes are *not* on loan, so, one may be inclined to wonder whether including these two attributes in every tuple wastes a lot of storage. There are two answers to that question. The first is that the question under current consideration deals with *logical* database design, and it is, therefore, premature to worry about storage utilization. The second answer (for those who might find the first one less than satisfactory) is that the implementors of a relational DBMS are free to represent null values however they wish, and there are ways to do this that involve minimal waste of space.

In its present form, the sample CATALOG relation contains another violation of 1NF. If a tuple is considered to represent a published work, then whenever a library owns multiple copies of one, the Bo r r owe r -No and Da t e -Du e attributes will each have to be capable of containing *sets* of values. This would violate the rule that attributes must be atomic. Again, it should be emphasized that the idea of having an attribute containing multiple values is not impossible to handle. The COBOL programming language, for example, permits so-called repeating groups of fields in records. However, there is clearly some additional complexity associated with this capability even in COBOL, and it would greatly complicate both the definition and implementation of some of the powerful data manipulation operations of the relational model. Thus, such constructs are ruled out by definition.

The alternative is to use a tuple to represent each distinct volume rather than each published work. In this case, the Ca l l No must consist of two parts—a catalog-no and a copy no—which *also* violates the restriction that attributes must be atomic! However, this violation can be removed simply by using Ca t a l og -No to identify the work and adding a new attribute, Co p y -No , to distinguish specific copies of it:

```
CATALOG {Catalog-No, Copy-No, Title, Author, Publisher,
Pub-City, Borrower-No, Date-Due}
```

Note that the key now consists of two attributes. Neither one alone uniquely identifies a tuple, but their combination does.

This relation is now in 1NF, but it still has a number of characteristics that would cause difficulties in use. For example, if a library has six copies of a book, there will be six tuples for it that will all have exactly the same contents for the Ca t a l og -No , Title , Author , Publisher , and Pub-City attributes. There is an obvious waste of storage space here and an even more serious risk that if any of these fields ever needed to be modified, some of the affected tuples might be missed, leading to inconsistencies. This is an example of what is generally called an update anomaly.

A 1NF relation may also be subject to deletion anomalies. If a volume is lost, stolen, or destroyed, it might seem reasonable to delete the corresponding tuple from the CATALOG relation. For the book referred to in the preceding paragraph, this can be done five times without losing any information about the work itself (author, title, publisher, etc.). However, when the sixth tuple is deleted, information is lost that refers not only to that particular volume, but to the work itself. At the very least, this makes the deletion of the sixth tuple different from the deletion of the preceding five, and it is a difference that is probably not intended. Informally, both types of anomalies can be attributed to the fact that the CATALOG relation describes two distinct things—published works and individual volumes that are instances of those works.

Second Normal Form (2NF)

Many update and deletion anomalies can be eliminated by converting a relation to 2NF. 2NF requires that all nonkey attributes must contain information that refers to the *entire* key, not just part of it. To convert the CATALOG relation to 2NF, it would have to be split into two new relations:

```
COLLECTION {Catalog-No, Title, Author, Publisher, Pub-City}
VOLUME {Catalog-No, Copy-No, Borrower-No, Date-Due}
```

Note that all information about a published work is now contained in a COLLECTION tuple that will not have to be duplicated, no matter how many copies of a book the library may contain. In conformity with the rules of 2NF, all of the nonkey attributes in COLLECTION refer to a Catalog-No, and all of the nonkey attributes of VOLUME refer to the combination of a Catalog-No and a Copy-No.

There is still a potential problem with the COLLECTION relation. If it is assumed that a publisher is located in only a single city or that the city of publication always refers to the location of the publisher's main office, then the fact that a publisher is located in a given city will be recorded in the tuples for each of that publisher's books. Again it can be seen that because a single fact is duplicated in many places, update and deletion anomalies can still occur.

This example also illustrates a third potential problem—insertion anomalies. It would be impossible to store the fact that a publisher was located in a certain city if the library did not currently have any books from that publisher in its collection. One might think that a COLLECTION tuple could be created with null values for the attributes other than Publisher and Pub-City. However, this would entail a null key value, and (as already mentioned) this is not permitted. Thus, it would be necessary to acquire a book from a publisher *before* there would be any place to store that publisher's location.

Third Normal Form (3NF)

The anomalies remaining in a 2NF relation can be eliminated by converting it to 3NF. The definition of 3NF is that the relation meet the requirements of 2NF, and, in addition, that each nonkey attribute refers directly to the key. In the example, it is true that Pub-City refers to Catalog-No, but it is a transitive rather than a direct referral. That is, Pub-City refers to Publisher, which in turn, refers to Catalog-No. Again, the solution is to split the offending relation into two new ones to give:

```
COLLECTION {Catalog-No, Title, Author, Publisher}
PUBLISHER {Publisher, Pub-City}
VOLUME {Catalog-No, Copy-No, Borrower-No, Date-Due}
```

If a publisher moved its head office from one city to another there is now only one field in the entire database that would have to be changed.

It can easily be verified that for each of these relations all attributes are atomic, all nonkey attributes refer to the entire key, and all such references are direct. This set of relations is therefore in 3NF. It is interesting to note that although 2NF depends on structural considerations only, the conversion to 3NF required knowing something about the *meaning* of the information. Specifically, the last modification made above was required because it was known that a publisher was always associated with a single city. Similarly, if it was known that *all* of an author's books were published by the same publisher, a similar modification would be needed to eliminate redundancy in the author-publisher data. However, under the more common assumption that an author may work with different publishers for different books, this design change is not required.

The normalization process, as discussed so far, has taken a single relation and transformed it into three others. The main result has been to eliminate redundancy, which is known to be responsible for many problems. In addition, normalization has made it possible to insert information about one type of entity, publishers, into the database independently of information about their books. The price that has been paid for these improvements is that retrievals that could have been accomplished with a simple selection operation before, now require a join as well. Thus, there appears to be a trade-off between design "correctness" and manipulation efficiency. The situation is not quite that simple. Although more operations will usually be required to process a query using a normalized database, the relations are individually smaller and, hence, are processed more quickly and economically. In any given case, the extra processing overhead owing to normalization can be calculated if enough is known about the size of the database and the processing requirements. There may well be cases where it is advantageous to leave part of a database in unnormalized form, although the risks of doing so must be considered carefully.

Functional Dependencies

2NF and 3NF can be defined concisely in terms of *functional dependencies*. An attribute (or group of attributes), Y, in a relation is said to be functionally dependent on another attribute (or group of attributes), X, if knowing the value of X is sufficient to determine the value of Y. In other words, there is only one value of Y associated with any value of X. The functional dependency of Y on X is written:

$$X \rightarrow Y$$

which is read: X functionally determines Y. It is obvious that the nonkey attributes of any relation are functionally dependent on the key.

It is now possible to specify that a relation is in 2NF if all nonkey attributes are *fully* functionally dependent on the key. That is, there must be no nonkey attribute that is functionally dependent on only a subset of the key. The original `CATALOG` relation violated 2NF because it contained functional dependencies that referred to only part of the key, such as:

        Catalog-No → Author

Such a result suggests that, perhaps, `Catalog-No` should be considered as a candidate key. However, closer inspection shows that this is unfeasible because a number of the other attributes are not functionally dependent on `Catalog-No` alone.

Similarly, 3NF is defined by the additional requirement that there must be no *transitive* functional dependencies. The first form of the `COLLECTION` relation violated 3NF as a result of containing the transitive dependency:

        Catalog-No → Publisher → Pub-City

Further Normalization

At one time, it was thought that the conditions of 3NF were sufficient to ensure that a relational database would not exhibit anomalous behavior. However, database designs have been discovered that meet all the requirements of 3NF, but are still subject to redundancy or other maintenance problems. Because the conditions that can give rise to these problems are somewhat complex, a concrete illustration will be presented rather than a general exposition. The illustration is based on a relation containing individual's preferences in food and wine:[1]

        LIKES {Name, Food, Wine}

For simplicity, assume that Name is adequate to identify an individual uniquely in this database. It seems clear that the only reasonable choice for a key for this relation would be the combination of all three attributes. Initially, assume also that the intention of this relation is to store two *independent* sets of facts about each individual—the foods and wines that the person likes. Because there are no nonkey attributes, the relation is obviously in 3NF. Nevertheless, it has some severe problems.[2] For example, there are at least three distinct maintenance strategies that would produce quite different contents for the `LIKES` relation.

---

[1] Unfortunately, the library database does not offer any unforced examples of the type of problem discussed in this section.

[2] This discussion is based on one in William Kent, "A Simple Guide to Five Normal Forms in Relational Database Theory," *CACM*, Vol. 26, No. 2 (February 1983), pp. 120–125.

Name	Food	Wine
Wiley	Pizza	
Wiley	Salmon	
Wiley	Omelet	
Wiley	Steak	
Wiley		Chablis
Wiley		Cold Duck
Wiley		Chianti

FIGURE 6–1

In the disjoint form shown in Figure 6–1, each tuple contains *either* a food or a wine. This is almost the same as using two separate relations, which is, in fact, what will ultimately be recommended as the solution to this design problem. The disjoint form contains many null values that may occupy space and that are certainly open to more than one interpretation. Does the null in column 3 of the first tuple mean that Wiley does not like any wines or that his wine preferences are stored elsewhere? Either interpretation is reasonable and unless all users of this database are aware of the convention being used, misunderstanding is almost certain to arise.

A second choice would be to eliminate, or at least minimize, the use of nulls by, as far as possible, storing both a food and a wine preference in each tuple. One possible result of this strategy is shown in Figure 6–2. A minor variation on this form would be to use repetition of some attribute value to avoid nulls as in Figure 6–3.

The last two possibilities are both open to the interpretation that the wine and food preferences within a given tuple are related—that is, that Wiley only likes Chablis with Pizza. Indeed, this is the most obvious interpretation. However, the original premise of this discussion was that the relation was to store *independent* wine and food preferences.

A third strategy is illustrated in Figure 6–4. There is no ambiguity about its interpretation, but this is achieved at the cost of a large amount of duplication.

Name	Food	Wine
Wiley	Pizza	Chablis
wiley	Salmon	Cold Duck
Wiley	Omelet	Chianti
Wiley	Steak	

FIGURE 6–2

Name	Food	Wine
Wiley	Pizza	Chablis
Wiley	Salmon	Cold Duck
Wiley	Omelet	Chianti
Wiley	Steak	Chianti

FIGURE 6–3

Any of the alternatives that involve duplication of data are subject to the same consistency problems described in the discussions of 2NF and 3NF. Adding a new item to Wiley's set of preferences would involve either inserting a new tuple, searching for one with a null value, or searching for one with a value that duplicates another tuple. Similarly, removing an item from the list of preferences would require either deleting a tuple or setting one or more attribute values to null. In the latter case, it would also be necessary to check that the modification did not produce a tuple that was an exact duplicate of one already in the relation.

The root of the problem discussed here is that the LIKES relation is attempting to represent two 1:N relationships. Of the many possible forms that such a relation could take, only the last one illustrated below is unambiguous as to meaning, and it is particularly susceptible to the defects that are the main argument for normalization. The solution, which may seem obvious, is to split LIKES into two new relations, each of which stores one of the 1:N relationships:

```
FOOD-LIKES {Name, Food}
DRINK-LIKES {Name, Wine}
```

Name	Food	Wine
Wiley	Pizza	Chablis
Wiley	Pizza	Cold Duck
Wiley	Pizza	Chianti
Wiley	Salmon	Chablis
Wiley	Salmon	Cold Duck
Wiley	Salmon	Chianti
Wiley	Omelet	Chablis
Wiley	Omelet	Cold Duck
Wiley	Omelet	Chianti
Wiley	Steak	Chablis
Wiley	Steak	Cold Duck
Wiley	Steak	Chianti

FIGURE 6–4

Name	Food
Wiley	Pizza
Wiley	Salmon
Wiley	Omelet
Wiley	Steak

Name	Wine
Wiley	Chablis
Wiley	Cold Duck
Wiley	Chianti

FIGURE 6–5

The example LIKES relation would be transformed into the two shown in Figure 6–5. Note that even though the Name attribute must appear in both relations, the total amount of storage required is greatly reduced. A comparison of the number of attribute values to be stored, shows that the version of Figure 6–4 requires

$$3 * F * W$$

whereas that of Figure 6–5 uses only

$$2 * (F + W)$$

where F and W are the number of Foods and Wines respectively. For four foods and three wines, the storage requirements for the two approaches are 36 and 14. As the numbers of foods and wines increase, the difference becomes increasingly dramatic. Of course, aside from the storage savings, the elimination of duplicate data removes the risk of inconsistency and the uncertainty about maintenance strategy.

The general lesson illustrated here is that a relation should not contain more than one 1:N relationship. Fourth Normal Form (4NF) is defined by that property in addition to the various requirements of 3NF. It is worth reemphasizing that the whole question of 4NF can only be discussed when the *meaning* of a relation is understood. Knowing a relation's structure, but not its contents, is insufficient to determine if it is in 4NF.

4NF deals with the elimination of redundancy caused by multiple 1:N relationships. Unnecessary redundancy can also occur for other reasons—for ex-

Name	Food	Restaurant
Wiley	Pizza	Roman Villa
Wiley	Pizza	Joe's Grill
Wiley	Salmon	Roman Villa
Wiley	Salmon	Joe's Grill
Wiley	Salmon	Star View
Wiley	Omelet	Roman Villa
Smith	Pizza	Roman Villa
Smith	Salmon	Roman Villa
Smith	Salmon	Chez Pierre
Smith	Salmon	Star View

FIGURE 6–6

ample, if a so-called symmetric constraint is present. This can be illustrated with the following relation:

EATS {Name, Food, Restaurant}

Because the problems being discussed now are associated with the semantics or meaning of relations, it is necessary to state precisely what this relation is intended to represent. In this case, the intention is that if the tuple {Wiley, Pizza, Roman Villa} appears in the relation, it means that Wiley eats pizza at the Roman Villa restaurant. If this is all that can be said, then the relation, which is clearly in 3NF, can not be improved further.

However, suppose the following rule is in effect:

> If an individual likes a certain food and patronizes a restaurant that serves that food, then the individual will eat that food at that restaurant.

Then, an instance of the EATS relation might appear as shown in Figure 6–6. Because of this rule, this relation can be replaced by the three relations of Figure 6–7. The advantage of the latter form is that each fact (for example, that Wiley likes Pizza or that Salmon is served at Joe's Grill) is stored only once. By contrast, in Figure 6–6, Wiley's liking for Pizza would be repeated as many times as there are restaurants serving that item. Furthermore, if by chance, the last of these restaurants should happen to close, there would be no way to retain the information that Wiley liked Pizza. The alternative of Figure 6–7, which is in 5NF, avoids both of these problems.

Informally, a relation may be said to be in 5NF if it *cannot* be reconstructed by a join operation on two or more smaller relations. It is easy to verify that if the three relations of Figure 6–7 were joined, the result would be precisely as shown

Name	Food
Wiley	Pizza
Wiley	Salmon
Wiley	Omelet
Smith	Pizza
Smith	Salmon

Name	Restaurant
Wiley	Roman Villa
Wiley	Joe's Grill
Wiley	Star View
Smith	Roman Villa
Smith	Chez Pierre
Smith	Star View

Restaurant	Food
Roman Villa	Pizza
Roman Villa	Salmon
Roman Villa	Omelet
Chez Pierre	Salmon
Joe's Grill	Pizza
Joe's Grill	Salmon
Star View	Salmon

FIGURE 6–7

in Figure 6–6, and that because of the previously stated rule, this correctly represents the actual situation. If that rule were not in effect—that is, if the fact that Wiley liked F1 did *not* imply that he would eat it at any restaurant he patronized that served it—then the join of the three smaller relations could include tuples that were contrary to fact. In such a case, a relation of the form shown in Figure 6–6, possibly possessing substantial redundancy, would be the only feasible approach.

5NF differs from 4NF only when there is a symmetric constraint on the data values, such as the one implied by the rule on food preferences and restaurants. In other words, although Figure 6–6 expresses several 1:N relationships, they are not independent of one another, so, the 4NF decomposition rule can not be applied. Figure 6–6 is, in fact, in 4NF, despite the fact that it exhibits considerable redundancy. In this case, the redundancy can only be eliminated by splitting the relation into three smaller ones, as shown in Figure 6–7.

DATABASE DEFINITION

The mechanics of defining a relational database are particularly simple because only one construct, the relation, is used to represent both entities and relationships. Defining a relation requires identifying it by giving it a name and then specifying the set of attributes that comprise it. Ideally, the attributes should be described by reference to abstract data types as discussed in Chapter 2. For example, attributes such as Birth-Date (for employees), Date-Due (for library books), and Departure-Date (in an airline reservation system) would all be instances of the Dates abstract data type. However, the capability to define attributes in this way is rare among current DBMS's. Thus, it would be more common to describe them in the more traditional way—that is, by giving each a name, type, size, format, and so on.

Although the abstract data type approach is appropriate for any data model, it is particularly relevant to the relational one because of the frequent need to compare an attribute from one relation with an attribute from another. Knowing that the two attributes are instances of the same abstract data type is sufficient to ensure that they can be meaningfully compared. Some relational implementations require that attributes be given the same name to show that they are comparable. This is not a good solution because it makes it impossible to use names that express the role that the attribute plays in each relation. Other systems allow comparisons between any attributes as long as they are of the same syntactic type. This, of course, leaves the DBMS powerless to detect absurdities, such as the one implicit in the query: "Find the names of all employees whose number of dependents is greater than their shoe size."

Representing Entities

This chapter illustrates the approach to relational database design that begins with an arbitrary initial version and refines it by applying the rules of normalization. Other approaches will be discussed in Chapter 8. A reasonable starting point for defining a relational database for the library example is the list of entities and attributes in Figure 2–9, which is reproduced in Figure 6–8 for reference. It is a trivial matter to transform this information into the initial set of relations shown in Figure 6–9. The underscored attributes constitute a tentative key specification for each relation.

The design should first be checked for compliance with the definitions of 1NF. There do not appear to be any attributes whose values are sets, but addresses for branches and borrowers would certainly have complex structure. This prob-

```
             LIBRARY:              Name
                                   Director

             BRANCH:               Name
                                   Address

             BOOK:                 Catalog-No
                                   Title
                                   Author
                                   Publisher

             BORROWER:             Borrower-No
                                   Name
                                   Address

             VOLUME:               Copy-No
                                   Date-Due
```

FIGURE 6–8 Library database entities and attributes.

lem could be dealt with by replacing each address attribute with others representing the standard components of an address, such as Street Address, City, State, and Zip Code. The value of this becomes apparent when one contemplates locating, for example, all of the branch libraries in Cambridge, Massachusetts. Given the 1NF address formulation, this can be done with a simple selection operation on City and State (as described in Chapter 3). However, with a single Address attribute, the retrieval program would have to examine the internal structure of each Address value to determine if it qualified.

A similar situation arises with respect to the attributes naming borrowers, authors, and library directors. These are all instances of person's names, which, like addresses, have complex internal structure. This could be handled using the technique just proposed for the address problem. However, the large number of names in the database and the fact that they are probably referenced in data manipulation much more frequently than addresses suggest another solution.

This proposal involves defining another entity-type, PERSON, and three new relationships. A PERSON can be related to a BOOK by virtue of having written it

```
        LIBRARY {Lib-Name, Lib-Director}
        BRANCH {Br-Name, Br-Address}
        BOOKS {Catalog-No, Title, Author, Publisher}
        BORROWER {Borrower-No, Name, Address}
        VOLUME {Copy-No, Date-due}
```

FIGURE 6–9 Initial relational database design.

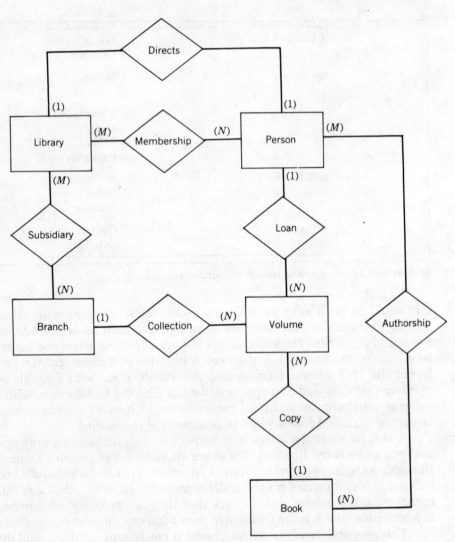

FIGURE 6–10 Revised entity-relationship (E-R) diagram for library example.

and to a LIBRARY by being its director and/or by having been issued with a borrower's card. The entity-relationships (E-R) diagram revised to illustrate this approach is shown in Figure 6–10. This change would be reflected in the database definition of Figure 6–9 by deleting the name attributes from the LIBRARY, BOOK, and BORROWER relations and adding a new relation, PERSON, corresponding to the new entity-type. This is illustrated in Figure 6–11 where ad-

```
LIBRARY {Lib-Name}
BRANCH {Br-Name, Br-Address}
BOOKS {Catalog-No, Title, BK-Publisher}
BORROWER {Borrower-No}
VOLUME {Copy-No, Date-Due}
PERSON {Prefix, First-Name, Middle-Name, Last-Name,
        Suffix, Address}
```

FIGURE 6–11 Revised library database definition—I.

dresses have been left in their original form to avoid complexity in the example that might obscure the essential points. The Address attribute has been deleted from the BORROWER relation because it is obviously more sensible to hold address information for individuals in the new PERSON relation. Storing each person's address only once helps to save space and reduce inconsistencies. However, note that this reduces the BORROWER relation to only one attribute, Borrower-No, which is useless on its own. This problem will be corrected shortly.

The existence of the PERSON relation not only makes it possible to eliminate duplication of addresses, but also greatly simplifies the problem of recognizing an individual in different roles, for example, finding all of the books taken out by library directors. If borrowers and library directors are not explicitly recognized as instances of Persons, there is a very good chance that they would be recorded differently in the LIBRARY and BORROWER relations, making it impossible to perform this retrieval accurately.

Representing Relationships

The relational database design of Figure 6–11 appears to obey the rules for 1NF and to represent all of the relevant entities to the extent required by the original E-R diagram. However, it is missing most of the information dealing with relationships. For example, it says nothing about which person wrote each book or about which branches are associated with each library. As mentioned earlier, there is no special construct in the relational model for representing relationships. Rather, this is accomplished either by creating new relations or by adding attributes to existing ones.

Consider first the three relationships defined for PERSON entities. The PERSON relation is modified by adding an additional attribute, Person-ID. This could be something like a Social Security Number or a special number defined for this application.[3] The important thing is that Person-ID must uniquely identify

---

[3] It should be noted in passing that the use of Social Security Numbers for such a purpose might be considered improper based on legal and/or privacy considerations.

```
LIBRARY {Lib-Name, Lib-Director-ID}
BRANCH {Lib-Name, Br-Name, Br-Address}
BOOKS {Catalog-No, Title, Author-ID, Publisher}
BORROWER {Lib-Name, Borrower-No, Borrower-ID}
VOLUME {Lib-Name, Br-Name, Catalog-No, Copy-No,
    Borrower-No, Date-Due}
PERSON {Person-ID, Prefix, First-Name, Middle-Name,
    Last-Name, Suffix, Address}
```

FIGURE 6–12 Revised library database definition—II.

each person in the database. It will be used both as the key in the PERSON relation and to refer to specific PERSON tuples elsewhere. For example, an attribute, Director-ID will be added to the LIBRARY relation. It will be defined on the same abstract data type as Person-ID, and its value will be the Person-ID of the library's director. The author relationship between a person and a book will be handled in exactly the same way by adding an Author-ID attribute to the BOOK relation. The fact that an individual has been issued a borrower's card by a particular library will be represented by adding two attributes to the currently meaningless BORROWER relation. One of these, Lib-Name, will identify the library issuing the card, and the second, Borrower-ID, will be the Person-ID of the individual to whom the card has been issued.

Other relationships are handled similarly. The library owning a branch is identified through a Lib-Name attribute in the BRANCH relation. The VOLUME relation is made meaningful by adding identifiers for library, branch, book, and borrower. The revised database definition, with appropriate changes to key specifications is shown in Figure 6–12.

The next step is to determine if there are any partial functional dependencies, that is, nonkey attributes that refer to only part of the key. This is, of course, possible only for a relation that has a compound key. In the BRANCH relation, both parts of the key are needed to identify a branch that is the item to which Address refers. It might seem that Borrower-ID in the BORROWER relation depends only on Card-No. However, this is not the case because libraries are assumed to issue cards independently of each other. Thus, the *combination* of Lib-Name and Card-No is needed to determine a Borrower-ID uniquely. It is similarly easy to verify that all of the nonkey attributes of VOLUME refer to a specific physical copy and, therefore, are dependent on the entire key. Thus, there are no violations of 2NF in this design.

Checking for 3NF involves looking for transitive dependencies—that is, situations where a nonkey attribute depends on another nonkey attribute, which, in turn, depends on the key. No such instances are apparent. It is interesting to note that there *would* have been a violation of 3NF rules if the Borrower Address attribute had been left in the BORROWER relation. In this case, the functional dependencies would be:

$$(Lib-Name, Card-No,) \rightarrow Borrower-ID \rightarrow Address$$

Thus, if addresses had not already been moved to the PERSON relation, there would be a clear signal at this point to move them. In any case, the revisions shown in Figure 6–12 are sufficient to meet the requirements of 3NF.

The next step is to check for multiple 1:N relationships within a single relation. None are present in this case, so, the design of Figure 6–12 can be considered satisfactory. It is worth emphasizing that this design was produced by a straightforward application of the normalization rules. Each rule identified specific flaws in the original design and offered general procedures for dealing with them. In a sense, it can be said that developing a relational database design with good operational properties is a much more mechanical process than it is for either of the other two models where designer insight and experience play a larger and more significant role.

A complete definition of the library database requires the addition of attribute definitions to the relation specifications of Figure 6–12. This is shown in Figure 6–13.

DATABASE MANIPULATION

Both the hierarchical and network database models are often described as navigational because they require (or allow, depending on one's point of view) the user to specify the detailed path to be followed in locating data objects. In these models, the basic retrieval facility consists of commands for locating individual records, although most commercial implementations also offer a higher level interface. In the relational model, by contrast, even the lowest level operations available to users deal with entire relations.

The most primitve operations defined in the relational model are those contained in the so-called *Relational Algebra*. Commercial relational DBMS's rarely give the user access to such low-level commands. Nevertheless, this chapter includes a description of the Relational Algebra because it gives useful insight into the workings of the model. The higher level languages that are more commonly found in commercial implementations are discussed in Chapter 12.

The Relational Algebra consists of a collection of operations, each of which takes one or two relations as its operands and produces a relation as its result. The fact that the result of an operation is the same kind of thing as the operands is a useful property of the Relational Algebra. In mathematics, this is referred to as the closure property, and its significance is that the result of one operation can be used as an operand for another operation. Ordinary arithmetic also exhibits

Relation Declarations		
Relation	Attribute	Abstract Data type
LIBRARY	Lib-Name (Key)	LIBRARY
	Lib-Director-ID	SSN
BRANCH	Lib-Name (Key)	LIBRARY
	Br-Name (Key)	STRING
	Br-Address	ADDRESS
BOOKS	Catalog-No (Key)	ISBN
	Title	STRING
	Author-ID	SSN
	Publisher	STRING
BORROWER	Lib-Name (Key)	LIBRARY
	Bor-No (Key)	LIB-CARD
	Borrower-ID	SSN
VOLUME	Lib-Name (Key)	LIBRARY
	Br-Name (Key)	STRING
	Catalog-No (Key)	ISBN
	Copy-No (Key)	INTEGER
	Bor-No	LIB-CARD
	Date-Due	DATE
PERSON	Person-ID (Key)	SSN
	Prefix	PREFIX
	First-Name	GIVEN-NAME
	Middle-Name	GIVEN-NAME
	Last-Name	LAST-NAME
	Suffix	SUFFIX
	Address	ADDRESS

FIGURE 6–13 Complete library database definition.

closure—that is, the result of any permissible operation on two numbers is another number. This is what makes it possible to nest operations and to combine them into complex sequences.

Set Operations

Because relations conform to the mathematical definition of sets (not to be confused with network model sets!), the standard set operators are all applicable to relations.

Abstract Data Type	Abstract Data Type Declarations Representation	Allowable Values
LIBRARY	CHARACTER (16)	{University, Municipal, Regional}
SSN	999-99-9999	Social Security Number
ADDRESS	(See note in text, p. 113)	
ISBN	9-999-99999-9	Intl. Std. Book Number
STRING	CHARACTER (*)	Any
LIB-CARD	INTEGER (6)	(100000-999999)
INTEGER	INTEGER (*)	Any
DATE	9999-99-99	Year-Month-Day
PREFIX	CHARACTER (5)	{Mr., Ms., Mrs., Miss, Dr., Prof.}
GIVEN-NAME	CHARACTER (*)	per list
LAST-NAME	CHARACTER (*)	per list
SUFFIX	CHARACTER (5)	{Jr., MD, Esq.}

FIGURE 6-13 (continued)

UNION

For the union operation to be defined on two relations, they must be of the same degree (i.e., have the same number of attributes) and corresponding attributes must be drawn from the same abstract data type. Relations that meet these conditions are said to be *union-compatible.*

If A and B are union-compatible relations, then A UNION B is the relation made up of all tuples that are in either A or B. Naturally, a tuple that is in both A and B will appear in the union only once in conformity with the rule that a relation may not contain duplicate tuples.

DIFFERENCE

The difference operation also requires that the relations be union-compatible. The result of A DIFFERENCE B is the set of tuples that are present in relation A, but *not* in B. Note that the order of specifying the two relation names is significant. A DIFFERENCE B is emphatically not the same as B DIFFERENCE A.

INTERSECTION

Intersection is also defined on two union-compatible relations. A INTERSECT B is the set of all tuples that are present in *both* A and B.

CARTESIAN PRODUCT

Two relations do *not* have to be union-compatible to be operands of a Cartesian-product operation. It is easiest to define by explaining how the result is constructed. Suppose that A is a relation containing nA tuples and B is a relation with nB tuples. Then, A CART-PROD B will contain $nA*nB$ tuples. Each tuple in the result will consist of the concatenation of a tuple from A with one from B, and all possible such concatenations will be included.

Examples

A few examples will make the power of these operations immediately apparent. Suppose that BOOK1 and BOOK2 are the BOOK relations for two separate libraries. Then:

> BOOK1 UNION BOOK2 will be a combined catalog for both libraries.
>
> BOOK1 DIFFERENCE BOOK2 will give the books that are available at the first library but not at the second, and
>
> BOOK2 DIFFERENCE BOOK1 will include those at the second but not the first.
>
> BOOK2 INTERSECT BOOK1 will show which books are available at *both* libraries.

By comparison with the hierarchical and network database models, the extraordinary simplicity and power of the Relational Algebra is immediately apparent (the reader is reminded that most commercial relational DBMS's consider the Relational Algebra to be at too low a level for end-users). Use of the Cartesian product operator can be illustrated more effectively after first introducing some other features of the Relational Algebra.

Special Relational Operations

The traditional facilities for manipulating mathematical sets include the ability to extract a subset defined by specified criteria. In the Relational Algebra, it is convenient to define two special versions of the subsetting operation.

SELECTION

The selection operation is used to construct a "horizontal" subset. That is, the result will contain all of the attributes of the operand relation, but only those tuples meeting a specified condition. The condition is normally specified in the form of a True-False expression that can be evaluated on a tuple-by-tuple basis. If the expression refers to more than one attribute, then all must be drawn from a common abstract data type. For example:

```
SELECT VOLUME WHERE (DATE-DUE < March 10, 1985)
```

PROJECTION

Projection constructs a "vertical" subset consisting of only the specified *attributes* of its operand relation. The result will contain a tuple corresponding to each one in the operand, except that any duplicates will be deleted of course. A list of all the publishers represented in a library could be produced by the operation:

```
PROJECT BOOK (PUBLISHER)
```

Most of the operations defined so far deal either with single relations or with two that are union-compatible—that is, they have the same structure. How are queries handled that require combining information from two different relations? For example, suppose that a library wanted a list of the names and addresses of its borrowers that also included their card numbers:

```
SELECT BORROWER WHERE (LIB-NAME=...)
```

would produce the subset of the total BORROWER relation that referred to the particular library. If that result is called TEMP1, then:

```
PROJECT TEMP1 (CARD-NO, BORROWER-ID)
```

gives a relation—call it TEMP2—in which the (unneeded) Lib-Name attribute had been dropped. However, replacing the Borrower-ID's with names and addresses requires referring to the PERSON relation. The only facility defined so far that would allow us to do anything at all with TEMP2 and PERSON is the Cartesian product. In fact, if the Cartesian product of these two relations is constructed, the result, TEMP3, will have the attributes:

```
TEMP3 {Card-No, Borrower-ID, Person-ID, Title, First-Name,
Middle-Names, Last-Name, Suffix, Address}
```

Note that to ensure that TEMP3 has unique key values, the key must be defined to include all the attributes that were part of the keys of the operand relations. Furthermore, TEMP3 is definitely *not* in 3NF.

TEMP3 certainly contains all the columns needed to answer the query. The problem is that it contains, in addition to all the tuples with valid data, a vast number that are irrelevant because *each* tuple from TEMP3 will have been matched up with *each* one from PERSON. It may be noted that the tuples of interest will have matching values in the Borrower-ID and Person-ID attributes. Thus, the SELECT operation could be used to identify the tuples where this condition holds:

```
SELECT TEMP3 WHERE (Borrower-Id = Person-ID)
```

Because the two attributes are both drawn from the same abstract data type, this operation is valid and produces the desired result.

JOIN

At this point, the reader may be losing enthusiasm for the Relational Algebra if, as it appears, a potentially enormous Cartesian product must be constructed whenever it is necessary to combine information from two nonunion-compatible relations. However, this is not the case. The join operation exists specifically to deal with cases where tuples from two relations need to be matched on the basis of specified attribute values.

For the query discussed above, the relation TEMP2 gives the Card-Nos that are wanted in the final result and Borrower-IDs that can be used to find the names and addresses in the PERSON relation. These can be directly related using a join:

```
JOIN TEMP2 (BORROWER-ID) = PERSON(PERSON-ID)
```

There will be a row in the result for each match between the Borrower-No of a TEMP2 tuple and the Person-ID of a PERSON tuple. The result will contain all of the attributes from both relations, except that because the Person-ID attribute would simply duplicate Borrower-ID, it will be dropped. This is the result that was desired, except that it still contains a Borrower-ID attribute that can be dropped using a final projection.

Technically, a join produces a subset of the Cartesian product of two relations. Although it may be difficult to find many situations where the Cartesian product, itself, is needed, the join is clearly of great value. There are actually many variations of join, depending on the condition used to perform the subsetting. The version just illustrated is referred to as the equi-join because tuples are combined on the basis of matching values in the specified attributes. This is the most generally useful type of join and the one most often implemented. However, joins based on any other Boolean comparison of tuples from two relations are possible in principle and may be useful under special circumstances.

DIVISION

As has been seen, the join operation is simply a convenient way to specify a function that could alternatively be accomplished through a combination of Cartesian product and selection. Division falls into the same class because it is equivalent to a projection on the intersection of the results of one or more selection operations. For the operation A DIV-BY B to be defined, the attributes of the relation B must be a subset of those of A. That is, if the set of attributes in relation A is denoted by {a} and the set of attributes in relation B by {b}, then it must be true that {a} = {a',b}. The result of A DIV-BY B will have the set of attributes {a'}— that is, those attributes that were present in A but not in B. A particular tuple, a', will appear in the result if the tuple a',b appears in A for every tuple, b, in B.

Some examples showing the use of the division operation are presented in Figure 6–14. It may also be noted that division is the inverse of Cartesian product in the sense that if C = A CART-PROD B, then C DIV-BY A gives B and C DIV-BY B gives A.

EVALUATION

The relational model was developed after the hierarchical and network models and differs from them in some important respects. The two earlier models have strong roots, both genealogically and functionally, in the commercial file processing world. Development of the relational model, on the other hand, took place away from the pressures and biases of the real world and represents a fundamentally different approach to database management.

The first thing one notices about the relational model is its simplicity and elegance. There is only a single construct, the relation, which is used to represent both entities and relationships. In real-world situations, it is sometimes quite difficult to decide whether to treat something as an entity or a relationship. Thus, it is quite appealing to have a data model that makes the distinction unnecessary. Treating relationships in the same way as entities also provides a natural way to represent attributes of relationships—something that can not really be done at all in the hierarchical model and that is rather artificial in the network model.

A second distinguishing characteristic of the relational model is the fact that data is manipulated in aggregates rather than one record at a time, and that the basic data manipulation functions are extremely powerful. This greatly simplifies the logic of database processing and facilitates the application of automatic query optimization techniques.

Probably the most often cited disadvantage of the relational model is its alleged inefficiency. To some extent, this impression is the result of a profusion of poorly implemented relational DBMSs. However, even the best of today's relational systems might not score well based on a narrow definition of

CATALOG

BR – NAME	BK – NO
BR1	BK1
BR1	BK2
BR1	BK3
BR1	BK4
BR1	BK5
BR2	BK2
BR2	BK4
BR2	BK5
BR3	BK1
BR4	BK2
BR4	BK4

BKS-1

BK – NO
BK1
BK2
BK3
BK4
BK5

BKS-2

BK – NO
BK2
BK4

BKS-3

BK – NO
BK3

CATALOG DIV-BY BKS-1

BR – NAME
BR1

CATALOG DIV-BY BKS-2

BR – NAME
BR1
BR2
BR4

CATALOG DIV-BY BKS-3

BR – NAME
BR1

FIGURE 6–14 Relation division examples.

efficiency. The philosophy behind this model intentionally trades machine resources for other benefits. As computers become increasingly powerful, and as the cost of hardware declines relative to other, predominantly human, resources, this trade-off becomes more and more attractive.

The last important property of the relational model to be mentioned is the fact that it is soundly based on an existing, and growing, body of theory. The importance of this cannot be overemphasized. It means that much knowledge about the behavior of relational database systems can be obtained by relatively quick, inexpensive theoretical studies. In the absence of such a theoretical base, it is necessary to rely heavily on actual experience for advancing knowledge. Experience is a costly way to learn. Furthermore, it is often impossible to be certain exactly why a given result occurred. Because of this property of the relational model, it is used for almost all database research. It has often happened that knowledge gained studying the relational model has been applied to increasing our understanding of the hierarchical and network models as well.

Although the relational model experienced early resistance in the commerical world because of the efficiency issue, it now appears to dominate the older alternatives. With its SQL/DS product for medium-sized installations and Database 2 for large ones, IBM has made the relational approach respectable. Its simplicity has also made it the natural choice for use in the rapidly expanding home and small office market where specialized staff support is not available. Networks and hierarchies will continue to exist for a long time, but the tide is shifting in the direction of relations.

TERMS TO UNDERSTAND

relation	Third Normal Form (3NF)
tuple	Fourth Normal Form (4NF)
normalization	Fifth Normal Form (5NF)
First Normal Form (1NF)	functional dependency
Second Normal Form (2NF)	

REVIEW QUESTIONS

1. Question 4 in Chapter 2 introduced the possibility of a data model in which relationships were considered to be just a particular type of entity. Could the relational model be considered an example of such a data model? Why or why not?

2. What are the advantages of having only a single representation for both entities and relationships? Are there any disadvantages?

3. Give an example of real-world situations that exhibit each of the following functional dependencies: (a) $A \rightarrow B$; $B \leftrightarrow A$; (b) $A \rightarrow B$; $B \rightarrow A$; (c) $A \leftrightarrow B$; $B \leftrightarrow A$.

4. What do the normal forms higher than 3NF have in common?

5. Why can keys not have null values?

6. Given an original example of a relation that is in 2NF but not 3NF. Describe how it would have to be modified to comply with the rules of 3NF.

7. Why is the result of a join not in 3NF?

8. Referring to the library example in this chapter, why cannot we just put the Bor-No attribute in the PERSON relation and dispense with the BORROWER relation entirely?

9. Describe how the operations of the Relational Algebra could be used to find the set of tuples that were in relation A but not in relation B. Assume that the two relations are union-compatible.

10. Consider the following relation:

Course	Instructor	Text
DBase 1	A	T1
DBase 1	B	T2

(a) Give *three* possible interpretations of this information; (b) What normal form is this relation in? How can you tell?; (c) For each of your interpretations in (a), show how the database could be redesigned to make that interpretation clear.

11. Design a 3NF relational database for the family tree of Chapter 2, Question 7. For each relation, list the attributes and underline the key. How do you know it is in 3NF? Specify an abstract data type for each attribute.

12. Design a 3NF relational database for the Last National Bank (LNB) (Chapter 2, Question 5).

13. Design a 3NF relational database for the university administration problem of Chapter 4, Question 5.

14. There is disagreement among database authorities concerning whether users should be allowed to specify the access path to be used in satisfying a query. What are the two sides of this controversy?

CHAPTER 7

DATA
INDEPENDENCE

It is, of course, an article of faith among advocates of the database approach that the separate files associated with individual applications should be integrated into a single whole. Integration is intended to reduce duplication, encourage sharing, and, in general, facilitate the rational management of information for the overall benefit of the organization.

Integration of data also creates new problems and increases the significance of some old ones. Three primary areas of impact may be noted:

- Access control
- Providing application-oriented views of data
- Limiting impact of changes

A rough-and-ready form of access control is implicit in the separate file approach because any given file is generally known and accessible to only a limited number of programs. With an integrated database, great care must be taken to ensure that data is not released to, or altered by, unauthorized people or programs. Similarly, when each application has its own files, the files are designed to contain precisely the information needed by the application, structured in the most appropriate way. A database, on the other hand, serves a number of applications. Its content and structure are determined on the basis of global criteria. From the point of view of an individual application, the database will contain much irrelevant information and probably less than ideal data structures. Finally, as applications are added or changed, changes to the content and structure of the database will undoubtedly be required. Because of the integrated nature of a database, applications not directly affected by the changes may still have to be altered.

These problem areas have been recognized for some time. Approaches to dealing with the latter two are generally covered by the term, "data independence," introduced in Chapter 1. Data independence may also be viewed as relevant to the access control area, in that it is concerned with protecting data used for certain applications from unauthorized interference by others. Most mechanisms used to achieve data independence work by introducing an element of isolation between applications and the database.

One such approach is the schema/subschema capability in the Data Base Task Group's (DBTG) network model. The schema is intended to be a description of the entire database, whereas subschemas are created to describe the views of the database relevant to particular users or groups. Users and applications programmers use the subschema as if it were a description of the real database. The Database Management System (DBMS) takes responsibility for performing the mapping required between this view and the database as it actually exists. The "view" facility in many relational database systems is used in a similar way.

The schema/subschema structure can be quite effective if there is sufficient mapping power in the subschema processor. When an application is added or modified in a way that requires a new view of the database, an existing sub-schema is modified or a new one developed. The subschema definition, using some Data Definition Language (DDL), must specify how each data object in the subschema relates to the underlying schema. Then, a machine-readable mapping is produced through a process similar to the compilation of high-level programming languages. The mapping is used by the DBMS to reinterpret subschema-oriented requests in terms of the schema itself.

As long as a new or altered subschema does not require any change to the schema, all mappings to other preexisting subschemas remain valid. Thus, applications using these other subschemas are totally unaffected by the change. Figure 7–1 illustrates this process. It shows the schema developed in Chapter 6 for the library example and a subschema for a comprehensive cataloging function. When

LIBRARY {Lib-Name, Lib-Director-ID}

BRANCH {Lib-Name, Br-Name, Br-Address}

BOOK {Catalog-No, Title, Author-ID, Publisher}

BORROWER {Lib-Name, Bor-No, Borrower-ID}

VOLUME {Lib-Name, Br-Name, Catalog-No, Copy-No, Bor-No, Date-Due}

PERSON {Person-ID, Prefix, First-Name, Middle Names, Last-Name, Suffix, Address}

Complete library system schema

BOOK {Catalog-No, Title, Author-ID, Publisher}

VOLUME {Catalog-No, Copy-No, Date-Due}

Subschema for branch catalog

BORROWER {Lib-name, Bor-No, Borrower-ID}

VOLUME {Lib-Name, Br-Name, Catalog-No, Copy-No, Bor-No, Date-Due}

PERSON {Person-ID, Prefix, First-Name, Middle Names, Last-Name, Suffix, Address}

New subschema for tracing lost books

FIGURE 7–1 Adding a new application.

```
┌─────────────────────────────────────────────────────────────────────┐
│  LIBRARY {Lib-Name, Lib-Director-ID}                                  │
│                                                                       │
│  BRANCH {Lib-Name, Br-Name, Br-Address}                               │
│                                                                       │
│  BOOK {Catalog-No, Title, Author-ID, Publisher}                       │
│                                                                       │
│  BORROWER {Lib-name, Br-Name, Bor-No, Borrower-ID}                    │
│                                                                       │
│  VOLUME {Lib-Name, Br-Name, Catalog-No, Copy-No, Bor-No,              │
│          Date-Due}                                                    │
│                                                                       │
│  PERSON {Person-ID, Prefix, First-Name,                               │
│          Middle Names, Last-Name, Suffix, Address}                    │
│                      Complete library system schema                   │
├─────────────────────────────────────────────────────────────────────┤
│  BOOK {Catalog-No, Title, Author-ID, Publisher}                       │
│                                                                       │
│  VOLUME {Catalog-No, Copy-No, Date-Due}                               │
│                      Subschema for branch catalog                     │
├─────────────────────────────────────────────────────────────────────┤
│  BORROWER {Lib-name, Br-Name, Bor-No, Borrower-ID}                    │
│                                                                       │
│  VOLUME {Lib-Name, Br-Name, Catalog-No, Copy-No, Bor-No,              │
│          Date-Due}                                                    │
│                                                                       │
│  PERSON {Person-ID, Prefix, First-Name,                               │
│          Middle Names, Last-Name, Suffix, Address}                    │
│                   New subschema for tracing lost books                │
└─────────────────────────────────────────────────────────────────────┘
```

FIGURE 7–2 Effect of schema modification.

another subschema is added for tracing overdue books, no change is required in either the schema or the previously existing subschema.

Occasionally, it may be necessary to change the schema itself to accommodate the needs of a new or altered subschema. In this case, *all* subschemas will probably have to be remapped. However, no action other than a recompilation is required for subschemas not directly affected by the schema changes. This is a relatively straightforward task. However, the reader should be aware that in many large organizations, the number of programs requiring recompilation could be in the thousands. This is, at least, a time-consuming and expensive process and one that requires tight procedural controls to ensure that it is done correctly. Figure 7–2 shows what would happen if a decision was made to issue library cards on a branch-by-branch basis. The schema is changed to include Br-Name in the BORROWER relation. This requires a corresponding change in the subschema for the overdue book application, but it does not affect the catalog subschema.

However, both subschemas would have to be remapped; the changed one for obvious reasons, and the other simply because its schema references will have to be somewhat different.

Schema changes are not as rare as might be expected. In current systems, the schema usually reflects closely the physical organization of the database. Thus, changing storage hardware to take advantage of technological advances will often require schema changes. Second, complete, organization-wide databases are almost never implemented in a single step. The process is usually an incremental one, both for budgetary reasons and to minimize risk and disruption of ongoing activities. Thus, at any given moment, the schema reflects the currently implemented portion of the entire database, and whenever applications are added in a new area, the schema has to be changed.

THE 3-SCHEMA FRAMEWORK

The schema/subschema approach does not provide a fully satisfactory approach to data independence because the schema is not usually sufficiently stable. Subschema changes can be easily isolated, but a schema change has widespread repercussions. A significant advance over this approach was suggested by the ANSI/X3/SPARC Study Group on DBMSs.[1] This study group developed a generalized framework for representing all aspects of the database management task. The framework identified three distinct spheres of interest, or realms, within the overall database environment.[2] The *external realm* is a simplified model of the real world as seen by applications. It contains any number of external views of the database, each of which is relevant to one or a group of applications. The entities, attributes, and relationships included in an external view are represented in an external schema.

The *internal realm* contains the internal view, which is a model of the data actually maintained in the database. This is described in the internal schema and includes details of storage hardware and strategies.

The *conceptual realm* contains a model of the real world as seen by the organization as a whole. This includes all those entities and relationships that are

---

[1] ANSI is the American National Standards Institute, which is responsible for establishing U.S. standards in many areas. ANSI/X3 is the designation for ANSI's Committee on Computers and Information Processing. SPARC stands for Standards Planning and Review Committee. One of the responsibilities of ANSI/X3/SPARC is the recommendation of areas within the computing field where standardization may be appropriate. Because of the amount of attention being paid to database concepts in the early 1970s, ANSI/X3/SPARC formed an ad hoc Study Group on DBMS's in 1972 to determine what needs for standardization were likely to emerge in this area.

[2] "Realm" has a specific technical meaning in the DBTG network model. However, this term was also used in its generic sense in the ANSI/X3/SPARC report, and we choose to remain consistent with their terminology. In this context, the word "level" could also have been used.

of interest to the enterprise. This model is called the conceptual view and it is described in the conceptual schema. Note that although there can be many external views, each oriented toward a particular clientele, there is only one conceptual view. The primary purpose of the conceptual realm is to provide the stable anchoring point that is missing in the DBTG approach. External views can be added or changed without any impact on the internal realm. Similarly, the internal schema can be altered to increase efficiency or accommodate new hardware without any impact on the external views. Mechanisms for controlling the content and use of the database are also included in the conceptual realm because they are independent of technology—at least in principle.

The ANSI/SPARC external schema is essentially equivalent to a subschema in the DBTG approach or a view in the relational model. The DBTG schema includes elements of the internal and conceptual schemas. However, it is impossible for an approach employing only two levels to provide the isolation between internal and external views needed for data independence.

The conceptual realm contains a model of the organization's complete database—even portions that may not be currently implemented. The internal realm contains a model of that portion that is implemented; the external realm contains a number of models, each offering a particular user-oriented view of the database. The reader may be wondering how these models relate to the data models described in earlier chapters. The answer is that any modeling approach may be used as long as it is capable of representing the relevant objects. It is even possible to imagine using different modeling approaches in the different realms as long as the DBMS has the capability of making the transformations between them. The entity-relationship (E-R) model seems especially well suited to conceptual modeling for example. The relational model might be chosen for use in the external realm because of its simplicity; the network model might be chosen for use in the internal realm because of its ability to specify details of storage structure and access.

THE CONCEPTUAL REALM

The conceptual level is concerned with the fundamental information needs of the organization quite independent of how data is collected, stored, or used. The tool for recording this information is the conceptual schema that is a model of the entities, attributes, and relationships of interest to the organization. Because of the global nature of this model, it is sometimes referred to as an enterprise schema. Very few organizations have such a model in any form, although as a result of the ANSI/SPARC proposal more and more are starting to construct one. Such enterprise schemas as do exist are relatively informal and often expressed pictorially. However, the ANSI/SPARC proposal envisions a quite formal conceptual schema stored in the database and processed by the DBMS.

Because the conceptual schema is intended to provide a stable anchoring point for the database environment, it is concerned with information content only. There is no reference to storage structures or access mechanisms. Ideally, design of the conceptual schema would be the first step in introducing database technology to an organization. The design of user views and physical representations could then be based on this more-or-less invariant foundation. As a practical matter, most large organizations made their initial commitments to the database approach *before* the idea of a conceptual schema had even been proposed. Furthermore, most of the widely used DBMS's were also developed prior to the widespread acceptance of the three-schema approach and hence do not include facilities for storing and processing a conceptual schema. Some recently introduced DBMS's have begun to support this capability, but this is of limited relevance to organizations that already have major investments in older systems.

There is not yet any universal agreement on exactly what should be contained in a conceptual schema beyond a definition of the entire database. It has been suggested that the conceptual schema should describe the basic functioning of the enterprise—not only data definitions, but also information on data flows and uses, validation procedures, access authorization, and so on. The conceptual schema would be expressed in a language developed specifically for this purpose and referred to as the Conceptual DDL (Conceptual Data Definition Language).

Although the conceptual schema is intended to be stable, it is not expected to remain unchanged forever. However, changes should be made only to reflect changes in the real-world enterprise or its environment. Care should be taken to perform the initial design as accurately as possible because changes to the conceptual schema may be expected to have widespread repercussions. It is possible to begin with a conceptual schema that does not cover the entire enterprise as long as interfaces are included to permit later extensions.

THE INTERNAL REALM

The internal realm is concerned with the database as it is physically stored and with achieving the greatest possible efficiency of operation. It deals with the representation of data-items, existence and maintenance of indices, and actual physical device characteristics. This is all described in the internal schema, which is written in an Internal DDL.

There is an interface, or mapping, between the conceptual and internal schemas that expresses how the objects in each are related. This mapping is used to determine how an item in the conceptual schema is actually stored and how it may be retrieved. Changes in storage technology, accessing strategy, or other matters that are the concern of the internal level require corresponding changes to the internal schema and to the mapping between the internal and conceptual levels. However, the conceptual schema, itself, is not changed, and, hence, there is certainly no requirement for changing any external schemas. Thus, changes at the internal level are entirely transparent to users.

One interesting aspect of the separation of a conceptual database definition from the description of its physical implementation is that it is possible to have objects in the conceptual schema that are not currently in the physical database at all! Their existence in the conceptual schema reflects the fact that they exist and are used in the organization, even though they are not yet part of the database. Thus, the conceptual schema is not constrained by where the organization may happen to be in its database implementation plan. Of course, any attempt to access something in the conceptual schema that does not physically exist will fail, but it is at least possible to design and test programs with full knowledge of what the database will eventually contain.

THE EXTERNAL REALM

The external realm contains the users' views of the database—one for each application area. Although there is only one conceptual schema and one internal schema, there may be many external schemas. Each external schema provides the view of the database appropriate for a particular set of applications. This does not mean that an external schema is merely a subset of the conceptual one. Objects in an external schema must be derivable from those in the conceptual schema, but the derivation process can be quite complex, involving computation and reorganization.

As an example, the conceptual schema for a university would undoubtedly contain objects representing students, courses, and grades. The external schema for the class scheduling application might be a hierarchy with students underneath courses, whereas transcript generation would require a hierarchy with course records underneath students. In addition, the transcript external schema would likely contain a field grade-point average. This field would probably not appear in the conceptual schema at all because it does not represent a concept that is fundamental to a university. Rather, it is derived by applying some formula (perhaps changing from time to time) to grades and course-credit values that are the fundamental quantities.

External schemas would be expressed in an External DDL and would, of course, have to based on some data model. As mentioned in the previous section, the data model used for external schemas would not have to be the same as those used in the other levels. Whether it would be possible, or even desirable, to have external schemas based on a variety of models is not addressed in the ANSI/SPARC report.

IMPLEMENTATION OF THE 3-SCHEMA APPROACH

It is important to emphasize that the ANSI/SPARC framework is merely a proposal. It does not reflect the structure of any current DBMS, most of which

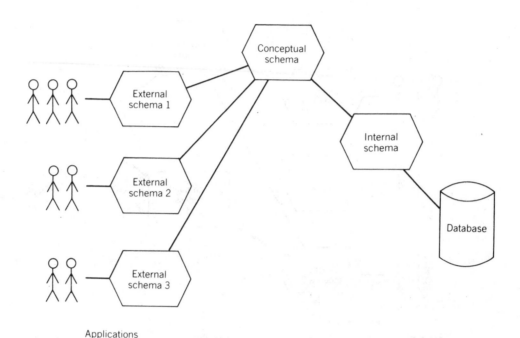

Applications

FIGURE 7–3 The three-schema model.

support a two-level approach based on the DBTG proposals. As mentioned previously, most large organizations began designing databases before the ANSI/SPARC proposal appeared with its emphasis on the conceptual schema as a foundation for subsequent development. Many firms have subsequently begun to construct conceptual models to guide their future database development.

The ANSI/SPARC framework can be summarized as shown in Figure 7–3. External schemas describe particular user views of the database. The internal schema describes what is actually implemented. Both of these are mapped to the conceptual schema, which provides a stable, high-level representation of the organization and its information needs. In the absence of the conceptual schema, mappings would be needed between the internal schema and *each* of the external ones. Any change in the internal schema would require alteration of all of these mappings. With the conceptual schema in the middle, a change to the internal schema caused, for example, by installation of new storage hardware or physical data organization requires changing only the single mapping between the internal and conceptual schemas.

In operation, an application program issues requests to the DBMS in terms of the objects defined in its external schema. This request is mapped to the conceptual schema, then mapped again to the internal schema for processing. If a user

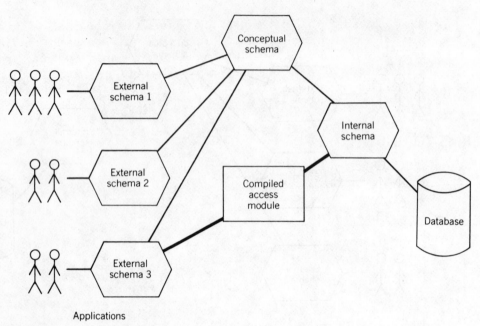

Applications

FIGURE 7–4 Three-realm model with access modules.

requests an item of data that is not actually stored, this second mapping will fail.[3] At some later time, when this data has been included in the physical database, a similar request will succeed. No alteration of the program will be required to take account of this addition to the database.

The reader who is greatly concerned about efficiency may be appalled at this double mapping on every data access. However, what has been described so far is the *basic principle* of data access in the ANSI/SPARC framework. It is not absolutely necessary that every access actually go through two distinct mappings. The model provides for the possibility that a pair of mappings—from external schema to conceptual and from conceptual to internal—could be processed once to produce a single access module that would generate requests directly to the internal realm (see Figure 7–4.) Of course, if either of the mappings contained within it were to change, the module would no longer work correctly and would have to be rebuilt by a process analagous to the compilation of programs. This procedure could be substantially automated by having the DBMS keep track of all existing access modules. Whenever any change was made to a schema, all mod-

---

[3] This does not necessarily mean that the program will abort. A good DBMS will advise application programs of the reason whenever it is unable to satisfy a request. User programs should be designed to interpret these messages and react accordingly.

ules that referred to that schema would be marked by the DBMS to indicate that they were no longer current. Any attempt to use a noncurrent module would cause it to be automatically reconstructed. Aside from possibly noticing a delay in response, the user should not be aware that anything unusual has occurred. A technique similar to this, although in a slightly different context, is used in IBM's Database 2 and (SQL/DS) relational DBMS's.

TERMS TO UNDERSTAND

data independence	internal schema
external schema	conceptual schema

REVIEW QUESTIONS

1. Within a single database, how many conceptual schemas are there? When is one changed or a new one created?

2. Answer Question 1 with respect to the internal schema.

3. Answer Question 1 with respect to the external schema.

4. Where are the schemas stored? How are they used?

5. What is the main reason for having conceptual schemas?

6. Outline the contents for each type of schema for the university administration database of Chapter 4, Question 5.

7. The process of linking a program to the (physical) data it needs is called binding. This can be done when the program is compiled, when it is executed, or at the moment the data is actually needed. Discuss the implications of these three approaches in terms of efficiency and data independence.

C H A P T E R 8

DATABASE DESIGN—II

TOP-DOWN VERSUS BOTTOM-UP

Most of the literature on database design recommends beginning with an analysis of the organizational function(s) to be supported, determining their information requirements, and then synthesizing these into a database structure. Although this must seem to be a highly rational approach, it fails to take into account that most organizations implementing the database approach already have a large investment in conventional files and programs. This neglect is intentional. Advocates of the top-down approach argue that existing systems were probably developed in an ad hoc manner without adequate planning or coordination. If these old systems are allowed to unduly restrict the design process. it may be impossible to produce a rational, integrated result.

One technique that might work for implementing the top-down approach would be to freeze development of existing file-based applications and continue to use them while a complete, new database-oriented system was developed and tested. When the new system was ready, all applications would be converted at the same time. Although this may seem appealing, it carries quite high costs and risk for all but the smallest organizations. Developing a complete, integrated set of applications programs at one time would be a large and enormously complicated task, with a high probability of failure. It also caries a high psychological price, in that there are no visible results until the very end. One rule of thumb of the information systems management literature is that projects should be chosen and scheduled so that successes can be regularly demonstrated. This is critical in maintaining the confidence of both users and higher level management.

For all of these reasons, database implementation most often employs an incremental, bottom-up approach. One application is selected for initial conversion, and if this is successful, the database is extended by stages into other areas. This means that for a long period of time, there will be many application programs using traditional files while others are accessing the database. During the transition period, there is likely to be considerable duplication of information between conventional files and the database, necessitating duplicate procedures for update, access control, and so forth. Because most organizations are still in this transition period, it is easy to understand why so few have succeeded in obtaining the benefits that are supposed to be associated with the database approach.

For organizations with a substantial portfolio of existing file-base applications, the top-down approach to implementing a database is likely to prove unfeasible. At the same time, the bottom-up, incremental approach carries a severe risk of producing a final database design that is far from optimal. The method suggested here combines elements of both approaches in an attempt to avoid both of these pitfalls. It begins with a top-down exercise to develop an overall conceptual schema. Actual implementation is then assumed to proceed on an application-by-application basis. The sequencing of applications for conversion to the database can take into account the strengths and weaknesses of existing systems as well as other, externally generated priorities. However, the existence of the overall conceptual schema is intended to assure that all of these individual implementation efforts are properly coordinated and result in the database design that best meets the organization's overall needs.

DATABASE DESIGN PROCESS

Implementation of an organizational database should follow the following sequence of steps:

1. *Develop a Corporate Data Model.*   A corporate data model (CDM) is a high-level, static abstraction of the organization. It shows the major functions performed and the flows of information in support of them. Note that this is quite a different notion from what is called a data model elsewhere in this book. In fact, CDM is simply the term usually used by practitioners for the enterprise or conceptual schema of the ANSI/SPARC framework.[1]

2. *Incorporate Database in Long-range Information Systems Plan.*   Organizations should employ some type of formal long-range planning for information systems development. This should provide for the regular review of existing applications as well as the development of new ones. The plan will normally cover a five-year time horizon. Detailed budgets and schedules will be provided for activities to be undertaken in the first year. The more distant future will be laid out in more general terms. The plan should be rolled forward annually so that it always provides a map of the organization's intentions as far into the future as is possible in an area as dynamic as information systems. As soon as the organization has made a commitment to adopt the database approach, this plan should be modified to show how and when each application will be considered for conversion to the database.

3. *Information Requirements Analysis (IRA).*   Each extension of the database to encompass a new application should begin with a careful analysis of the information needed. For each data element identified, the analysis should specify its definition, format, accuracy and timeliness requirements, usage, and relationship to other data elements.

4. *Logical Database Design.*   Database design is usually divided into two stages. This first one is concerned with determining the actual contents of the database, the relationships that will be represented, the access and integrity constraints, and the views that will be available to various users. This stage is

[1]ANSI/SPARC: see footnote 1, Chapter 7, p. 131.

entirely independent of limitations imposed by hardware or a particular database management system.

5. *Physical Database Design.*   This stage transforms a logical database design into a form that is acceptable to the hardware and to the Database Management System (DBMS) that will be used. Storage structures and access mechanisms are also selected with an eye toward optimizing performance.

Converting an application to use a database will almost certainly require redesign and reprogramming. This can be done in a minimal way, in which case the database will simply be used to simulate the old separate files, or it can be more extensive to take advantage of the additional capabilities offered by a database environment. Either way, the usual sequence of developing and approving specifications for the new programs, followed by their implementation and testing, will be followed. The reader is referred to any standard text on systems analysis and design for a fuller discussion of this process. The following chapter will discuss some of aspects of systems development that are different in a database environment.

Data Dictionary

The basic premise of this book is that a database is a tool that can assist in making organizations more effective. If this is true, then it should apply to data processing organizations as well as other kinds. That is, it ought to be possible to improve the effectiveness of a data processing department by providing it with a database that contains all of the important information required for decision making, just as might be done for a factory or sales department.

The database that supports the information processing function is called the data dictionary. As the name suggests, the data dictionary was originally conceived as simply a list of all the data elements maintained by an organization along with their official definitions. Initially, it was believed that such lists could easily be maintained manually—in a notebook for example. However, it quickly became clear that this collection of information was both larger and more dynamic than originally thought, and a number of computer-based packages were developed to assist in storing, updating, and retrieving it. Once the information was available in machine-readable form, many other uses were found for it. It turned out that this expanded form of data dictionary is most useful, not only to people who work with the database, but also to the DBMS itself. In some cases, the data dictionary packages acquired facilities that made them seem almost like small DBMS's themselves. At this point, it became obvious that the data dictionary could be, and should be, managed, using the same software as was used for applications databases. This not only eliminated the need to acquire, maintain, and learn two separate complex packages, but also greatly simplified communication between the data dictionary and the DBMS.

Data dictionaries are discussed in detail in Chapter 10. All that is needed at this point is an awareness of the idea of a database to help manage the database. The data dictionary should be the first database application in any organization, and it should be used to store and manage all of the information produced during the process of designing other database applications. (Note that because the data dictionary is simply one piece of the overall corporate database, it will include a description of itself!)

The remainder of this chapter will consist of more detailed examination of the steps in designing a database.

The Corporate Data Model (CDM)

According to the ANSI/SPARC framework and most other modern views of database design, construction of the CDM should be the first step in implementing a database for an organization. As previously discussed, most organizations will not be in a position to implement a complete database at one time. The number of programs that would have to be converted and the mass of data to be transferred will normally make this an unreasonably risky and expensive undertaking.

Organizations usually begin to think seriously about the database approach when faced with implementing an application where this technology seems to offer a significant advantage. A DBMS is acquired and installed initially for just this one use, usually with the intention of extending it to other areas later. When the time comes to implement the next database application, it will be most surprising if the existing design, which was oriented toward one particular use, can be extended gracefully. Redesigning and reloading the database at this point is usually an unthinkable alternative, so, what often happens is that a completely separate database is designed and implemented for the new application. Eventually, the organization finds itself with a number of completely separate databases, each supporting a distinct set of tasks. This is obviously not the way database technology is intended to be used.

The way to avoid this situation is to design each piece of the database with full awareness of how it will eventually link to all the other pieces. This is precisely what the CDM is intended to accomplish. It presents a high-level view of the ultimate organization-wide database. With this as a starting point, it should not be difficult to identify suitable pieces for the initial as well as each subsequent implementation step and to ensure that each piece will be compatible with the other pieces.

In practice there are two reasons why development of a CDM is not the usual first step in implementing a database. First, a substantial majority of organizations large enough to use the database approach effectively began to do so before the idea of a CDM had been conceived.[2] Many of these organizations are now attempting to construct CDM's in order to document what has already been implemented and as a guide to rational future expansion.

Second, there is little support in existing database management software for the CDM concept, although it is starting to be recognized in some of the newest DBMS's to appear in the marketplace. In principle, the CDM should be expressed in a machine-readable Conceptual Data Definition Language (Conceptual DDL) and should be stored in the data dictionary. If this is done, then the external and internal schemas prepared in subsequent steps can be directly related to the CDM as discussed in the preceding chapter. If the DBMS does not include facilities for this, then the CDM must be kept outside the database environment, usually on paper. Although it can still be useful as a design and control tool, this will happen now only if appropriate administrative procedures exist to ensure that subsequent steps refer to, and are consistent with, the CDM.

Information Requirements Analysis (IRA)

One often finds discussions of logical database design beginning with, "Once the requirements are known. . . ." This neatly assumes away one of the most critical aspects of the problem.

Because database design is normally carried out within a functioning organization, information requirements analysis (IRA) is usually conducted by examining what is already going on. One way to view information requirements is in the form of the hierarchy shown in Figure 8–1. An organization consists of users, each of whom performs a set of tasks, each task requiring various items of information. One approach begins at the top of this hierarchy and works downward to determine the information needs. This is an inherently logical approach, but tends to be expensive and time consuming. Also, because this type of analysis is done without any consideration of the organization's existing information systems, it may well result in a set of recommendations for something that is quite different from what is already in place.

Such a recommendation would have to be considered carefully, making use of the well-known theorem comparing the value of birds in the hand to those in the bush. That is, even though some alternative set of information systems might be more effective than the current ones, the current ones already exist. People presumably know how to use these systems to perform their jobs. It may, there-

---

[2] The question of whether database technology is only appropriate for large organizations will be discussed in a later chapter. There is no doubt that DBMS software can be purchased along with an adequate hardware base for a price well within the reach of any commercial enterprise and many individuals. However, there is more to the successful installation of a database environment than hardware and software.

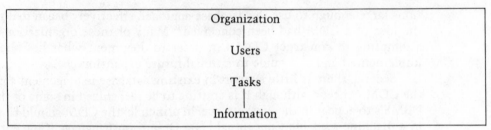

FIGURE 8–1 Information requirements hierarchy.

fore, be preferable to continue to use some or all of them and use development resources for other projects rather than to replace existing systems to achieve minor improvements.

The opposite approach starts at the bottom by looking at the organization's existing stock of information and attempting to trace where and how it is used. The main liability of this method is that it may be too strongly influenced by existing systems and may miss useful possibilities that are not included in them. Most organizations use a combination of the two in the hope of making the most of what they already have while not closing the door to other, perhaps innovative, ways of performing a task.

The bottom-up approach begins with the existing information systems—manual as well as computerized. Existing data collection forms and reports are gathered and examined. The first objective is to determine all of the individual data elements that are used by the organization. As these are discovered, they are entered in the data dictionary. Each entry is accompanied by a definition of the data element and a specification of its syntax. For existing automated systems, much of this information may be extracted from the system documentation if it has been prepared and maintained with sufficient care. Manual systems, however, rarely have adequate formal documentation. When the written documentation is nonexistent or insufficient, personnel familiar with the system should be interviewed to find out what each data element is.

As this information is collected, the analysts should be constantly looking for cases where the same name is used to describe different things and where different names are used for essentially the same thing. This often happens when the data elements are part of systems developed at different times or by different groups. In the first case, new names must be assigned to one or more of the elements to prevent confusion. In the second case, it will often be possible to use one of the elements in place of all the others or to define a single new element to be used in place of all of them.

The simplication thus achieved can be quite significant. Until embarking on a data dictionary project, few organizations realize how many different data-items they use. One public utility found that, even after elimination of duplicates, there were 1300 distinct data elements that were defined for a customer record, 700 for an employee. (It is, of course, unlikely that all of these elements would be present in the record for any single customer or employee.)

Once a set of data elements has been defined, the next step is to trace the path of each through the organization's information systems from initial collection through maintenance and use to eventual archiving or purging.

If the organization has a well-developed mature set of information systems, this analysis might be expected to produce an accurate description of its actual information needs; because the survey is based on documentation and forms that should be readily available, it is a relatively easy analysis to perform. In practice, things are usually not this simple. The formal information systems of an organization often contain information that nobody actually uses, and it would be surprising if some users could not be found who supplemented the information provided through formal channels with informal sources of their own.

Top-down IRA begins by identifying the potential users. These might be specific individuals, but more often they would be positions in the organization chart. The users may be at any level of the organization and may span more than one level.

Then, at least two individuals holding each affected position should be interviewed.[3] The first objective of the interviews is to develop an understanding of the tasks performed. Then, the information requirements of each task need to be identified. In some cases, this may be perfectly obvious. In others, it may be deduced from an understanding of how the task is performed. For example, if one of an individual's responsibilities is managing a raw materials inventory and the standard Economic Order Quantity formula is used, then the information requirements can be determined directly from the formula.

In many other cases, however, especially in tasks calling for human judgment, there may be no direct way of obtaining the information requirements. The usual approach, in these cases, is to ask the user what information he or she needs; although this may seem simple, it is subject to a variety of pitfalls. This topic is more appropriately treated in a text on systems analysis. A few comments will be offered here to suggest some of the dimensions of the problem.

In the first place, although nearly all authorities agree that users should participate in information system development projects, the users, themselves, are not always anxious to be included! They often do not know much about information systems and may be reluctant to exhibit their ignorance. They may be especially resistant to accepting responsibility for decisions that they do not fully understand. Also, it must always be remembered that user groups have their

---

[3] A database may sometimes be implemented to serve a specific single individual. In that case, of course, only that person need be interviewed at this stage.

regular responsibilities that cannot be ignored simply because there is an information systems development project underway. It is, in a very real sense, an addition to their duties that cannot be handled properly unless extra resources are provided. Finally, the quality of user personnel assigned to this task is important. When asked to nominate someone to work with the system developers, a manager will often be tempted to pick the person whose loss will cause the least interruption in his or her operations. This is usually a junior person or one who is new to the group. This is precisely the wrong kind of person to provide meaningful user input. Ideally, the user representative should have both experience and seniority, but managers tend to be quite reluctant to give up such people, even on a temporary basis.

There is also some evidence that when asked to state what information they need for a particular task, users tend to reply by describing the information they currently use. This should not be surprising because the user *has* to perform the task in the current environment and must, somehow, evolve a method for doing it with the information that is available. Thus, the user's first inclination often is to equate what is needed with what is available.

When pressed by the interviewer to describe the "ideal" set of information for the task, users will often greatly expand the original list, dreaming up all sorts of things that might be useful under various particular circumstances. Such answers cannot be accepted uncritically, not only because there is cost associated with collecting and providing information, but also because of the phenomenon of information overload, which suggests that decision performance may actually go down as more and more information is provided.[4]

The top-down approach to determining information requirements has much to recommend it in its tendency to minimize bias caused by past behavior and to focus on the basic functions that the database is intended to support. However, because of its demands on user (often managerial) time, it can be a lengthy and expensive process. Again, users are not always in a position to elucidate clearly their own information needs. Most organizations try to combine this approach with the bottom-up one, which begins with the existing information and traces where and how it is used.

Logical Database Design

In this step, the designer uses the previously accumulated knowledge about information requirements to produce a logical specification of the database. The exact form of this specification will vary depending on the technique used. Any of the standard data models could be used as vehicles for logical database design. If it is

---

[4]This is caused partly by the additional time required to absorb an increased amount of information and partly by the difficulty of selecting the essential "wheat" from a larger pile of "chaff."

performed using the same data model that will ultimately be used to implement the application, then the physical design step may become almost trivial. However, there are some good reasons not to always take advantage of this apparent simplification. Of the three most common data models, only the relational one is really well-suited for use as a logical design tool. The hierarchical model is inherently too limiting; the network one, excessively preoccupied with technical details that are more properly considered in the following stage. Even the relational model is handicapped by the lack of a clear and unambiguous way to represent semantic information, that is, information about what the data means. For this reason, the entity-relationship (E-R) model or one of the newer ones incorporating semantics is a better choice.

Logical Design Using the E-R Model

The most common approach to logical database design in the context of the E-R model, called *view synthesis* (Figure 8–2), begins from the users' perspective. An E-R model is prepared for each user view that the database is to support. Then these diagrams are combined in a relatively mechanical way to produce a unified E-R model capable of supporting all of the views. At this point, the complete E-R diagram can be drawn and reviewed for completeness and consistency. When the designer is satisfied that the E-R diagram is correct, the final step consists of specifying the attributes of each entity-type and relationship-type and identifying the appropriate abstract data types for each.

Production of the user views is usually a relatively ad hoc process that depends heavily on the skill and experience of the designer. Of course, the fact that the view-level E-R models are relatively small and are focused on a single application area helps to reduce the complexity of the design task. More formal methods for developing E-R models have been proposed, intending both to reduce the significance of subjective factors and to make sure that nothing of importance has been inadvertently omitted from the final design. One of these is the E-R expansion method.[5] This method consists of the following six steps (illustrated in Figure 8–3):

1. *Determine Requirements.*   The designer reviews the output of the IRA and any other documentation available that describes the objectives of the new system. This helps the designer to build up a mental model of what needs to be included in the database. This is used as a starting point. Subsequent steps help to identify anything that may have been omitted in this first, relatively intuitive stage.

---

[5] Ilchoo Chung, *An evaluation of entity-relationship (E-R) modeling performance among cognitive styles and three methods of designing E-R diagrams,* Unpublished Ph.D. dissertation, University of California at Los Angeles, 1983.

Entity-relationship (E-R) diagrams for individual user views

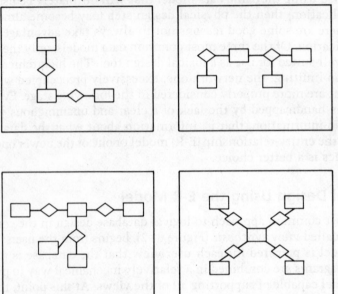

Synthesized composite entity-relationship (E-R) diagram

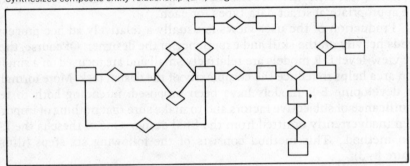

FIGURE 8–2 Entity-relationships (E-R) view synthesis.

2. *Generate a List of Entity Types.* The designer attempts to write down a complete list of the types of things that must be represented in the model. In this example, libraries, branches, books, and borrowers would seem to be the obvious entity-types.

3. *E-R Expansion.* The entity-types from Step 2 are analyzed one at a time. The name of the selected entity-type is entered in the center rectangle of an E-R expansion worksheet, such as the one shown in Figure 8–4. Next, all other

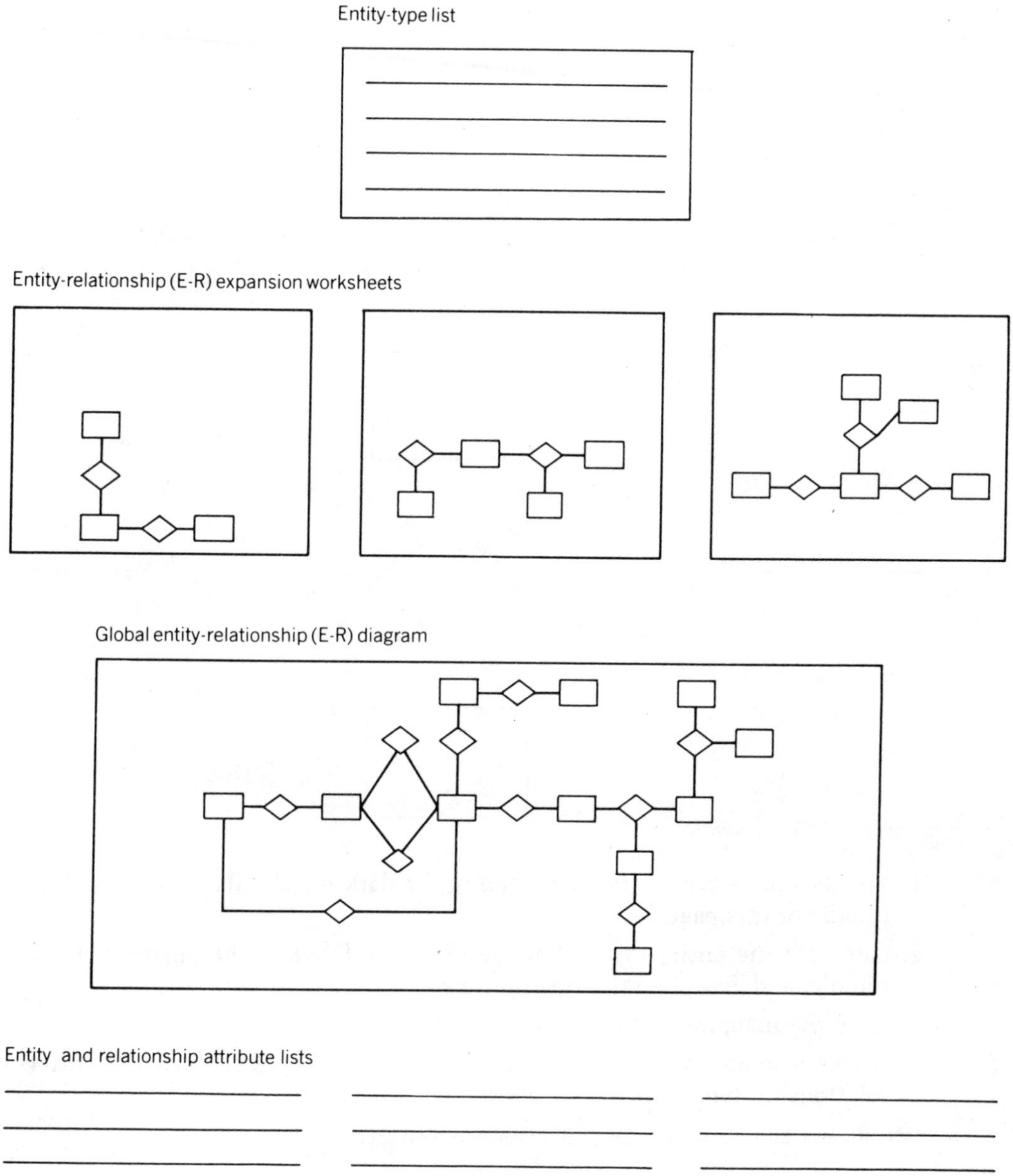

Entity-type list

Entity-relationship (E-R) expansion worksheets

Global entity-relationship (E-R) diagram

Entity and relationship attribute lists

FIGURE 8–3 Entity-relationships (E-R) expansion method.

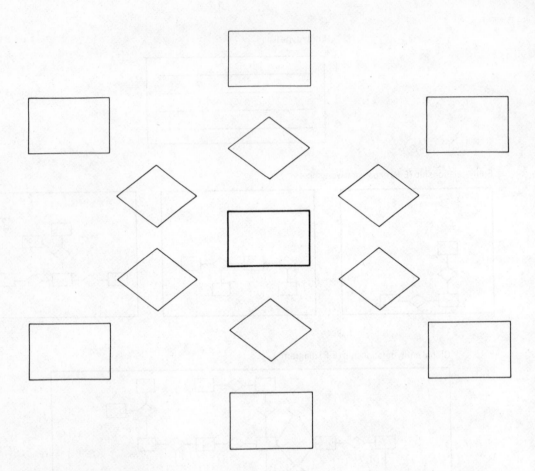

1. Put the entity-type *to be expanded* in the dark rectangular box located in the middle of this page.
2. Generate the entity-types that are *closely related* to the entity-type in the middle, and give the relationship-type.
3. Give the mapping ratio (e.g., 1, *N*, or *M*).
4. If you generate more entity- or relationship-types, please draw the entity- or relationship-type symbols by yourself.

FIGURE 8–4 Entity-relationships (E-R) expansion worksheet.

entity-types that are directly related to the selected one are entered in rectangles around the outside of the worksheet. The entity-types entered here can be ones from the list developed in Step 2, but the process of expanding one entity-type may also remind the designer of others. Each of these "outer" entity-types implies the existence of a relationship type. The last task in the expansion of an entity-type is the naming of these relationship-types and, for each one, the specification of the associated roles and mapping ratios. A completed E-R expansion worksheet for the VOLUME entity-type is shown in Figure 8–5.

4. *Draw the Global E-R Diagram.*   This step integrates all of the E-R expansion worksheets to produce a complete E-R diagram. The process is purely mechanical and is capable of being automated. The first E-R worksheet is copied onto a large sheet of paper. Then the remaining worksheets are examined one by one, and any entities and relationships not already included in the diagram are added to it. Needless to say, it will usually be possible to make the resulting diagram much more comprehensible by redrawing it to reduce crossing lines, and so on. Figure 8–6 shows the result of integrating the expansion worksheets for the library database.

5. *Critically Review the E-R Diagram.*   A picture of the complete logical database structure now exists for the first time. This should be examined for any obvious errors or omissions. Questions to ask include:

- Do the entity types shown in the diagram really exist? Can instances of each be identified?
- Are there any redundant relationship-types?
- Are there any missing relationship-types?
- Do the mapping ratios correspond to the real world?
- Are there any missing entity-types?

Any changes suggested by this review should be made on the E-R diagram and the review cycle repeated until no further changes are needed.

6. *Assign Attributes.*   Each entity- and relationship-type is examined and a list is made of all the attributes (properties or characteristics) that will need to be included in the database. The data dictionary should contain most of the information needed for this task.

   Finally, each attribute must be assigned to a abstract data type. The appropriate collection of abstract data types is highly dependent on the application. Figure 8–7 lists some that would be useful in most business environments. Recall that abstract data type assignments will be used to determine if it is permissible to compare values of two attributes. For two attributes from a common abstract data type, the role specification will indicate whether the comparison is sensible.

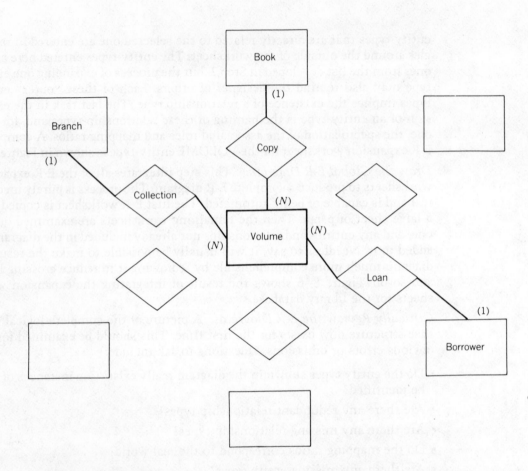

1. Put the entity-type *to be expanded* in the dark rectangular box located in the middle of this page.
2. Generate the entity-types that are *closely related* to the entity-type in the middle, and give the relationship-type.
3. Give the mapping ratio (e.g., 1, *N*, or *M*).
4. If you generate more entity- or relationship-types, please draw the entity- or relationship-type symbols by yourself.

FIGURE 8–5 Worksheet for VOLUME entity-type.

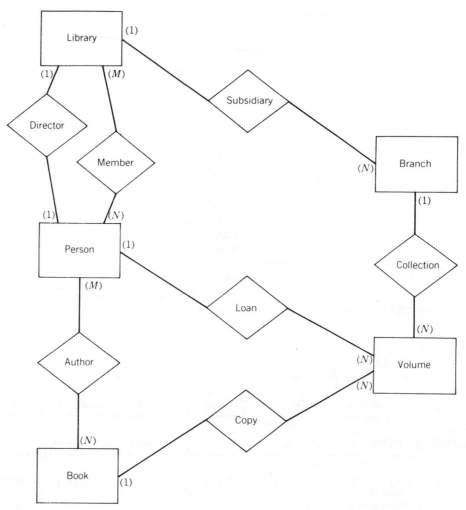

FIGURE 8–6 Complete library entity-relationships (E-R) diagram.

It is possible to represent an E-R model as a set of tables that look very much like relations. Figure 8–8 shows the tabular representation of the VOLUME entity-set. The only thing that is not quite consistent with the usual way that a relation is depicted is that each column has two levels of heading. The first level, Attribute Name, describes the role that the column plays in the relation. The second, Abstract Data Type, specifies the underlying set from which the values of that attribute are taken. This is an important distinction that is not usually made in the relational model.

Character String Attributes

- Person's Names
- Place Names
- Dates
- Colors
- Application specific:
  - Departments
  - Products

Numeric Attributes

- Money Amounts
- Times of Day
- Social Security Numbers
- Telephone Numbers
- Application specific:
  - Employee Numbers
  - Part Numbers

FIGURE 8–7 Some generally useful abstract data types.

VOLUME

Attribute name	Lib-Name	Br-Name	Cat-No	Copy-No	Bor-No	Date-Due
Abstract Data Type	LIBRARY	STRING	ISBN	INTEGER	LIB-CARD	DATE
Entity-occurrences	Univ	Science	1-123-12	3	236348	1985-10-04
	Municipal	Main	1-123-12	1		
	Municipal	Main	5-443-81	1		
	Municipal	East	0-648-40	2	766432	1985-11-01
	Univ	History	1-228-65	1	794362	1985-10-14
⋮	⋮	⋮	⋮	⋮	⋮	⋮

FIGURE 8–8 Tabular representation of VOLUME entity-set.

COLLECTION

Entity-name	LIBRARY	PERSON	
Entity's role	Issuer	Holder	
Ident. attribute	Lib-Name	Person-ID	Bor-No
Abstract Data Type	LIBRARY	SSN	LIB-CARD
Relationship-occurrences	Municipal	312-44-5742	212604
⋮	⋮	⋮	⋮

FIGURE 8–9 Tabular view of COLLECTION relationship-set.

The tabular depiction of the VOLUME—BRANCH relationship is shown in Figure 8–9. Once again, additional heading information is present. The top row specifies the entity types that are relevant to the relationship. The next row indicates the specific role that each entity-type plays. The next two rows specify roles within the entity-type or relationship-type and abstract data type, just as in the case of an entity relation. These tables provide a concise representation of the E-R model suitable for storage in machine-readable form. This completes the logical database design task.

Physical Database Design

There are two main tasks associated with physical database design. The first is the translation of the logical design into something that is compatible with the DBMS that will be used. The second is the modification of the design to achieve optimal performance. Because both of these tasks depend critically on the choice of DBMS, they can only be discussed here in fairly general terms.

The following sections describe the conversion of E-R models to relational or network form.[6] Then, some techniques for optimizing a database design will be discussed.

Relational Database Design

As noted, an E-R model in tabular form is already nearly a set of relation specifications. One relation will be defined for each entity-type in the E-R model. The name of the relation will be the name of the entity-type. The only

---

[6] The hierarchical model will not be explicitly considered in this section. As discussed in earlier chapters, it suffers from some basic flaws which have led database researchers to pay it less attention than the other two.

modification that is required deals with the handling of attribute names and value-sets. In most current systems, these two concepts are not clearly separated. The result, in some cases, is that attributes in separate relations must be given the same name to be able to compare them. This, of course, totally obscures the role that the attribute plays in each relation.

It is perhaps somewhat more common to allow attribute names in relations to be freely chosen and to permit comparison of any pair of attributes that are compatible on a syntactic level, that is, any two character strings or any two numbers. Some vendors of relational database systems have announced plans for systems that would support the generalized value-set concept. If such a system is not available, then the necessary changes in the E-R entity descriptions will result in some loss of information.

A straightforward approach to relational database implementation will also have one relation for each relationship type in the E-R model. The name for the relation should normally be constructed from the role names in the E-R table; if allowed, the entity-type names should be concatenated with the attribute names to make it perfectly clear which entities are involved. The modification associated with handling value-set information is exactly the same as for entity-sets.

In Chapter 6, much was made of the issue of normalizing an arbitrary relational database to convert it to a form that would not exhibit anomalous behavior in the face of insertions, deletions, and updates. What role does normalization play in a relational design produced via the E-R process? A general treatment of this question is beyond the scope of this book. However, a few informal observations will be offered without being proved. First, no relation in what might be called E-R form will violate 1NF. Second, because of the way E-R relations are constructed, each describes precisely one thing—either an entity or a relationship. It will be recalled that this was our informal criterion for 2NF.

It is more difficult to show that a set of relations produced by the E-R approach is in 3NF, but the reader is invited to verify that this is certainly the case for the example used in this chapter. One way of comparing the normalization approach to the E-R model would be to observe that the former begins with an arbitrary set of relations and uses some semantic information to transform them into a new set with suitable properties. This might be described as a bottom-up approach. The E-R model, on the other hand, could be considered as a top-down approach because it begins with the fundamental things of interest—entities and relationships among them—and uses the semantic information to organize the data elements into relations that represent these fundamental things.

In some cases, the E-R approach will result in some decomposition that is not required to ensure 3NF. When this is observed, it is usually possible to explain it on the basis of some semantic significance that is not taken into consideration by the normalization process.

Network Database Design

There are two rather distinct approaches to getting to a network database design from an E-R model. It is possible to make the transformation directly or one may first generate a relational design as described above, then convert it to an equivalent network.

It might seem that one can get from an E-R diagram to a network database design simply by constructing a record-type for each entity-type and a set-type corresponding to each relationship-type. It is correct that there will be a record-type for each entity-type. However, the Data Base Task Group (DBTG) concept of a set is much more restricted than the E-R relationship, so, much more care must be taken in transforming these.

The following limitations must be noted: A DBTG set can represent *only* a $1:N$ binary relationship. Any other type, such as an $M:N$ relationship or one among more than two entity-types, requires the creation of a record-type to represent the relationship. This will become a member in sets owned by each of the relevant entity record-types. A relationship record-type is also needed in any case where there are attributes associated with the relationship. In the case of a relationship between two entities of the same type (such as marriage), a relationship record-type will be needed, and there will be two set types: one owned by the entity record-type with the relationship record-type as member and one going in the opposite direction.

Figure 8–10 illustrates some typical E-R fragments and the equivalent Data Structure Diagrams. The latter, of course, are directly implementable in a DBTG system. The marriage example requires some further explanation. Two sets are employed with the same owner and member-types. One of these is used to connect a PERSON record to all the MARRIAGE records in which that person participated as husband. The other set connects a PERSON to all the MARRIAGEs in which that person was the wife. Each MARRIAGE record will be a member of precisely one HUSBAND set and one WIFE set, and, thus, will relate the two PERSONs who participated in that marriage. It is obvious that except under extraordinary circumstances, no PERSON record will have nonempty HUSBAND *and* WIFE sets. Furthermore, if a list of someone's spouses is desired, it is necessary to determine the sex of that person to know whether to search the HUSBAND or WIFE set. The awkwardness of this construction is obvious but also unavoidable because of the rule that a record cannot be a member of more than one set of a given type.

We have seen how an E-R diagram can be converted to a Data Structure Diagram by adding relationship record-types to deal with the E-R relationships that do not map directly into DBTG sets. An even simpler, although probably less efficient, approach would be automatically to create a record-type for *every* rela-

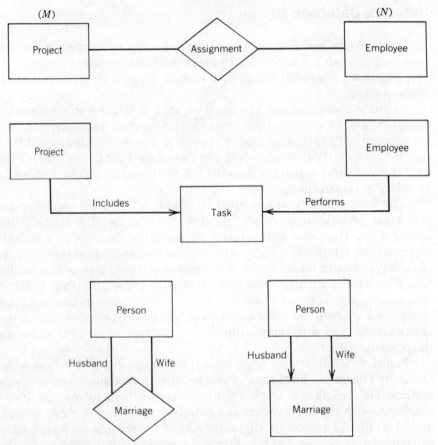

FIGURE 8–10 Network equivalents of typical entity-relationship (E-R) forms.

tionship-type as well as for every entity-type. DBTG sets are then defined following the lines already present in the E-R diagram, with the entity record-type always playing the role of the owner and the relationship record-type as the member. This will generally result in a network with more record- and set-types than the other approach.

There is another approach to the design of DBTG databases totally independent of the E-R formalism that deserves mention.[7] This developed out of the observation that there were various approaches available for designing relational databases with desirable properties and (at the time) few commercial relational

---

[7] Larry Clough, William D. Haseman, & Yuk HoSo, "Designing Optimal Data Structures," Proceedings of the National Computer Conference, AFIPS Press, 1976.

DBMS's. Was it perhaps possible to take a relational database design in 3NF and convert it automatically to a network design without losing the desirable properties inherent in the original design?

An algorithm was developed that takes a set of relations and automatically performs this conversion. Basically, it extracts common groups of attributes that may occur in several relations and uses them to define a record-type. The remaining attributes in a relation constitute another record-type. Set-types are created by looking at the functional dependencies between the groups of attributes. If a group of attributes that have been combined in a record-type, *A*, determine another set in record-type, *B*, then a set-type can be defined with *B* as the owner and *A* as the member. If *A* determines *B* and *B* determines *A*, then either can be the owner of the set. If there is no functional dependency between *A* and *B*, then there is, in fact, a many-to-many relationship between them. In this case, it is necessary to construct a dummy record-type that can be owned by both *A* and *B*.

Although the network thus developed will have the good properties of a 3NF relational design, there is no guarantee that it will be optimal in any sense. The developers of this algorithm proposed to use linear programming techniques to refine the initial design. The objective function to be minimized would be the sum of the storage and processing costs. Formulating this for a real problem requires knowing the numbers of each type of record as well as considerable information about the types and frequencies of queries. The fact that such information is not usually available during the database design process has made it difficult to apply such optimization techniques.

DATABASE OPTIMIZATION

Database systems have a reputation for being quite inefficient. There is no doubt that they tend to be large programs and to require a lot of processor capacity. However, if they work as they are intended to, the user gains considerable benefit from having a DBMS, so, it is possibly unfair to speak of inefficiency. Nevertheless, there are clearly significant savings to be achieved by making DBMS operation as efficient as possible. Database efficiency improvements fall into two classes—those that may be considered enhancements to the database design and those that have to do with the procedures used to manipulate the database.

Database Design Modifications

The addition of extra indices would be an example of something that might be done during the database design process to improve performance. In any database system supporting the concept of keys, an index will normally be maintained on the values of the key data element(s). This allows efficient retrievals where the key values are known because the index can be used to find the relevant records without any additional searching. Many systems permit the database designer to specify that additional indices should be created and maintained for nonkey data elements that are the basis for frequent retrieval requests.

Indices are not automatically created for all data elements because there are costs associated with having them. The amount of additional storage required for an index would normally be small by database standards. However, whenever a database update operation results in changing the value of an indexed data element, the index must be updated as well. Deciding whether or not to create additional indices depends on knowing something about the relative frequency of updates and retrievals. If retrievals are far more numerous than updates, then an index may be effective. If updates occur about as often or more often than retrievals, then the extra work required to maintain the index will probably outweigh the value of having it.

This illustrates one of the main general difficulties associated with trying to optimize database performance. It is impossible to judge the effectiveness of a proposed enhancement without knowing quite a bit about the usage environment. Because the act of installing a database system alters the way users behave, it is difficult to obtain the information needed to make optimization decisions before the system is operational.

Other types of design-time optimization tend to depend on the particular data model that is being used. With a relational system, there is not too much else that can be done because this model puts a strong emphasis on isolating the user and even the designer from internal operational details. There is, however, at least one other area where the designer can exercise some discretion.

The relational database design produced either by the E-R approach just described or the normalization process of Chapter 6 tends to contain a large number of small relations. This is necessary to reduce redundancy and keep the meaning of each relation unambiguous. However, producing the answer to user queries will often require that two or more of these small relations be joined together. This can be a major part of the cost of a retrieval operation. Many of these joins could be avoided if the designer is willing to include some non-3NF relations in the basic design. Like the question of additional indices, this basically comes down to trading retrieval efficiency for extra work when the database is updated. No general rule can be given. It depends on the detailed circumstances.

The network database designer has available a much wider range of choices. This may, however, be a mixed blessing because the uncertainty about user behavior (just mentioned for the relational system) is also present with any other database model. Among the alternatives that the network designer can consider are a wide variety of storage structures and access mechanism for sets. Set members can contain both next and prior pointers or only one of them. Alternatively, sets may be implemented through a list of member pointers stored with the owner, and indices can also be used instead of simple lists. It is also possible to include a direct pointer to the owner record in each member. Generally speaking, the more pointers provided, the better will be the performance on retrieval operations. Extra pointers may also facilitate the insertion or deletion of set members. On the other hand, pointers often have to be changed as a results of database updates, so, the more of them there are, the more work is required to maintain them.

Although it has been suggested that additional indices do not usually incur much of a storage penalty, this may not be true for some of the more sophisticated set implementation strategies. There have been some attempts to estimate the amount of storage needed in a DBTG database for pointers and other overhead functions; in many cases, it appears that this may exceed the amount of storage needed for the actual data. Increasing the size of the database in this way not only increases direct costs for storage, but also slows down input-output speed measured in *records* per second.

The designer of a hierarchical database can consider additional indices, subject to the same caveats discussed earlier. There are also a few other options available that can affect performance. IBM, the leading supplier of hierarchical database systems, has produced a program called the IMS Database Design Aid that simulates the performance of a given design under a specified usage load. This program does not actually perform any optimization, but it can be used to try out various alternative designs and to test their sensitivity to changes in load.

Postdesign Optimization

This chapter is primarily concerned with the task of initially designing a database. However, there are some further issues relevant to the performance improvement question that will be included here to keep the entire optimization discussion in one place. Once a database design has been finalized and the data loaded, performance improvement basically revolves around the question of finding the most efficient route to the data required by each query. Aside from a few generally applicable principles, this really comes down to looking at the specific configuration of the database and selecting the shortest path. Thus, one important question deals with *when* the access path selection is made. The two choices are: when the retrieval program is written or when it is executed. The other major question is whether the access path decision is made by the DBMS or by some person—either user or programmer.

One of the basic precepts of the relational model is that access path decisions should be made by the DBMS and, ideally, not until the query is processed. It is claimed that, in theory at least, this should be the optimal approach. Waiting until execution time to make the access decision means that it can take into account the exact state of the database at that moment. Placing responsibility on the DBMS could be viewed merely as a convenience to users, but actually it should be interpreted as an assertion that the system is better able to make these decisions than a human being. Accepting this argument requires a certain amount of faith. In today's world, the state of automatic access path selection algorithms is relatively primitive. However, advocates of this approach believe that it will eventually lead to greater efficiency than can be achieved by human intervention.

With network and hierarchical DBMS's, the access path decision is typically made by the programmer at the time a retrieval program is written. Advocates of this approach claim that a person who understands the database structure can choose a path more effectively than any automatic algorithm. This is almost certainly true at the moment, but there is little reason to believe that automatic path selection will not eventually surpass the manual approach, especially because it has the luxury of waiting until the last moment to make the decision. Databases evolve over time; even if a programmer makes an access decision that is absolutely optimal when it is made, there is no reason to think that it will remain optimal indefinitely. Furthermore, access path selections hidden in programs tend to be taken for granted and may not be reviewed as often as they should be.

The one important advantage of choosing an access path early—that is, prior to execution time—is that it saves a lot of computation during the running of the application. It is similar to the distinction between compiled and interpreted programming languages. There has been some recent research that indicates that the best solution to this dilemma may be the dynamic compilation of database operations.[8] In this approach, the database request is left in symbolic form until the moment of execution. At that point, however, it is compiled and then executed rather than being directly interpreted. The experiments in which this approach gave good results were carried out in a relational system where individual database queries usually involve retrieving large volumes of data. In network or hierarchical systems where retrieval tends to proceed on a record-by-record basis, the performance improvement would probably not be as great.

A similar approach is taken by the IBM relational systems, Database2 and SQL/DS, where access modules are compiled in advance but where they may be discarded and replaced dynamically if the system recognizes that they may no longer be valid.

TERMS TO UNDERSTAND

top-down approach
bottom-up approach
corporate data model (CDM)
data dictionary

information requirements analysis (IRA)
view synthesis
E-R expansion

[8] Michael Stonebraker et al., "Performance Enhancements to a Relational Database System," *ACM Transactions on Database Systems*, Vol. 8, No. 2 (June 1983), pp. 167–185.

REVIEW QUESTIONS

1. Contrast the top-down and bottom-up approaches to database design.

2. Discuss the advantages and disadvantages of the various approaches to determining information requirements.

3. Consider the university administration problem described in Chapter 4, Question 5. Develop user views for three applications: transcripts, student timetables, and class lists. Apply the view synthesis method to produce a logical database design for this application.

4. Consider the university administration problem described in Chapter 4, Question 5. Make a list of the key entities and then use the expansion method to produce a logical database design.

5. Why might the view synthesis and entity-relationship (E-R) expansion methods produce different logical database designs? (If you have done the two preceding questions, use your answers to explore this question.)

6. Why should relations produced from an entity-relationship (E-R) model always be in 3NF? Is it possible to say anything about higher normal forms in this context?

7. For each of the three basic data models:

   What are the major postdesign adjustments that can be made to increase efficiency?

   What usage information is needed to make these adjustments?

PART II

DATABASE ADMINISTRATION

C H A P T E R 9

INFORMATION RESOURCE MANAGEMENT

BACKGROUND

When an organization first acquires a Database Management System (DBMS), it usually finds it necessary to add a position to the data processing department staff. As a technical specialist in database management, this person is responsible for:

Installation of the DBMS software and integrating it with the operating system.

Acting as an in-house consultant to users and system developers on DBMS usage. In this capacity, the database expert leads training sessions and assists in the design of databases and application programs to use them.

Keeping the DBMS operational. This involves analyzing trouble reports from users and either fixing the problems (if local in origin) or referring them to the vendor.

Attempting to maximize database efficiency through appropriate choices of data structures and access mechanisms and ongoing performance monitoring.

As organizational experience with DBMS's grows, it becomes clear that making the database concept work requires more than simply mastering a complicated technology. A basic premise of the database approach is that data will be shared among applications, and sharing implies coordination and compromise. One user group will want employee numbers stored in binary form to facilitate sorting, whereas another will want them stored as character strings to eliminate the need for conversion on input and output. One group will need to access personnel records on a random basis and will want them stored in a way that makes this type of access efficient. Another group will need to process them sequentially and will not want to pay the price that goes along with a random ordering.[1] Someone has to decide what actual formats and data structures will be used. Policies and procedures have to be established and enforced to ensure that these decisions will not be circumvented, and users whose applications become less efficient because of them must be compensated.

Although there is a technical component to this task, performing it satisfactorily requires skills that are usually associated with managers rather than technicians. In addition, these decisions need to emanate from a point in the organizational hierarchy that will have the authority and/or prestige to ensure compliance.

---

[1] It is important to understand exactly what is implied in these examples. Any good DBMS will allow each of these users to view his or her information in the desired way, no matter what the physical database actually looks like. However, a cost-and-performance penalty will have to be paid by those whose desired view is significantly different from the way the data is really stored.

The answer that has been proposed for these problems is a new staff function called information resource management (IRM). The essence of this idea is that information is a basic organizational resource, like money or people, and that like these, it should have a professional, high-level management group that is responsible for its effective use throughout the organization.

Whenever the creation of a new management position is proposed, it is natural that existing managers will be concerned about the possible loss of authority. This is especially true if the new function impinges on an area perceived by managers to be critical. Information would certainly seem to be in that category, and this may be one reason why so little progress has been made in implementing IRM concepts. However, there is a precedent in an equally critical area—personnel management.

Until the emergence of personnel administration as a distinct specialty, line managers typically had complete control over hiring, evaluating, and firing their own employees. It may be presumed that managers guarded this authority jealously in the belief that control over personnel was a critical element in accomplishing their responsibilities. The idea of a corporate personnel function has now become very well accepted. Experience has shown that the concern about loss of control was largely unwarranted. Establishment of corporate personnel departments did not generally remove the right of managers to make their own staffing decisions. Its effect, rather, was to provide a set of policies and procedures for achieving consistency in the way these decisions were made throughout the entire organization. Also, the personnel department became responsible for keeping informed on the latest techniques and making them available to line managers. This saved the line managers the time and effort that would otherwise be required to keep abreast of developments in an area distinct from their main concern.

The IRM function should operate in a similar fashion. That is, it should not, in most cases, take over the actual making of information management decisions. Rather, it should establish policies and procedures to guide managers, users, and system developers so that *their* decisions will be consistent and compatible and employ the best in currently available technology.

There is considerable confusion in the literature about the nature of this task and even about its name. The earliest discussions referred to the function as Data Base Administration (DBA). Later writings introduced the term, Data Administration (DA). There has been little agreement among authors as to how these two positions relate to each other. Some authors use the terms interchangeably. A number of others assign technical responsibilities to the DBA, whereas the DA deals with planning and policy formulation.[2] James Martin accepts this distinc-

---

[2] For example, see *Guide International* "Establishing the Data Administration Function," (June 1977).

tion, but proposes that there should be multiple DBA's, one for each of an organization's databases.[3] Yet a fourth view gives the DBA complete control over the data stored and accessed under control of a DBMS, but if the job is extended to cover other data as well, the title is changed to DA.[4] The term "data resource management," was introduced by Richard Nolan.[5] He argued that data should be considered an organizational resource because it had characteristics of cost, value, and scarcity similar to the more familiar material, financial, and human resources. Managing any resource involves planning for, allocating, and conserving it. Therefore, data resource management was defined as the function handling these tasks with respect to data. In more recent years, there has been a tendency to substitute the word "information" for "data"—probably to suggest a greater involvement with management support and high-level decision making. This chapter will use the term "IRM," to encompass the full range of tasks associated with managing information as a resource.

The following section describes the most important IRM duties and classifies them in a variety of ways. Then, a number of alternatives for placing IRM in the corporate hierarchy are examined. Options for the internal organization of the IRM group are considered after that. As part of that discussion, positions that might fit various definitions of DA or DBA are identified. It might seem that managing information as an organizational resource implies centralization of authority. The final section extends the concepts of IRM to decentralized organizational environments. Throughout the chapter, recent survey data about how IRM is actually implemented will be compared to what the normative literature says should be done. It will be seen that there is a great disparity between theory and practice in IRM. This is, very likely, one of main reasons why the alleged benefits of the database approach have been so illusive.

TASK CLASSIFICATION

An excellent examination of both the theoretical and practical aspects of the IRM function has been carried out by J. L. Weldon.[6] Much of the analysis in this chapter follows the approach developed in her study. Most lists of IRM responsibilities are extensive. Weldon observed that the full set of IRM tasks can be classified using a two-dimensional framework. One dimension, implied by our previous discussion, represents the degree of technical content. Some IRM tasks

[3] James Martin, *Principles of Database Management*, Prentice-Hall, 1976.

[4] David Kroenke, *Database Processing*, 2nd Edition, Science Research Associates, 1983.

[5] Richard L. Nolan, *Managing the Data Resource Function*, West Publishing Co., 1974.

[6] Jay-Louise Weldon, *Data Base Administration*, Plenum Press, 1981.

	Applications	Systems
Administrative	Corporate data model development	Hardware/software selection
	Determine goals and priorities	Policy formulation: -Backup/recovery -Coding standards
	Policy formulation: -Access authorization -Data standards	
Technical	Data dictionary maintenance: -Create data definitions -Define user views DB documentation Education	DBMS support Physical DB design DBMS performance monitoring and enhancement

FIGURE 9–1 Information resource management (IRM) task classification.

are highly technical, others have a strong administrative character. The second dimension distinguishes tasks that relate primarily to the users of a database from those associated with the hardware/software environment. Weldon calls these dimensions Administrative/Technical and Applications/Systems. Figure 9–1 lists some key tasks in each of the four quadrants of this framework.

IRM groups can also be classified according to the role they play in the organization. Weldon distinguishes four possible IRM roles: advisory, support, consultant, and management.

The advisory IRM role is concerned with administrative tasks, such as planning, research on database technology and policy formulation. Weldon suggests that this concentration on administrative tasks is appropriate for organizations that are preparing for the adoption of the database approach but that do not yet have a DBMS installed as well as for those decentralized data processing organizations where the administrative tasks are handled by the central staff and the technical tasks are performed by the decentralized groups.

The support role of IRM is a logical outgrowth of the technical database specialist described at the beginning of this chapter. It views IRM as a repository of expert knowledge about the database. This knowledge is provided to system designers and users in much the same way that data communications expertise is usually handled. This type of IRM deals mainly with the tasks in the Technical/Systems quadrant of Figure 9–1.

Consultant IRM may be involved with the full spectrum of tasks. As the name implies, the consultant IRM has no direct authority but acts as an advisor to system developers and data processing management on matters concerned with using database concepts.

The management IRM role is similar to the consultant role, except that the IRM group is given the authority to create and enforce standards on the system developers.

DUTIES AND RESPONSIBILITIES

The IRM function can include a wide range of tasks. In the last section, they were classified in several ways. Here, a chronological approach is taken, and (assuming that the group is established before any other database activity is underway) the key IRM tasks associated with the stages of database planning, design, implementation, and operation are described.

Planning

Ideally, the IRM function should be established before the DBMS has been acquired, in fact, even before the decision to acquire one has been made. Every organization uses information and, therefore, should be able to benefit from managing its information handling activities as effectively and efficiently as possible. At this early stage, the Information Resource Manager should be concerned with collecting information about the organization's information usage and about relevant technology. To the extent possible, projections about the future should be made in both areas to be used in later planning. The information about data usage will be stored in a data dictionary for future reference.

Specific IRM responsibilities during the planning phase include:

Gather information on current state of DB technology.

Prepare forecasts of technical developments expected over organization's planning horizon.

Gather information on current information requirements.

Prepare forecasts of expected changes in information requirements—both volumes and types.

Work with users and system designers to develop realistic objectives for database applications.

Prepare a long-range plan for developing database applications, taking into account both organizational priorities and technological constraints.

Standards must be developed covering all aspects of data handling.

It is worth noting that a definition of IRM or DA that refers only to managing data already in a computerized database does not provide explicitly for these essential planning tasks.

Design

Once an adequate picture of the organization's information usage has been built up, IRM is responsible for the development and maintenance of the corporate data model (CDM), also called the conceptual schema or the enterprise schema. It is the overall framework into which all database applications will fit, and it should be completed prior to attempting any specific applications.

When a database application is being implemented, the IRM function plays two roles. It supports the work of the system designers by providing consultation on how to use the database facilities most effectively. It also must evaluate the resulting design for compatibility with the existing database. Any requests to add something to the database or change something that is already there must be approved by IRM. In the absence of this function, the system designers and their managers would probably make these decisions considering only their own particular needs. The key advantage of having them made by IRM is that this group should have both the capability and the motivation to take an overall organizational perspective. IRM is also in a position to know what other projects are underway that might provide useful opportunities for integration.

IRM bears virtually the entire responsibility for the physical database design.

Implementation

The IRM function is responsible for maintaining the integrity of the database and for controlling access to it. In carrying out these responsibilities, it develops the procedures that will be followed by the data collection and computer operations groups, and it will probably also provide training and performance monitoring to ensure that the individuals involved understand the procedures and follow them.

A key task under this heading consists of specifying the procedures to be followed in recovering from errors of various types and the steps to be taken when it is necessary to recover a damaged database. Carefully developed and enforced procedures for data entry and update as well as standards for checking out new or modified programs can significantly reduce the need to invoke database recovery procedures.

Another area of operational responsibility for the IRM function is the control of access to the database to prevent unauthorized users from doing anything to it and authorized ones from going beyond what they are supposed to do. This aspect of the IRM function is the subject of Chapter 13.

Performance monitoring to maximize efficiency is a final operational responsibility of the IRM group. It is responsible for adjusting storage structures and access methods as usage patterns change, as well as for evaluating alternative hardware and software options.

Operation

In the final stage, the IRM function is concerned with getting the maximum benefit out of the organization's investment in a database. To a large extent, this is accomplished through liaison with current and potential user groups, determining their needs and letting them know about new facilities as they become available. The IRM group, because of its responsibility to be aware of information usage throughout the organization, should be able to identify situations where a database project that is being undertaken for one purpose can also serve others.

IRM also establishes the standards governing database usage and acquires or develops tools to help users such as specialized query languages (Chapter 12), automated database design aids (Chapter 8), and, of course, the data dictionary (Chapter 10).

ORGANIZATIONAL POSITION

There is clearly a strong interrelationship among the role given to the IRM function, the tasks it is expected to perform, and its position within the overall organization structure.

Historically, the technical support role was the first to be recognized in most firms. The obvious place for technical support is within the Data Processing Department. In organizations with a functional approach to organizing the Electronic Data Processing (EDP) Department, a technical support Information Resource Manager will usually report to the Manager of Support Services, who, in turn, reports to the Department Director (Figure 9–2). This places IRM on a par with data communications support and such other functions as documentation and education.

An IRM group in this location is reasonably well situated to perform tasks in the Technical/Systems category. It is a poor position, however, from which to carry out the administrative IRM functions because it is too far down in the organizational structure to exert the necessary authority over system developers. It is also probably buried too deeply within EDP to carry out the user-oriented tasks effectively.

Surveys of real organizations show that this is, by far, the most common place for the IRM function to originate. However, unless it manages to migrate upward, it will have a hard time expanding beyond the technical support role.

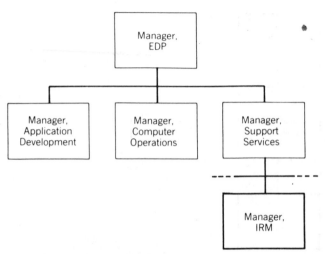

FIGURE 9–2 Functional/support information resource management (IRM).

A slight variation on this arrangement is often found in data processing organizations that are organized by application-area or project. In this case, as shown in Figure 9–3, the IRM group reports to the project or application-area manager. This position has all of the weaknesses discussed above, and it virtually guarantees that the scope of work will be restricted to the particular area. In fact, firms with this organization will probably have a separate IRM function in each application-area.

The main problem with both of these structures is that the IRM function is too far down to perform its administrative tasks effectively. This difficulty can be partially overcome by having the Information Resource Manager report directly to the Director of EDP. There are several paths along which the function can develop in this location. In one version (Figure 9–4) the Information Resource Manager becomes a member of the staff of the EDP Manager. This has the advantage of placing IRM closer to the seat of power, but of course, staff positions carry no direct authority and must accomplish their tasks through persuasion.

This position is particularly appropriate for the advisory IRM role, and, as such, it may be the initial location of the function rather than the result of a reorganization—especially in organizations that have come to database technology more recently and, thus, have been able to take advantage of the experience of their predecessors.

It is also possible to find IRM reporting to the Director of Data Processing in a line capacity. This gives the group greater direct authority than the staff alternative. Weldon found two variations on this approach: one in which the IRM func-

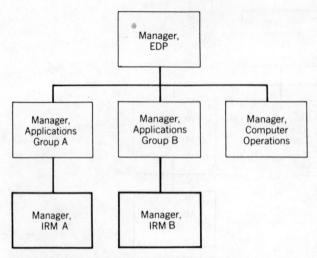

FIGURE 9–3 Project/support information resource management (IRM).

tion is at the same organizational level as the Manager of Application Development; the other where the IRM function is one level higher (Figure 9–5).

The most interesting thing to note about all of the alternatives described so far is that they view IRM as being within the Data Processing Department. In fact, surveys suggest that over 90% of all IRM groups are located there. This is explainable on historical grounds because early IRM groups tended to arise out of a DBMS support function, which clearly belongs within EDP.

However, there are two major problems with this location for IRM. First, it tends to focus attention on information stored in machine-readable form and processed by computer. Manual information systems and nonmachine-readable

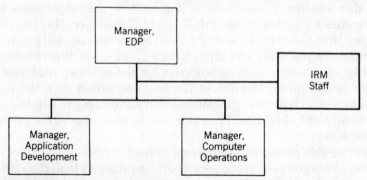

FIGURE 9–4 Information Resource on the Electronic Data Processing (EDP) manager's staff.

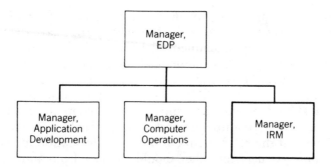

(A) Information resource management (IRM) parallel to applications development

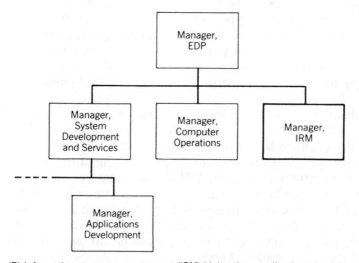

(B) Information resource management (IRM) higher than applications development

FIGURE 9–5 Information resource management (IRM) as a line
responsibility.

data are almost certain to be ignored. Second, an IRM function within the Data
Processing Department is going to have a difficult time influencing user behavior. It surely will not have line authority over user departments from this location. In addition, for a variety of historical reasons, the Data Processing Department often does not have the credibility with users that would allow it to
influence them without formal authority.

Restricting the IRM function to deal only with machine-readable data is
almost certainly not desirable. The objectives of rational information management are just as applicable to manual systems as to computerized ones. In fact, it
has already been suggested that one of the key IRM decisions is the choice of

storage medium and processing mode for each type of information. One recent survey found that less than 25% of the responding firms gave the IRM group any responsibility at all for nonmachine-readable data. In the same survey, only one third of the firms even put all machine-readable data under the control of the IRM function. In the others, IRM tended to be restricted to dealing with information stored under the control of a DBMS. In such an organization, the decisions as to whether data should be stored manually or in computer-readable form and whether to incorporate it into a database will probably be made by application system designers. If the full benefits of rational information management are to be realized, these are decisions that should be made from an organization-wide perspective, that is, by the IRM group.

If IRM is to have responsibility for all of an organization's formal information systems, regardless of technology, then it certainly should be located outside of the EDP Department. In fact, it is not hard to make a case, in theory, that EDP should report to IRM rather than the other way around! One occasionally sees titles on organization charts that suggest movement in this direction. However, it is likely to be some time before organizations fully recognize the appropriateness of this arrangement and settle the very substantial power shifts that are implied.

The problem of IRM-user relations suggests a similar solution. In many organizations today, relations between EDP departments and their users are far from what they ought to be. There are many reasons for this. Schedule delays, budget overruns, and generally overenthusiastic selling of the wonders of computers have all contributed to giving EDP departments low credibility in many firms. These have often been compounded by communications difficulties (excessive use of data processing jargon) and, frequently, at least a perception of arrogance on the part of the EDP personnel: "We know what you need." For all of these reasons, user personnel in many organizations are wary of anything that comes out of their EDP departments.

Finally, EDP personnel have sometimes been characterized as having a primary loyalty to, and interest in, their profession rather than their employer. They tend to be highly mobile, changing jobs frequently to work on interesting projects or systems. In such an environment, they often do not know, or care, very much, about the noncomputer-oriented parts of their organizations. Individuals who fit this description would probably not be good at, or interested in, the nontechnical aspects of IRM, and people who are interested in those things would probably find that they did not fit well in a typical data processing organization.

All of these arguments are intended to support the idea that much of the IRM function—specifically the administrative and applications tasks—can be most effectively carried out by a group external to the EDP department. Where then should it go? One survey respondent reported that his firm, after two unsuccessful attempts to establish IRM within the Data Processing Department, was now proposing to set it up within the corporate planning function.

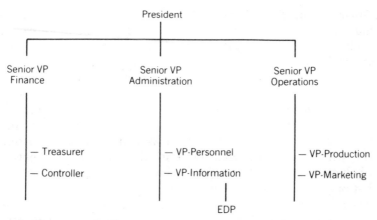

FIGURE 9–6 "Ideal" approach to information resource management (IRM).

In many ways, this seems to be a reasonable choice—at least at the beginning. Although corporate planning is a staff function without any direct authority, this should not be much of a handicap during the early IRM activities of planning and policy formulation. However, once the planning is completed, there might be some difficulty in ensuring that the policies and procedures that had been developed were actually being followed on a day-to-day operational basis.

A clue to what might be the best location for these responsibilities can be found by recalling that IRM is intended to accord to information the same kind of formal management attention that is given to other basic resources, such as money and personnel. This is recognized by an organization chart like the one in Figure 9–6 with a Corporate Director of Information at the same level and with comparable responsibilities as the directors of Personnel and Finance. Note that the EDP Department is shown as reporting to the Director of Information—a complete reversal of the usual current situation! This is intended to recognize both that EDP can be viewed as one of the tools used to manage information rationally and that, as computing technology stabilizes and continues to decline in cost, the need for high-level management attention to it for its own sake should decrease.

The organizational arrangement of Figure 9–6 seems well suited to handling all IRM tasks in the Administrative/Applications quadrant and a significant fraction of those in the Administrative/Systems and Technical/Applications classes. However, there is still a set of tasks that are either highly technical or so closely related to the hardware/software environment that they clearly belong within the EDP Department.

This dilemma can be solved by splitting IRM responsibilities between two separate groups. One will occupy the location shown in Figure 9–6 and perform the policy-making, priority-setting, and planning functions. The other will fit in the spot indicated in Figure 9–5 and be responsible for the more technical matters. This solution suggests that it will not be necessary to undergo any wrenching relocation of existing arrangements. The first of these two groups is largely nonexistent today. Its tasks, to the extent that they are performed at all, tend to be handled in a relatively ad hoc fashion. As their importance becomes clearer, it may be expected that specialized positions at the appropriate organizational level will be created. The second group is already quite common. It is primarily concerned with the technical, DBMS support tasks, and it is located within the EDP Department, which is just the right place for those particular functions. Thus, one way of characterizing the situation today with respect to IRM would be to observe that one, relatively small, part of the task is currently being handled— and in approximately the right way. The other, larger and more important, part is simply not yet being handled in a coordinated way in most organizations.

INTERNAL STRUCTURE OF IRM

One of the difficulties that has always been associated with actually implementing IRM is the wide range of skills required to perform all of the tasks. Obviously, a high level of database technology expertise is required for the tasks in the Technical/Systems category. On the other hand, many of the other responsibilities require general mangement skills, including, in particular, outstanding skill in negotiation and mediation.

This combination of skills is quite rare, and if IRM is viewed as a single position, it is clearly going to be almost impossible to fill. However, as already discussed, there are good reasons to split IRM into an administration function located high in general management and a technical one within EDP. Because the first of these is virtually nonexistent today, the best models for how it should be organized are probably the equivalent staff functions in other areas.

DA or DBA groups do already exist in a large number of organizations. They are usually organized along functional lines as shown in Figure 9–7, although in many firms the small size of the DA staff requires that there be some doubling up of functions.

The DB design group works with users and system designers in the development of logical database designs and has primary responsibility for physical database design. The data dictionary group supports the data dictionary software[7] and is responsible for entry and maintenance of its contents. Because efforts to de-

---

[7]In the past, the data dictionary has usually been implemented by using a special software package for that purpose. It is obviously more appropriate to think of the data dictionary as just one more application supported by the DBMS, but this facility is just starting to appear in commercial systems.

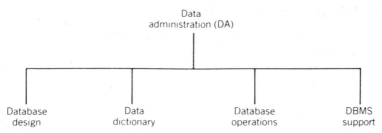

FIGURE 9–7 Typical current data administration (DA) group.

velop database standards and policies often begin with data element names and definitions, this group is also the logical one to handle that task.

The database operations function is responsible for defining standard procedures for using the database. This includes the areas of database security, access control, and data integrity. Responsibility for implementation and operation of procedures for database backup and recovery also fall here.

The database support group is responsible for technical support of the DBMS. In addition to the usual duties associated with supporting any large software system, this group will also be responsible for monitoring the performance of the DBMS and tuning it to achieve maximum efficiency. In some organizations, this function will be assigned to the operating systems maintenance group rather than to DA.

This structure does not assign any specific responsibility for long-range database planning and the development of a CDM or enterprise schema. The planning function would usually fall on the head of the DA/DBA group. Development of a CDM would probably be handled as a special one-time project, with personnel assigned to it from the other functions and, possibly, from outside the group. This is a good example of a task that properly belongs in the "other" part of the IRM function—the part that does not exist.

Nothing has yet been said about the connection between the administrative and technical parts of IRM. Again, the best place to look for guidance is similar relationships in other functions. For example, in the personnel area, individual line managers are usually still responsible for day-to-day supervision, performance evaluation, and career development of their employees. The effect of a corporate level personnel department is felt in the thick manual of procedures prescribing how these tasks are to be performed. Such a department probably also plays a role in training the people who will be carrying out its policies and in monitoring them.

In the IRM area, the administrative group will play a similar role, establishing policies, procedures, and standards, training users and EDP personnel in them, and monitoring compliance. It will also serve as a court of last resort to settle disputes between user groups or between users and EDP.

DECENTRALIZED AND DISTRIBUTED IRM

Until recently, economies of scale in computing equipment and the highly competitive market for qualified personnel provided strong incentives to centralize data processing functions. The database concept, with its emphasis on integrating all data into a common pool, provided a further argument for centralization. Unfortunately, centralized data processing operations often seemed either unwilling or unable to provide adequate service to its full range of clients. In response, users began to demand more local control over their own computing.

With the development of commercially practical large-scale integrated circuit technology, the economics of computer hardware underwent a significant change. This made it perfectly feasible in an economic sense to replace a large centralized computing system with a number of smaller ones. As a result, two distinct alternatives to the traditional centralized data processing function became viable.

In an organization practicing *decentralized* data processing, individual units are given responsibility for their own computing. These units may be defined on a functional basis, by product line, by geography, or in any other way that may make sense for the particular firm. The usual guideline is that the structure of data processing should follow the structure of the organization it is intended to support.

Distributed computing and/or database management is something quite different. It is a technique for taking advantage of the changing economics *without* altering the basic organizational arrangements used to provide data processing services. In this approach, processing power and data storage are spread through the organization—wherever they are needed. However, all of this is planned and controlled in the traditional way. In fact, although decentralizing data processing is basically an organizational change, distributing it is simply a technical one, and users should not be affected by it at all, except that they will (hopefully) benefit from higher quality, lower cost service.

What are the implications of these strategies for development of IRM? If management is really highly decentralized, it almost certainly means that each of the individual units should have its own EDP and IRM groups. However, even the most decentralized organization requires that top management be able to exercise some degree of coordination. Thus, there is bound to be a data processing function at that level and an IRM function as well. Furthermore, headquarters and subsidiary data processing cannot be fully independent of each other because there is a definite need for top management to obtain information from the decentralized units in a compatible manner.

This is greatly facilitated if all of the various computing departments are compatible with each other at the hardware and systems level. To achieve this, it is not uncommon for the data processing group at headquarters to establish standards that must be followed by the other groups. Much the same thing could be done in the IRM area. That is, the policy formulation would be done at headquarters for the entire organization, but the technical work required to implement these policies in each subsidiary unit would be handled at the local level.

In any decentralized organization, it can be argued that there is little need for integration of the information systems. The decision to adopt the database approach will usually be made independently by the decentralized units, and the result can be a number of totally separate and incompatible databases. This approach allows for some attractive simplification because all the planning functions can be done considering only the needs of a single unit.

Many organizations, whether or not they are really this decentralized, currently find themselves in this position as a result of implementing database technology on an application-by-application basis. This is unlikely to be a good idea because it makes difficult the coordination that must be required at some point. However, in the short run, it often seems to work. For example, a company that chooses personnel management for its first database application and inventory control for the next is unlikely to find many requirements for exchange of information between them. It is situations such as this that are responsible for the references in some of the database literature to having multiple DBA's.

From the point of view of IRM, a *distributed* database is equivalent to a centralized one. It is still managed as an integrated whole and viewed as one by the users, despite the fact the actual data may be widely dispersed. Of course, the planning function becomes significantly more complex because of the additional decisions that have to be made concerning how to distribute the data. Chapter 14 is entirely devoted to the topic of distributed databases.

It is worth pointing out that in a highly decentralized organization each unit would have its *own* database rather than having a single, unified one for the entire firm. This allows the database in each unit to be tailored to its specific circumstances, thereby achieving one of the main objectives of decentralization. However, it also carries some disadvantages. Each unit that adopts the database approach will have its own system and require its own staff. This is certain to be more expensive than a single system and support staff for all. In addition, separate databases for each unit means that there will not be sharing of information among them. In many cases, this is irrelevant because the decentralized units are virtually independent companies, but it is an issue that must be evaluated in each specific situation.

TERMS TO UNDERSTAND

information resource management (IRM)   data administration (DA)
database administration (DBA)

REVIEW QUESTIONS

1. There are several different opinions as to the role and responsibilities of the data administration (DA) function. Describe three distinct alternatives and explain the rationale for each.

2. What skills are required to be a successful Information Resources Manager? Why?

3. Nearly all organizations that have an information resource management (IRM) or data administration (DA) function place it within the Data Processing Department. Why has this happened? What are the advantages of this location? What are the disadvantages?

4. How can an information resource management (IRM) group located within data processing achieve its objectives when it does not have authority over user departments?

5. Propose and defend a set of criteria to be used by a database administrator in responding to a user's request to add (or delete) a field in the database.

6. You are the head of a database design team presenting a proposal to top management recommending the creation of a Data Administration (DA) office. At the end of your presentation, one of the vice presidents comments that this new office seems to duplicate activities that are already being handled by existing groups. How would you respond? What would you say in reply to another vice president who asks what the consequences might be of *not* establishing this new function. What should you do if top management decides not to accept your recommendation?

7. How might the information resource management (IRM) function be carried out in a highly diversified and decentralized company? What role, if any, should be played by corporate headquarters?

8. How might the information resource management (IRM) functions be accomplished in an organization that is too small to have a full-time, formal position. (Hint: Consider how such organizations handle other resource management problems.)

CHAPTER 10

THE DATA DICTIONARY

Almost as soon as the first databases went into service, it became apparent that there was a need for a formalized means of finding out what was in the database. For example, analysts and programmers developing a new application needed to know if information they required was already in the database and, if so, how to access it. Managerial users faced a similar problem. They had query languages available that were supposed to make it possible for them to go directly to the database to obtain needed information. However, they generally lacked the detailed knowledge of database contents and structure needed in order to know exactly what to ask. The solution to these problems was the provision of a Data Dictionary/Directory (DD/D), which listed all of the elementary data-items in a database together with their definitions and accessing information. The DD/D served as an index (in the usual, noncomputerized sense of the term) to the database, allowing users to determine what information is available. It also helped to clarify the precise meaning of terms. For example, did an element called SALARY contain monthly or annual figures? Did the element ADVANCED-DEGREES contain yes/no, the number of them, or the actual details?

The earliest such compilations were constructed in the late 1960s. At that time, it was thought that the DD/D would not be particularly large and would not change frequently. Thus, implementation often took the form of a manually updated, hard copy document. Many organizations were surprised to find out how poor a choice this was. Companies of only moderate size found tens of thousands of distinct data elements in their records. Different groups often had different names for the same thing or used the same name for different things. The process of finding and reconciling these inconsistencies was time consuming and arduous. It quickly became clear that this was a task for which the computer itself could be used and a number of programs were written and marketed for maintaining data dictionary information.

The data dictionary concept has come a long way since then. Today, it is most concisely described as the database for the Information Resource Management (IRM) function. That is, it stores information about all the entities of concern to IRM and supports decision making in this area in much the same way that decisions in other management areas are supported. To a large extent, the market for specialized data dictionary software is drying up as it becomes clear that this should be viewed as just one more part of the corporate database. The same facilities that are used to manage the marketing data or the personnel data can also be used to manage the IRM data.

There is, in actuality, one important difference between IRM data and data used by other groups. A database is usually thought of as containing information about the entities of interest to an organization—products, customers, employees, and so forth. The data in the IRM database, on the other hand, describes data. It is, in a sense, one level more abstract than the rest of the database. The term "metadata" is often used to indicate this, although a strict constructionist would probably claim that this is an inappropriate use of the prefix, meta.

In any case, this distinction has two interesting consequences. The first is that because the DD/D describes the database and is, itself, part of the database, the DD/D must describe itself. Beginners often find this confusing, but it need not be. Consider a relational example: the database contains a number of relations describing the entities and relationships of concern to the organization. Each of these relations consists of a number of columns or attributes. Now imagine that two additional relations are created. One, called RELATIONS, is used to describe all the relations in the database; the other, called ATTRIBUTES, is used to describe all the attributes in the database. The RELATIONS relation, for example, contains all of the attributes needed to describe a relation, such as its name, contents, keys, location, and access restrictions. It has one tuple describing each relation in the database. In particular, this means that it has a tuple describing the ATTRIBUTES relation as well as one describing itself. Similarly, the ATTRIBUTES relation contains a tuple for each attribute in the database and columns for all of the necessary information about an attribute. The attributes of the ATTRIBUTE relation, itself, are described here, along with all the others.

The second way in which the IRM database is unusual is that it is accessed on a routine basis by the database management software, itself, as well as by human users. Database Management Systems (DBMS's) have always had to have information about the structure and format of the data as well as access control specifications. In modern systems, the data dictionary portion of the database serves this function, thus making it unnecessary to have special mechanisms.

This chapter will begin by describing the contents of a modern data dictionary. It will be seen that the concept has potential far beyond a mere list of data element definitions. The next section will examine how the data dictionary fits in a modern data processing environment. A variety of users, both human and computer-based, will be identified and their relationship to the data dictionary examined. Finally, the linkage between the data dictionary system and the DBMS will be discussed.

CLASSES OF DATA DICTIONARIES

Current data dictionary systems vary greatly in the facilities provided and research in the area has proposed additional features that are not yet found in any commercially available systems. This wide range of capabilities can be described using a model consisting of four concentric rings. The innermost ring provides the most basic functionality, and each of the others includes the features of all rings within it. The four rings (illustrated in Figure 10–1) are:

1. *A Data Dictionary.* Although the term "data dictionary" is casually used to refer to everything discussed in this chapter, it will be given a specific, technical definition for the purposes of this model. The data dictionary describes

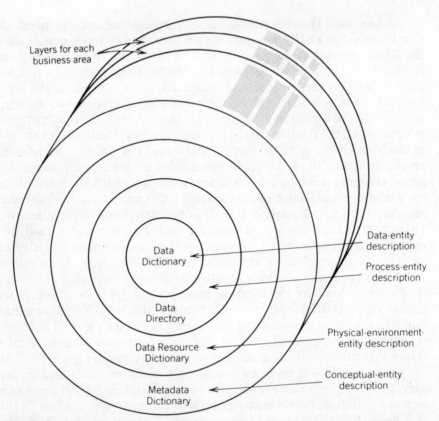

Layers for each
business area

Data-entity
description

Process-entity
description

Physical-environment-
entity description

Conceptual-entity
description

Data
Dictionary

Data
Directory

Data Resource
Dictionary

Metadata
Dictionary

FIGURE 10–1 Structure of a data dictionary system.

data objects in terms of their intrinsic attributes, such as name, type, size, format, and definition.

2. *A Data Directory.* A data directory includes additional information about data objects, such as where they are stored and used and their relationships to other data objects. It also describes processing units, such as programs, modules, and system, and it relates processing units to data objects.

3. *A Data Resource Dictionary.* The data resource dictionary adds information about the systems environment to the data directory's description of the data elements and processing units. Such information, including hardware characteristics and data usage patterns, is used primarily by technical personnel and the computing system itself to select efficient ways to execute user requests.

4. *A Metadata Dictionary.* The preceding rings capture all information required to describe the actual data processing environment. The metadata dic-

tionary adds the capability to describe conceptual objects required for representation of the corporate data model (CDM) or conceptual schema.

The metadata dictionary, if it exists, always describes the entire organization. The part inside that, the data resource dictionary, can be implemented for only a particular functional area or application. When databases for different functional areas are implemented independently at different times, they may each have their own data resource dictionary. In such a case, the metadata dictionary should be the means of unifying these separate systems.

Data Dictionary

The data dictionary is concerned with describing all of the data objects in a system. The smallest, but most numerous, of these is the data-element, sometimes called a field or a data-item. "Serial Number" or "Quantity-on-Hand" are common examples of data-elements. The next larger object is the logical data aggregate. This is defined as a collection of data-elements for which it is convenient to have a single name. "Address" consisting of the data-elements Street Address, City, State, and Zip Code is an example of a logical data aggregate. "Street Address," itself, might be another logical aggregate, consisting of the elements Street Number, Street Name, and Apartment Number. Because the data dictionary will already contain detailed descriptions of the individual data elements, it need not specify anything about a logical data aggregate, except to identify the data elements that compose it.

The next unit to be described in the data dictionary is the "Physical Segment," which in many systems is called a record. A Physical Segment is the smallest accessible unit of information on a physical storage device. All of the fields comprising a Physical Segment will, themselves, be described in the data dictionary. In addition, there must be an entry for the Physical Segment itself because it can have attributes, such as the specification of a key, that are not attributes of any of the constituent data elements.

The fourth level in the data classification hierarchy is a collection of physical segments called a File. It is possible for a File to contain more than one type of Physical Segment. The most complex data object is a "Database." This is defined as a collection of data-elements, aggregates, and physical segments relevant to a particular business function.

Basic differences among these types of data objects make it difficult to define a set of attributes for the data dictionary that will apply to all of them. However, five classes of attributes can certainly be identified:

1. *Name Attributes.*   Every data object must have a unique identifier that can be used to distinguish it from all others. To guarantee this uniqueness, the identifier should probably be assigned by the data dictionary system itself. It

should also be possible to associate with the data object any number of synonyms, or alternative names, that will not necessarily be unique throughout the entire system but that are unambiguous in the context of a particular system or computer program. This capability is needed to allow for conventional usage and to comply with naming restrictions in programming languages.

2. *Content Attributes.*   Content attributes consist of descriptive information to aid in understanding the data object. The main component is a free-form textual description of the object intended to explain it to human users. There should also be a status attribute that could take on values, such as "proposed," "current," or "superceded." This would allow the data dictionary to be truly complete by including not only a description of what the database looks like currently, but also of its past and possible future content.

3. *Structure Attributes.*   Structure attributes are used to describe how lower level data objects are combined into higher level ones. Structure attributes for any nonelementary data object would specify what its constituents were and how they were organized. They would also specify key(s) and, where appropriate, the sorting sequence.

4. *Integrity Attributes.*   Most integrity attributes apply to data elements only. They describe the legal set of values in enough detail that generalized programs could be used (e.g., by a DBMS) to check data for validity before accepting it. If the DBMS supports the value-set concept described earlier, the appropriate reference would be included here. Otherwise, more detailed information would have to be supplied, such as the allowed character set, the length of the data element, a structural description (using something like a COBOL picture clause), and edit rules to be applied to the value of the element.

5. *Security and Privacy Attributes.*   Security and privacy attributes provide information needed by access control functions to determine whether a request for information is legitimate. They could include parameters specifying what a requestor would have to be, have, or know to gain access. The person or group responsible for this data object and the one responsible for the entry and maintenance of the actual values should also be identified here.

The basic data dictionary just described is a database about data. Although considerable work might be required to collect all of this information in a large organization, it is not a task calling for much technical sophistication, and the computer program to manage this information need not be complex at all. Of course, simply having all of this information written down or in a machine-readable file does not mean that the integrity or access control specifications will be automatically enforced. However, it serves a valuable documentation role and is the necessary first step to a more sophisticated management of the information resource.

Data Directory

What has been described so far is a facility for maintaining a fairly complete description of *data*. The data directory adds to that information about *users* of the data and about the relationships between data and users. The term "user" is employed here in a general sense—it means not only people, but also any entity that uses data. In particular, three distinct classes of user entities can be identified:

1. Human users.
2. Computer programs and their component pieces, modules, and subroutines.
3. Procedures that specify actions to be performed on or with data. These can be stored in any form and can be intended for manual as well as computerized execution.

The relationship between data and user is reflected in three other entity-types that collectively are called data interchange entities:

1. *Transactions.* A transaction associates a unique occurrence of some data object with a particular event. In this sense, a transaction might seem to be a logical data aggregate and, therefore, something that should be included in the data dictionary. This is not exactly correct. There *is* a logical data aggregate associated with a transaction, possibly called a transaction record. However, the significant thing about a transaction is that it is related to a process. For example, receiving an order for merchandise is a transaction. There is a set of data associated with such an order, but the transaction, itself, also defines a set of actions that must be taken to accept the order and arrange for production, shipping, and billing as required.
2. *Reports.* A report is an aggregation of data objects for the specific purpose of providing information to a human user.
3. *Documents.* In a sense, a document is the opposite of a report. (The alternative term "source document" may help to emphasize this.) A document is a collection of data objects whose purpose is to initiate some processing function.

The main additional capability provided by including user and data interchange entities in an IRM database is the ability to investigate how data objects flow through the system. If the format of the Postal Code data element must be altered, for example, it is important to be able to determine the identities of all programs that use it and of all reports and documents in which it appears. Similarly, when a request is made to alter some program, the data directory provides an immediate means for assessing the impact of the change by identifying the data elements that will be affected and the other programs with which this one interacts.

Data Resource Dictionary

The data resource dictionary adds to the information already compiled some description of the processing environment. This is used during the design and operation of information systems that refer to the database. In particular, the contents of the third ring would include:

1. Information on the location of data objects at the hardware level, that is, specific identification of the disk module, cylinder, and track or tape reel on which particular data are stored. This information is stored here so that users do not have to be aware of it. It is also used to support some performance-optimizing functions.
2. Statistics on usage frequency, access patterns, and other variables that can be useful in selecting storage devices and access paths.
3. Documentation on the physical characteristics of information processing entities, such as computers, disk drives, and people.
4. Performance characteristics and usage protocols for telecommunications systems and networks.

It will be noted that some of this information is relatively static, whereas some is quite dynamic. In fact, some of these attributes, particularly those related to usage patterns, must be updated constantly and automatically as a routine byproduct of using the data. The reason for having all of this relatively technical information will be discussed in the section on data dictionary users.

Metadata Dictionary

The metadata dictionary is the outermost ring in the data dictionary system. The ones described earlier all contain information that helps to design and use information systems and to make them as efficient as possible. The objects described have been concrete—files, programs, computers. The subject matter for the metadata dictionary is more abstract, that which has been referred to in previous chapters as the corporate data model, enterprise schema, or conceptual schema.

All data and all uses of data within an organization should be described at this level whether or not the process is currently computerized. If the organization is collecting or storing data in anticipation of future use, that should also be described, even if the information is not being used now at all. As previously discussed, the role of this level is to provide a framework on which to hang specific information systems so that they will be compatible with each other and with the basic needs of the organization.

The main additional requirements of the data dictionary System at this level are the need to represent conceptual entities, such as "employee," "department," or "order," and the relationships among them. Events and processing functions also need to be representable and linked to the conceptual entities. For example, "Order Arrival" is an event that will cause a function "Order Processing" to be performed by a certain "Department," and so on.

DATA DICTIONARY USERS

The data dictionary system supports a wide variety of individuals and functions. There are three main classes of human users:

Those who *use* data to accomplish some task. This group is sometimes referred to as end-users.

Those whose job is the *provision* of information to end-users. This group includes information systems development personnel as well as those involved in computer operations and data entry.

Those responsible for *controlling* data, including Information Resource Management and data processing functions.

There is another group, auditors, who can usually be considered as end-users of information, but who may sometimes be involved in controlling it as well. In addition to these human roles, the data dictionary can also be used by a variety of computer programs. Each of these groups will be discussed in turn.

End-Users

On a routine basis, perhaps the most frequent use of the data dictionary by end-users is to find out where to look to obtain desired information. A user needs information about some subject to deal with a problem that has arisen. He or she knows that there will be some relevant information in the database but probably not exactly what. Furthermore, to construct a request acceptable to the DBMS, the user will have to use terms that are known to the system; to make any sense of the response, the user will also have to know the exact definitions of the data objects that are being manipulated. The need for this type of information was recognized quite early, and most of the original, manual data dictionary systems were designed to meet this requirement.

End-users are also often involved in planning for new information systems and modifications to existing ones. In this capacity, they will use the data dictionary to help determine the scope and impact of proposed changes. Finally, it has been suggested that a complete metadata dictionary can play a significant role in the training of new employees by providing a model of the organization, showing the sources and uses of information, and indicating who is responsible for what functions.

Information Providers

The information providers category includes systems analysts and programmers who are involved in creating new information systems as well as data entry and computer operations personnel who deal with them on a day-to-day basis.

The systems analyst is responsible for the design of new information systems and modifications to existing ones. During the design of a new system, the conceptual schema provides the basic framework that can be used to define boundaries and interfaces. The analyst then develops a more detailed conceptual model of the area that is to be automated, specifying the events, entities, and processes that are involved. All of this information should be immediately entered into the data dictionary system, whose facilities can then be used to check for consistency and compatibility with already existing systems. Standard systems analysis reports, such as information flow diagrams and function matrices—which specify who is involved in performing what functions—can be generated from the data dictionary. These are used in reviewing specifications for the new system with the users to verify correctness. Throughout this work, the data dictionary serves as a clerical aid, storing all of the design specifications, checking them, and preparing standard reports.

The data dictionary is especially useful when modifications to existing systems are under consideration. It can perform impact analysis on a proposed change to determine what other systems, programs, or files will be affected. Such analysis is critical to performing an accurate cost-benefit assessment of the change as well as to estimating the amount of work that will be required to implement it. It can also be used to verify that the change is consistent with the organization's conceptual schema.

Programmers use the data dictionary system to reduce the amount of tedious clerical work that must be performed as well as to minimize errors. At a minimum, reference to the data dictionary can be used to obtain the correct names, types, and formats for program variables. In a more sophisticated approach, the data definition section of a program could be generated automatically from the data dictionary. This guarantees that all programmers working with the same data will have the same definition of it. It also enhances programmer productivity by reducing or eliminating a major part of the program development task. With modern programming languages, the data definition portion of a program will often exceed in length and complexity the part that actually does the processing. The programmer's use of standardized routines for input, output, and data validation will also be facilitated by having the necessary size, format, and edit criteria extracted automatically from the data dictionary.

It will have been noticed in the discussion of the data resource dictionary that much of its contents are particularly relevant to data processing operations. It provides documentation in a single place and in a standardized form that describes the characteristics of processing resources and the requirements of jobs.

The description of a job could include information about who was authorized to initiate it and who was entitled to receive the output. The data resource dictionary is also the logical place to store access control information, some of which will be processed automatically by various operating system routines but which may have a manual component as well.

Computer operators require information about device requirements of jobs, parameter values that are to be specfied, action to take when various error messages are received, and procedures for backup and recovery. To the extent that this information is formally maintained today, it is usually in procedures manuals that sit on the computer operator's console. They are often not complete or up to date, and they are usually heavily supplemented by informal, word-of-mouth guidelines. The data resource dictionary provides a formal, disciplined approach to collecting and maintaining all of this essential information.

Information Controllers

The relevance of the data dictionary system to control of the database must surely be obvious. It fills a need analagous to what an inventory management system does for a production manager. In fact, there are many similarities between the task of managing a physical inventory and that of managing the information resource.

The data dictionary automates much of the clerical work of IRM. Simply having all of the data definition information in machine-readable form greatly simplifies the task of keeping it up to date. It also means that many of the routine questions that have to be answered about the database can be handled by some type of automatic manipulation of the data dictionary rather than requiring time-consuming and error-prone manual responses.

The data dictionary is the repository of security and integrity specifications, which will be used by the DBMS to control access. It also maintains the usage statistics needed for performance tuning.

Another control-related function of the data dictionary is invoked when changes to the database definition itself are being considered. For example, it should be possible to store more than one version of a database definition so that the processing facilities of the data dictionary system can be used to evaluate proposed changes before they are implemented. In addition, saving old definitions can be of great help to auditors, who may need to know exactly what the database structure was at some previous time.

The data dictionary system also helps to enforce database standards. If data definitions in programs are generated automatically from the data dictionary, then adherence to the standard is guaranteed. Where automatic compliance is not feasible, the data dictionary can hold a standard version against which to compare those in applications programs.

Other Data Dictionary Usage

The data dictionary system also has an important role to play in the process of selecting a DBMS, that is, if the data dictionary has been set up prior to this selection. If it does exist, it can be used to generate requirements for the DBMS, including estimates of volumes of data to be stored, types of relationships that must be represented, types and frequencies of queries, and performance requirements.

The data dictionary is also valuable in educating users about the database. It provides a coherent, simplified picture of the entire database and ensures that all terms have been defined and are used in a consistent way.

Nonhuman Users

In addition to assisting people in their use of a database, the data dictionary is also used directly by such other machine-based functions as the DBMS, compilers, and high-level applications development systems. There are two basic roles that the data dictionary can perform in this environment. When new applications are being developed, much of the information needed to describe data can be extracted directly from the data dictionary. This eliminates the need for manual preparation and entry of this data, increasing productivity and reducing errors. On a continuing basis, the data dictionary can be the source for parameters needed by standardized routines to perform many of the basic data processing functions, such as data entry and validation, access control, and output formatting.

DATA DICTIONARY/DBMS RELATIONSHIP

An important key to the effectiveness of a data dictionary system is the nature of its connection to the DBMS. Three basic configurations are possible (Figure 10–2). They vary in the closeness of the linkage between the data dictionary and the DBMS and also in whether the data dictionary plays a passive or active role in DBMS operations. The fully independent one is typical of early implementations. In this case, the data dictionary is managed either manually or using a piece of software dedicated specifically to that task. In the second alternative, the data dictionary is managed as just one more application of the DBMS. In the third approach, the data dictionary is tightly integrated with the DBMS.

The main advantage of the independent data dictionary is that it can be implemented with relatively little investment. In particular, it is not necessary to wait until a DBMS has been selected before starting to compile the data dictionary. The main disadvantage of this approach is that it is completely decoupled from the DBMS. All of the functions that assume that the DBMS can directly

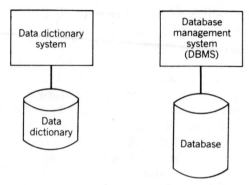

(A) Independent data dictionary

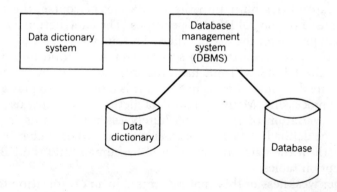

(B) Data dictionary as Database management system (DBMS) application

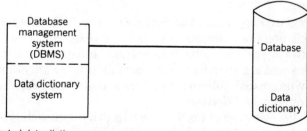

(C) Integrated data dictionary

FIGURE 10–2 Data dictionary/Database Management System (DBMS) relationships.

query the data dictionary are difficult, if not impossible, to implement with this arrangement. In addition, because the data dictionary is controlled by separate software, there is one more piece of software that has to be purchased, maintained, and learned.

Setting up the data dictionary as a DBMS application eliminates all of the problems associated with having a separate piece of software. Software acquisition and maintenance costs are reduced. Data dictionary usage is also simplified because the same procedures and commands that operate on any other database can be used on it as well. There are weaknesses with this approach however. First of all, if the data dictionary is treated as just another application, then it only exists if the organization decides to implement it. The DBMS can not assume that the data dictionary will be implemented. Even if it does exist, its form and content are also whatever the organization wishes them to be. Under these circumstances, the DBMS cannot rely on using the data dictionary for its own data description needs and, therefore, must include specialized facilities for this purpose. The capabilities built into the DBMS are, of course, the ones that will actually be used to control DBMS operations. The data dictionary application, if it exists, will just be for the use of others. This, inevitably, creates the possibility of inconsistency between the two sets of data description information. It also means that the DBMS will not have the intimate relationship with the user-accessible data dictionary that is needed if it is efficiently to play a dynamic role in database processing. Many current data dictionary systems use this approach or a simple variation of it. It is absolutely essential, if this is to work, that procedures be defined and enforced to ensure that when a change is made, it is recorded both in the data dictionary used by humans and the DBMS's internal data description tables.

Another weakness of this approach arises in an organization that is running more than one DBMS on the same hardware. There are many conceptual reasons why this ought not to occur, but as a practical matter, it does. In such a case, the interface between the data dictionary and the DBMSs, other than the one on which it is implemented, are exactly equivalent to the independent alternative discussed before.

In the integrated approach, the data dictionary is an inseperable part of the DBMS. There is no data description stored anywhere else; thus, the DBMS and other users always see the same information. Integrity constraints and other processing rules that are specified in the data dictionary are not just stored there for retrieval by interested humans. They are actually used directly by the DBMS in processing queries and updates.

The main disadvantage of both of the latter two approaches is that an organization must acquire a DBMS before it can begin to compile its data dictionary. Because it has already been argued that the data dictionary is an important tool in DBMS selection, there is a clear conflict. There are two possible ways to resolve this. One is that the future may see a reduction in the diversity among DBMS's—a point that will be treated in the discussion on DBMS standardization in the next chapter. However, even in the absence of official standards, there is some evidence of convergence toward generally accepted objectives with respect to capabilities and interfaces. Greater commonality among DBMS's would reduce the significance of the selection process.

The other approach, which may seem more relevant at present, would be to acquire a DBMS for use in compiling the data dictionary—but with full awareness that some other system might be adopted before any actual applications are implemented. There are obvious disadvantages to this approach. It implies, for example, or at least condones, the acquisition of two DBMS's. On top of the initial cost, there would be two systems to install, maintain, and learn to use effectively.

However, the picture may not be quite this bleak. The DBMS requirements for just a data dictionary are not particularly severe. The amount of data would not be great, and one would not expect to see a heavy volume of either queries or updates. This is such a reduced version of the general database management problem that it could easily be handled by relatively stripped down, simple, and inexpensive systems. Choosing one of these at the very beginning of a database project and using it just to support the early planning also has the advantage that employees could begin to gain experience with the database environment before the decision on a production system had to be made. This is similar to the idea of prototyping information systems where users are given a rough, inexpensive prototype of a system early in the development cycle and their experience with it plays a valuable role in designing the ultimate system.

TERMS TO UNDERSTAND

data dictionary	metadata dictionary
data directory	information providers
data resource dictionary	information controllers

REVIEW QUESTIONS

1. What is the difference between the data dictionary and the data directory? Why is this distinction made in discussing the structure of a data dictionary system?

2. What problems might one face when trying to decide on standardized names for data elements?

3. In what part of the Data Dictionary/Directory (DD/D) would one find the following?: (a) The number of times a particular field was accessed in the

previous month. (b) The maximum number of characters allowed for in the field containing "Employee Address." (c) The availability of indices or inverted lists. (d) Whether or not a particular user ID can be used to access a given type of information. (e) Conceptional schema. (f) Information on a proposed system.

4. The integrated data dictionary appears to dominate the other two approaches discussed in the chapter. Why? What is its main disadvantage?

5. Outline some of the ways in which nonhuman users can make use of a data dictionary. Why is this useful?

6. Discuss how the data dictionary can be used to increase the productivity of both end-users and application-system developers.

DATABASE MANAGEMENT SYSTEM (DBMS) SELECTION

There are few decisions that an organization makes within the realm of information processing as momentous as the choice of a Database Management System (DBMS). It is one of the largest decisions in terms of direct financial expenditure, with only a mainframe hardware acquisition likely to involve as great a single commitment. Even more important, the choice of a DBMS will ultimately affect almost every aspect of the organization's information processing. Thus, the total financial obligation will greatly exceed the outlay for the DBMS itself, and the risk associated with the decision spans the entire range of data processing activities.

Anyone who reads the popular magazines in the personal computing area will have noted the widespread availability of low-cost DBMS's in this market. It may be wondered, then, why database system selection is treated as such a major issue in the large systems community. Probably the most obvious discrepancy concerns cost. If DBMS's for personal computers can be sold for only a few hundred dollars, why do the most popular ones for large systems carry price tags a thousand times greater? Why, also, do these expensive DBMS's seem to strain the capacity of even the largest mainframe systems when their cheaper relatives run comfortably on far less powerful hardware? Finally, why is it that most of the personal computer DBMS's use the relational database model, whereas in the large system arena, it is considered still somewhat experimental?

A full discussion of the microcomputer DBMS issue is beyond the scope of this chapter. However, a few brief comments are required here to justify the preceding claims about the cost and risk of DBMS selection and to motivate the elaborate decision process that is about to be described. To a great extent, the three questions raised in the last paragraph are all manifestations of one reality— much more is expected of a DBMS running in a large business organization than of one used for hobby purposes or household management.

The first difference is in the size of the database that must be managed. Personal-use databases are rarely more than a few hundred thousand characters in size. Commercial ones can easily be larger by four or five orders of magnitude. Personal systems are usually just that—intended for use by a single person. All of the problems of multiple simultaneous access simply do not arise. Commercial systems, on the other hand, often have thousands of concurrent users. This not only places greater demands on the processing facilities, but also means that great care must be taken to coordinate the database activities of all the different users. Similarly, the general area of backup and recovery, which is of crucial importance in a large commercial system is often given little attention in the microcomputer versions.

This chapter is written for large organizations with big databases serving many different applications and users. For such firms, it is impossible to exaggerate the significance of the DBMS decision. The requirements are quite demanding and the cost of correcting an error later is high. For smaller and simpler environments, these considerations become progressively less important until, at the level of the home hobbyist, they are almost totally irrelevant.

DATABASE MANAGEMENT SYSTEM (DBMS) STANDARDS

If all DBMS's provided the same functions and the same interfaces, selection would be much simpler. One could then focus entirely on factors such as cost, efficiency, and reliability. Under these circumstances, the risk of choosing incorrectly would also be greatly reduced because switching from one DBMS to another would be relatively simple. Considerations such as these have been responsible for the long-standing interest in standardization of DBMS's.

The impetus for standardization can be traced to the CODASYL Committee that developed the network database model. CODASYL had previously sponsored the development of COBOL. COBOL remains an attractive choice for business programming, even though it contains many deficiencies. One reason for COBOL's popularity is the fact that it is regulated by international standards. This means that programs written in standard COBOL can be moved from one installation to another and even from one type of computer to a completely different one with a minimum of fuss. It has also encouraged the development of a large community of skilled COBOL programmers.

The CODASYL Committee felt that the same benefits ought to be realizable in the database area; when their network proposal was first publicized, it was intended for consideration as a draft standard. This suggestion met with considerable opposition for a variety of reasons. Some people simply did not like the CODASYL proposal. As discussed in Chapter 5, the CODASYL DBTG network proposal is based on strong beliefs about what is important in a DBMS, and these are not universally accepted. Other opposition was based on the view that it was inappropriate to adopt *any* standard at such an early point in the history of the field. It was considered possible, even likely, that much better approaches remained to be discovered, and it was feared that early standardization would tend to choke off additional research. Another factor that probably worked against acceptance of the CODASYL proposal was the position taken by IBM. Although almost all of the other major computer manufacturers participated in the CODASYL project, IBM remained on the sidelines. There are a number of possible explanations for this, ranging from antitrust concerns to a reluctance to disclose the directions being taken by internal database research projects. In any case, even though IBM did not overtly oppose the CODASYL effort, its lack of endorsement probably influenced many others to hold back.

In the interim, there has, of course, been a considerable amount of additional research, most of which has focused on the relational model and its derivatives. There has also been additional study of the standardization question itself. It was relatively easy, even back in the 1960s, to determine what the standard for a programming language would have to contain—a complete specification of the language's syntax and semantics. It is, by no means, as obvious what should be included in a database standard. One school of thought has emphasized the various language aspects of a DBMS. Thus, it has been proposed that a standard specification might be written for data definition languages and data manipulation languages. The DBTG proposal also envisioned a Device/Media Control Language for relating logical constructs to actual physical facilities. Note that standards of this type describe the interfaces between the DBMS and such other entities as users and the computer's operating system. They do not specify the internal workings of the DBMS. As described earlier, the committee established by ANSI/SPARC[1] suggested that interfaces were the appropriate things to try to standardize.

However, it is usually accepted that language standards would have to imply a standard data model as well. The lack of consensus as to the superiority of any one data model has inhibited much progress on the language standardization issue. In the meantime, another ANSI/SPARC study group was set up to investigate standardization possibilities within the relational database model.[2] This group noted that there were more than 70 DBMS's on the market claiming to support the relational model. Although all these systems exhibit certain similarities, there are substantial differences among them. It was felt that an official definition of the relational model would give implementors a clear indication of what was expected and potential customers a set of criteria to use in evaluating the vendor claims to relationality. The study group proposed that an initial relational standard should concentrate on the basic concepts of the model, the functions to be performed and the interfaces between a relational DBMS and the outside world. It was specifically recommended that the standard exclude the internal architecture of a DBMS, language syntax, and issues that are not data model dependent, such as those of concurrency and security.

Another useful area for standards-related research is the relationship *among* the different data models. Because each model has its own terminology, conceptual similarities among them are often obscured. An interesting approach to revealing commonalities among the three well-known data models is reflected in the Universal Database Language (UDL) of C. J. Date.[3] UDL is based on the observation that a relation may be considered a special case of a hierarchy and a hierarchy, a special case of a network. The second of these should be evident to

---

[1] ANSI/SPARC: see footnote 1; Chapter 7, p. 131.

[2] M. L. Brodie & J. W. Schmidt (Editors), *Final Report of the ANSI/X3/SPARC DBS-SG Relational Database Task Group*, Doc. No. SPARC–81–690. In *ACM SIGMOD Record*, Vol. 12, No. 4 (July 1982).

[3] C. J. Date, *An Introduction to Database Systems*, Volume I, 3rd Edition, Addison-Wesley, 1981, chap. 27.

anyone who has read this far—a hierarchy is a network in which each record occurrence belongs to exactly one set. The correspondence between a relation and a hierarchy is not as obvious. However, a hierarchy consisting only of root segments can be viewed as equivalent to a relation. The major contribution of UDL is that it introduces a single set of concepts, terminology, and functions that can be applied to all three models.

Although there has been little progress toward official standards in the database area, there is some evidence of movement toward informal ones. The network database model was supported from the beginning by most of the non-IBM vendors as well as by many user organizations. Probably expecting that it would achieve early acceptance, many of the vendors began developing database products that conformed to the DBTG proposal. Although the standardization drive did not ultimately succeed, a number of commercial DBMS's were produced based on these specifications. These are not absolutely compatible with each other, but they come close enough so that converting from one to another ought not to be too difficult. The incompatibilities arise from two main sources: some details were intentionally left to the judgment of the DBMS implementors to allow for the most efficient possible implementation. Other portions of the specification were unintentionally ambiguous and susceptible of more than one reasonable interpretation. This is inevitable when something as complex as a DBMS must be described in ordinary language.[4] In fact, one function of the national and international standards organizations is to resolve these ambiguities before adoption if possible, afterward when necessary. Despite these minor inconsistencies, there is great similarity among the various DBTG-based systems on the market; therefore, at least some of the objectives of standardization have been achieved.

In the relational sphere, formal standardization work is still at a very early stage. However, IBM has done a great deal of internal work on these systems, and it has released several commercial relational database products. Because of the dominant position of IBM in the data processing market, their systems often take on the character of de facto standards. There is some sign of this in the database area. Most of IBM's relational offerings use Structured Query Language (SQL). One of IBM's main competitors in this area, the ORACLE system, also uses SQL; in fact, it has undertaken to maintain compatibility, even though IBM's SQL is still being revised from time to time. This development strongly suggests that SQL will attain the status of an unofficial standard whether or not the formal standardization procedures are ever invoked.

---

[4] One way to attack this problem is to use specialized formal languages to express standards. For an introduction to this approach and a good list of references, see Lamersdorf, Winfried, "Comparison of Four Relational Data Model Specifications," in *ACM SIGMOD Record*, Vol. 13, No. 3 (April 1983), pp. 18–31.

DATABASE MANAGEMENT SYSTEM (DBMS) EVALUATION

The lack of database standards greatly complicates the problem of choosing a DBMS. After the organization's requirements are understood, the range of available DBMS products must be surveyed to determine the one with the best overall match. In carrying out this process, the evaluator must not only deal with significant differences in capability, but also with the problem of specific terms being used by different vendors to mean quite different things.

In today's world, the process usually begins by choosing the data model that seems most appropriate and then proceeding to a detailed evaluation of only the candidates that support the selected model. In the future, it is possible that standardized user-level languages, such as Date's UDL, may make the internal data model of a DBMS totally irrelevant to users.

Once a model has been selected, the evaluation procedure concentrates on comparing commercially available systems that implement that model. The remainder of this chapter is devoted to discussing methodologies for performing this comparison. However, it may seem that this approach neglects the possibility of *building* a DBMS rather than acquiring an existing one. In principle, this is an alternative that is always available. In practice, it would take some *very* unusual circumstances to make it a sensible choice. At the beginning of the database era, firms sometimes found it necessary to build their own DBMS's because they had requirements that could not be met by the available commercial products. This is highly unlikely to occur today, and the gap would have to be enormous to justify the expense and risk of developing a unique DBMS.

The construction by users of large pieces of system software (like DBMS's) is generally not recommended. When undertaken by a hardware or software vendor, there is an opportunity to spread the large investment that is required over a large number of purchasers. However, when a firm elects to develop something like a DBMS by itself, it must be prepared to bear the entire cost. It also must be prepared to wait a considerable length of time before the finished product is ready for use and to devote considerable management attention to staffing and running a high-risk, high-cost project in an area that is peripheral to the company's main interests.

A company that develops its own DBMS must also expect to live through a long period when the software will be quite unreliable. This is unavoidable with software of this size and complexity. However, when one buys a package commercially, most of the bugs should already have been discovered (by previous purchasers!). Furthermore, someone else, the vendor, is responsible for fixing those bugs that are encountered, whereas with an in-house system, the work must be done locally. A final factor militating against the development of unique DBMS's is their effect on application developers. One of the most significant factors limiting development of database applications is a shortage of trained staff. Organizations using popular commercial DBMS's can, at least, attempt to recruit staff from the pool of people experienced with the chosen system. However, an organization that has developed its own DBMS must be prepared to undertake all of the training needed by both users and system maintainers. It is also possible that good people will be less inclined to work in such an environment because of the reduced transferability of their skills and experience.

Throughout the rest of this discussion, it will be assumed that the choice has been made to acquire a DBMS in the commercial marketplace rather than to construct one independently. Through most of the 1970s, many users of IBM equipment with large amounts of data to manage found that once they had ruled out building their own systems, the selection process was virtually complete because there was only one candidate available that combined the ability to manage a large database with the necessary attention to backup, recovery, and other supporting services. This was, of course, IBM's own Information Management System (IMS). Thus, despite its well-known conceptual inadequacies and poor efficiency, it was adopted by many large users, virtually by default.

The situation is vastly different today. As a result of the maturing of the DBMS field, a wide range of products are now available, and there can be a great payoff associated with making the correct choice. There are many DBMS vendors competing for the business of users of IBM (and compatible) equipment. There are also a number of DBMS's that have been implemented on a variety of different manufacturers' hardware. Thus, it is possible to imagine replacing a computer with a totally incompatible one from a different vendor without having to change the DBMS.[5]

The techniques available for selecting DBMS software are basically the same as those used for other large software procurements, and even for choosing new hardware. However, because of the particular nature of a DBMS and its role in the organization, the applicability of these approaches needs to be carefully reviewed.

BENCHMARKING

One highly recommended approach to buying anything is to try it out first. Most people would not dream of buying a car without taking it for a test drive. On the other hand, rarely is it possible to test a car for a long enough period or under a wide enough range of conditions to be really sure that it will perform satisfactorily. That this approach seems to work all right for buying cars may be due to the

---

[5] Of course, the DBMS program itself would almost certainly have to be replaced when the hardware environment changed, but if one converts from, say, IDMS on an IBM computer to IDMS on one from Sperry, the applications programs and database will not have to be redesigned, nor will the personnel require retraining.

fact that there do not tend to be great differences between models in the same type, size, and price group.

Test driving or benchmarking, as it is called, is also a well-known technique for evaluating computer systems, where the differences among competitive products can be much greater than is typically the case with automobiles. A benchmark is an application, or a portion of one, that all by itself accounts for a large fraction of the total workload or is typical of the range of applications encountered. Once the benchmark has been implemented, its performance can be evaluated along whatever dimensions are considered relevant. One might look at the size and cost of the hardware configuration, the transaction processing rate, ease of use, and level of vendor support, among many other things.

If the test application is correctly chosen, benchmarking can provide a basis for rational decision making not matched by any of the alternative mechanisms. There are, however, a few general disadvantages. One is that it is obviously time consuming to implement an actual application or even a significant part of one. It is also costly. Furthermore, if the test is to provide a valid measure of the performance of each candidate system, the distinctive features offered by each must be utilized effectively. Thus, the benchmarking must be done by people who know the systems well. It would be quite unusual to find this level of expertise concerning each of the candidate systems in the customer organization. Often, it is not even possible to get the necessary information from the vendors prior to making an acquisition commitment.

One possible solution to this problem is to have the benchmarks prepared by the vendors themselves. Whether the vendors would be willing to do this clearly depends on the value of the contract. It has been done with some success by the U.S. Government when multiple system contracts worth enormous amounts of money were at stake. In such cases, a vendor might well invest many man-years and hundreds of thousands of dollars in preparing a benchmark. Clearly, this degree of investment could not be expected for the smaller contracts that are more usual in the commercial marketplace.

Even if the vendor is willing to prepare a benchmark application, there are things of which to be wary. Although the vendors must take full responsibility for knowing how best to exploit their own products, they may not fully understand the application. This can result in benchmarks that do not take advantage of certain features in the application and therefore make a system look worse than it should. Alternatively, a benchmark may indicate better performance than it should if it fails to take account of subtle constraints in the problem. Both of these types of errors can occur at the same time. Thus, even though benchmarks make it possible to directly measure performance, there is no certainty that measurements on the benchmarks are a good indication of how the actual systems, properly implemented, will perform.

The usefulness of benchmarking in general can be summarized by noting that it provides an actual working system that can be measured in any desired way, but it is time consuming and expensive to undertake and the results will only be valid to the extent that the problem is properly understood and the capabilities of each candidate fully utilized.

All of these comments certainly apply to the use of benchmarking to evaluate DBMS's. In addition to the usual programming work that is part of any benchmark, it is also necessary to design a suitable test database and fill it with data. We have discussed the database design process in earlier chapters, and it should be clear that a considerable amount of work must be invested if it is to be done properly. This is especially true if the systems under consideration do not all employ the same database model.

In addition to the usual uncertainties associated with benchmarking, there are some unique problems in applying it to DBMS evaluation. Performance of a DBMS may depend significantly on the overall transaction volume or on the relative frequency of different types of transactions. Errors in estimating these may seriously distort the results. Benchmarking a DBMS also requires that a database be constructed. Such test databases are usually much smaller than the corresponding real ones. The performance of any DBMS is affected by the size of the database, and the sensitivity to this parameter may be much greater for some systems than for others. Thus, a system that is significantly better than another in processing a test database may have a much smaller relative advantage for databases of realistic size.

In summary, benchmarking is a time-consuming and expensive technique that purports to provide the most accurate possible basis for comparing systems. However, as has been seen, there are a number of factors, some general and some specific to the DBMS area, that can make benchmark results much less valid than might be expected.

MODELING AND SIMULATION

These are two approaches that use mathematical techniques to predict the performance of a real system. The real system need not even exist as long as an adequately detailed description of it is available. Thus, these techniques can be applied to evaluating candidate designs in order to select the best one for implementation. Constructing a mathematical model of something involves developing equations that describe its performance in terms of various parameters. For example, in a model of a database management system, one equation might state that the total time for a retrieval transaction is the sum of the times for query interpretation, data fetching, and processing required to manipulate the data. The equation for data fetch time might relate it to the amount of data to be read, to the number of different files accessed, and various physical characteristics of the storage hardware.

The performance of an actual or proposed system is estimated by "plugging in" parameter values that describe the workload, the DBMS, and the processing environment. The computation required to solve a model of this type is usually quite small. Often, it is not even necessary to use a computer. There are cases, though, where the equations may not be directly solvable at all. Then, numerical methods can be used to approximate the solution to any desired degree of accuracy. In this case, substantial amounts of computer time may be required.

By inserting sets of parameter values that describe different DBMS's, a model can be used to compare their performance. It is also possible to alter parameter values that describe the workload and/or the environment to see how dramatically performance would change under different assumptions.

The main problem with this approach is that it is usually only possible to capture the gross characteristics of anything as complex as a DBMS if the models are to remain mathematically tractable. It is difficult to design models that are detailed enough to be useful and still capable of being solved. It is also difficult to demonstrate that such models are valid. Ideally, this should be done by comparing predictions of the model to measurements made on the real system.

However, much of the value of these models comes from their ability to *predict* the performance of systems *before* resources have actually been invested in constructing them. When it is impossible to validate a model by comparing it to reality, it is necessary to rely on intuitive tests of reasonableness and sensitivity analysis. The reasonableness of a model is assessed by varying input parameters systematically and checking to see if the output predictions change in the expected ways. Of course, tests of this type are not foolproof. Sometimes, real systems do not behave in the way that would be expected on the basis of intuition.

Sensitivity analysis looks at the magnitude of changes in the output caused by changes in input values. If the important conclusions do not change under a wide range of values for some input variable, then it is not too important whether or not the value of that variable is known exactly. If the output is found to be especially sensitive to certain parameters, then extra work can sometimes be done to try to refine the input values.

Modeling is often a relatively quick and inexpensive way of estimating the performance of a system. Its main disadvantage is that the simplification required to construct the model may obscure important properties of the systems being modeled. Because of the degree of mathematical sophistication needed to develop these models, they are not widely used for procurement decisions in the commercial world. However, they have been used with considerable success in academia to study the behavior of general classes of DBMS's.

An interesting characteristic of mathematical models is that one need not understand exactly how the system being studied works internally as long as equations can be written that relate the output to the input. Sometimes, the total behavior of a system is too complex for such equations to be written or solved, but the functioning of its constituent pieces can be individually described in detail. In these cases, a special type of modeling, known as *simulation* may be helpful.

A number of specialized programming languages exist for construction and exercising simulation models. Typically, the system being simulated will be described in terms of events (e.g., the receipt of a database query), resources (e.g., central processors and disk drives), and flows of information and/or physical materials.

Once the simulation model has been constructed, the simulator (program) generates streams of transactions in accordance with specified parameters. Each of these transactions is then traced as it proceeds through the various stages of the model. After a large enough number of transactions have been traced, it is possible to compute statistics that describe the overall behavior of the system.

A key difference between simulation and other types of models is that the former often employ probabilistic descriptions of the transactions or of the system—or both. Thus, each run of a simulation may give slightly different results. A conventional mathematical model, using equations that describe the system relationships directly, will always give exactly the same answers (unless, of course, the system exhibits some uncertainty in its actual behavior).

Simulation has been applied to studying the behavior of individual DBMS's. However, using this technique to choose between alternative systems would require constructing a model of each. The effort involved in developing the detailed knowledge of their internal workings and constructing the simulation models would be very great, indeed.

FEATURE ANALYSIS

Feature analysis is the most common approach to selecting database systems in real organizations. The cost and time required can be matched to any external circumstances by choosing the level of detail of the study. It also does not require any particular mathematical skill or computational resources.

The basic approach is as follows: first, a list of features that can be used to characterize a DBMS is compiled. This list refers to DBMS's in general and does not depend at all on the conditions in the organization doing the study. A number of examples of generalized feature lists can be found in the literature. Part of one possible list is shown in Figure 11–1 to suggest what might be included.

The second step is to evaluate each candidate DBMS. Each feature on the list

(A) VENDOR SUPPORT

1. Training
2. Documentation
3. Technical Support
4. Vendor Credibility
5. User Experience

(B) EASE OF USE

1. Initial Implementation
2. Database Design Change Facilities
3. Continuing Use

(C) SYSTEM REQUIREMENTS

1. Hardware
2. Software

(D) COMPLETENESS

1. Security Features
2. Utilities
3. Data Structures Supported
4. Query Facilities
5. Report Writer Facilities
6. Batch/Online Capability
7. Communications Interface
8. Language Interface
9. Data Dictionary Capability
10. Usage Statistics
11. Support for Data Independence

(E) INTEGRITY

1. Checkpoint/Restart
2. Backup/Recovery

(F) PERFORMANCE

1. CPU Usage
2. Channel Usage
3. Tuning Flexibility

FIGURE 11–1 Partial Database Management System (DBMS) feature list.

is checked to see if it is present at all, and if it is, a score (on a scale of, say, 1 to 10) is assigned reflecting the quality of the feature. At this stage, it would be possible to simply add up the scores and get a rating for each DBMS as a whole, but this generalized rating would not be especially useful for decision making because it does not take account of the organization's particular needs. For example, facilities for dealing with unanticipated ad hoc queries may be important in some organizations. However, because such features will probably adversely affect updating and routine sequential processing, they may actually be detrimental to other organizations.

These considerations are dealt with in the third step, which involves reviewing all of the items on the feature list from the using organization's viewpoint. Characteristics of the organization, its data, and the intended applications are used to assess the importance of each DBMS feature. One simple way to do this is just to categorize each one as essential, desirable, irrelevant, or undesirable. Alternatively, a weight can be assigned reflecting the importance of each feature. A scale of -10 to $+10$ might be used in this case to allow for the fact that some features might actually be detrimental. If the numerical weighting system is used, features receiving high weights should be checked to determine if they are absolutely essential. The purpose of assigning weights is to ensure that the final scores will count features that are important to the organization more heavily than less important ones.

The final step in the procedure consists of developing a score for each system. This is done by first eliminating systems that are missing any of the essential features. Then, if numerical weights have been assigned to features, the score for a DBMS is computed simply by multiplying the score for each feature by its weighting factor, and then summing the results. See Figure 11-2 for a partial example. If numerical weights were not assigned, a rough score can be produced by giving the essential or desirable features a weight of $+1$ and the undesirable ones a weight of -1. Irrelevant features are given a weight of 0.

There are several reasons for the popularity of this approach. Probably the main one is its simplicity. No special skills or resources are required, and anyone can understand how the method works. It also has the appearance of being a rational, quantitative technique. Finally, the process can be expanded to include one or more levels of weighting and aggregation in between the detailed features and the overall DBMS score as shown in Figure 11-3. This may be helpful in determining the best set of weights, and it also helps in interpreting the final score by indicating the general areas in which a particular system is strong or weak. Such analysis is useful when a selection decision must be justified.

There are also disadvantages to this method. The most important one is that, despite its appearance of rationality and objectivity, it is just about as subjective as a totally ad hoc decision because all of the crucial numbers—both feature scores and weights—are produced by human estimate. A cynic might suggest

Feature	Weight (1–10)	Exists (Y/N)	Quality (1–5)	Weighted Score

DBMS: _____

Vendor: _____

Evaluated by: _____ Date: _____

FIGURE 11–2 Feature analysis worksheet.

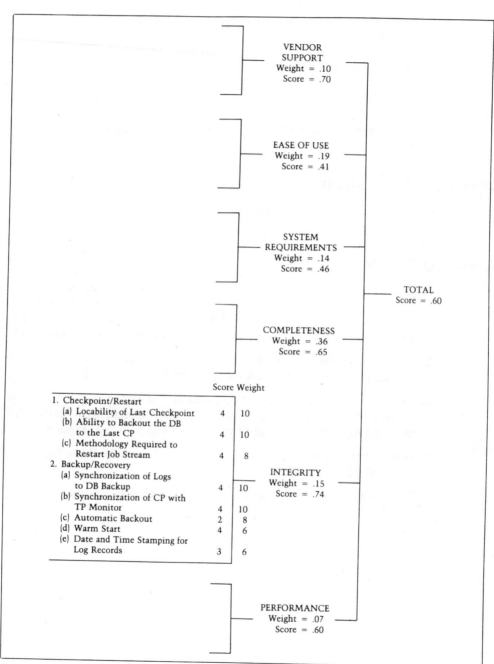

FIGURE 11-3 Expanded feature analysis approach.

that one of the reasons for the popularity of this method is that it can be easily manipulated to give any result that may be desired. Unless all of the candidate systems are evaluated by the same individual, or by a group working *jointly*, it is also possible for differences in interpretation to pollute the results. One evaluator might give a score of 8 to a particular system's data dictionary facility, for example, whereas another evaluator, with different experiences or standards, might give the same facility only a 5.

This approach is easy to use and understand. But, unless it is handled carefully, it will not provide the objective reliability that is needed.

TERMS TO UNDERSTAND

standards   feature analysis
benchmark

REVIEW QUESTIONS

1. List at least five reasons why a company should not want to construct its own Database Management System (DBMS). Are there any circumstances under which development of a unique DBMS can be justified? Is your answer to this question any different today than it would have been 10 years ago? Why?

2. What is the difference between modeling and simulation? For what problems is each best suited? What skills are required to use each?

3. Suppose you were interested in evaluating a Database Management System (DBMS) query language on user-friendliness. Construct a feature list for this task and indicate the weights you would apply to the items on your list.

4. Why is benchmarking not often used to select a Database Management System (DBMS)?

5. What is the major weakness of the feature analysis method?

CHAPTER 12

THE USER DATABASE MANAGEMENT SYSTEM (DBMS) INTERFACE

The usefulness of a database to an organization depends on a number of factors. The amount, relevance and quality of the data are all obviously important. The range and power of the data manipulation facilities also play a major role. This chapter deals with yet a third dimension of database usability—the facilities provided for expressing the user's desires to the database management software. It is widely accepted today that the user interface is an important part of any system. It is particularly critical for databases because of the wide range of sophistication, interest, and experience present in the user community and because of the high degree of complexity of some database operations. Because of the wide diversity among database users and applications, there is probably no single Database Management System (DBMS) interface that is optimal for all and features that are desirable in one context may be disadvantageous in another.

Although this chapter is concerned with all aspects of the interface between the DBMS and user, an emphasis is placed on language because this is the aspect of the interface that is most controllable. Other interface characterisics that deal with the physical channels used for input and output and the speed of communication are usually determined outside the database environment.

The chapter will begin by developing two frameworks. The first will be used to describe the requirements placed on a DBMS interface in terms of characteristics of users, their jobs, and the tasks they perform. The second framework consists of a number of dimensions useful for characterizing DBMS—user interfaces. There is an obvious connection between these two frameworks: certain interface properties are well suited to each requirement, others are not. Following the discussion of these two frameworks and their interaction, a selection of database languages will be described and related to the frameworks. The languages have been chosen to illustrate a range of interesting alternatives.

A REQUIREMENTS FRAMEWORK

Many attempts have been made to classify the different ways in which people interact with databases. The discussion presented here is based in part on previous work by Everest[1] and Schneiderman.[2] This framework consists of five dimensions:

- Cognitive style
- Training
- Frequency of use
- Programming
- Task complexity

[1] Gordon Everest, *Database Management*, McGraw Hill, 1984.

[2] Ben Schneiderman, "Improving the Human Factors of Database Interaction," *ACM Transactions on Database Systems*, Vol. 3, No. 4 (December 1978), pp. 417–439.

The first dimension, cognitive style, is specifically a property of an individual; the other four refer to the individual's usage of the database.

Cognitive Style

Much research in Management Information Systems (MIS) has attempted to relate information systems characteristics and effectiveness to the cognitive style of the users. Although cognitive style is inherently a complex concept, some useful work in the field has been done using highly simplified models.[3] These often refer to a spectrum of cognitive styles that ranges from analytic to heuristic. An analytic thinker tends to solve problems by developing algorithms, or sets of rules, which (if followed) will produce the desired answer. At the other extreme, a heuristic person looks first at the data and often uses particular examples to aid in understanding the general situation. Researchers in this area take pains to emphasize that neither of these extremes can be considered better than the other—in general. However, particular styles may be advantageous in the performance of certain types of tasks. It is often suggested that analytic thinking is especially valuable in tasks like production management, where the problem is highly quantitative and many formal solution methods are known. A heuristic person, on the other hand, may be more effective on strategic planning tasks, where there is little reliable data and few good models. For the purposes of this discussion, the key finding of cognitive-style research is that the performance of any decision maker can be improved by providing access to information in a manner that is compatible with the individual's mode of thinking. Therefore, one way to categorize database languages and interfaces would be according to the type of cognitive style for which they are best suited.

Training

Users also vary in the amount of training they can be expected to undergo in the use of the system. People in clerical jobs are usually expected to follow prescribed procedures and, therefore, normally attend training sessions before starting to work. The relatively low wage rate for this kind of work and the need for all the people performing a task to do it the same way make such training essential. At the other extreme, high-level executives tend to receive little formal training in their work. The distinction here, though, is not between low and high levels in the corporate hierarchy. In some cases, the nature of the application makes training of users impractical. Many systems intended for use by the general public would fall into this category. Examples could include automated library catalogs

---

[3] For a good introduction to this topic see Robey, Daniel & William Taggart, "Human Information Processing in Information and Decision Support Systems," *MIS Quarterly*, Vol. 6, No. 2 (June 1982), pp. 61–73.

or databases accessed through videotex facilities. It is not difficult to design a system for users who will have little, if any, formal instruction, but the result will be quite different from one where elaborate training can be given.

Frequency of Use

Frequency of use is another dimension that can be used to categorize database users. This dimension is not entirely independent of the preceding one. Where frequent use is expected, it is usually easier to justify training. However, there is a subtle difference. The frequent user will probably have little difficulty remembering how to use the system once this knowledge is acquired. The intermittent user has to face the problem of forgetting and relearning. Experiments have shown that the procedures needed to use some database languages are remembered much more easily than others. A single individual may perform different roles at different times and, thus, may have different requirements.

Programming

User roles can also be characterized according to whether or not they involve computer programming in the traditional sense. It is not necessarily the case that a nonprogramming user is a person who does not know how to program, merely that programming is not required in that particular role. Each end of the programming dimension can be further categorized. It is useful to distinguish, for example, between nonprogramming roles where the user simply initiates canned functions for specific, preplanned tasks and those that require a more sophisticated ability to manipulate the database. Everest uses the term "parametric nonprogramming user" for the first of these, whereas the latter group are referred to as "generalized nonprogramming users."

The parametric nonprogramming user (PNU) is the simplest of all user roles. However, it deserves careful consideration because it probably accounts for the largest share of all database transactions in most organizations. In fact, in real-time systems, such as airline reservations or banking, virtually all transactions come from PNUs. The PNU selects a transaction type by pushing a specific button or typing a short code. Depending on the requirements of the transaction, the user may also enter parameter values. For example, a balance inquiry in a banking system will require entering the account number and, perhaps, type.

The main advantage of parametric, nonprogramming usage is that there is relatively little need for training and little opportunity for errors because the user's actions are so highly constrained. Because the PNU works in such a highly structured environment, he or she may often be totally unaware of whether or not a general purpose database system is being used. Somebody else, either a programmer or a generalized nonprogramming user (GNU), will have prepared the actual procedure needed for each transaction-type, and these will all appear as basic system functions to the PNU.

Although the PNUs training is primarily directed toward the application area, the GNU is expected to have some knowledge of the content and structure of the database. He or she also must learn to use a special language for expressing database queries. An individual who is proficient in one of these query languages has much greater ability to manipulate the database than one who is restricted to preprogrammed parametric queries. This is the type of usage that is generally considered appropriate for managers. Unfortunately, managers often have neither the time nor the motivation to learn the query language. One way of dealing with this challenge is to develop query languages that are as close as possible to ordinary English, and much effort has been expended in this direction. A later section of this chapter discusses the role of so-called "natural" language in database manipulation.

An enormous variety of languages have been developed for the GNU. At one extreme, these languages are similar to conventional programming languages; at the other extreme, they resemble ordinary English. There are not, as yet, any official standards governing query languages, although there seems to be some informal concensus developing around IBM's Structured Query Language (SQL). There is a fine line to be drawn between generalized nonprogramming use of a database and programming use of it. Many of the generalized query languages have manipulative power and complexity equivalent to standard programming languages.

Programming users are characterized by their use of the database through programs written in a conventional programming language. Again, it makes sense to consider a spectrum of programming usage. At one end, the applications programming user (APU) is concerned with using the database in the context of a specific application. He or she knows the precise content and structure of the relevant portion of the database. At the other extreme, the GNU writes database processing programs that are intended to be useful in a variety of situations. Usually, these programs must be capable of querying the DBMS to determine the content and structure of the database.

The distinction between APU and GPU is similar to that between applications programmers and systems programmers. Program modules written by the latter will often be used as building blocks in the programming of applications. As an example, in the specific context of database processing, an APU using a relational DBMS to develop an employee directory might have to retrieve specific attributes from an EMPLOYEE relation and print them in a specified format. The APU would know the name of the relation and the name and format of each of its attributes. A contrasting GNU-task would involve writing a program to print out the contents of a relation—any relation. This program would have to know how to extract the necessary names and descriptive information from the DBMS and

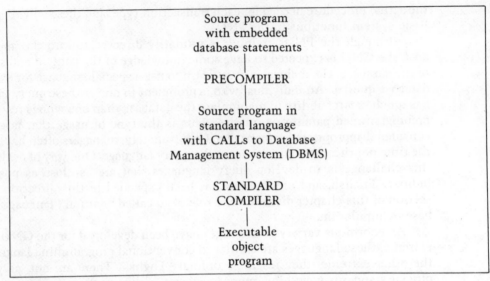

FIGURE 12–1 Use of a preprocessor for database manipulation.

would also have to select appropriate output formats for the particular data. The additional level of generality makes this type of programming somewhat more demanding than that involved in developing an application where the structure of the data is well defined in advance. It also seems reasonable that the GPU should be more concerned with efficiency than the APU because generalized routines are more likely to experience frequent usage.

There are two obvious approaches to manipulate a database through a general-purpose language such as FORTRAN or COBOL. The first is to use the subroutine calling mechanism present in virtually all high-level languages to connect to the data manipulation functions. The other is to modify the language itself to include database operations.

In practice, these tend to work out to about the same thing. No standard programming language has yet been officially modified to include database capabilities.[4] However, a number of DBMS's simulate this capability. The programming language used by the programmers is one of the standard ones augmented by an additional set of operations that perform database functions. After the program is written, it is translated by a preprocessor—supplied by the DBMS vendor—that replaces all of the nonstandard statements with CALLs to subroutines. Figure 12–1 illustrates this process.

---

[4] Recall that the network database model was developed by a CODASYL committee whose charter was to investigate the addition of database capability to COBOL.

Task Complexity

The final dimension in the requirements framework deals with the complexity of database use. The vast majority of users need to perform only relatively simple operations. Illustrations in the context of the library database might include changing a borrower's address, finding out who has borrowed a particular book, or producing a list of books due on a specific date. Other users have more complicated information needs. Determining, for example, the borrowers who have read *all* of the books by a certain author requires surprisingly complex manipulation of the database. (Try it using, for example, the relational algebra to get a good idea of what is involved.) Most languages and interfaces are adequate for simple queries. For such applications, the selection should probably emphasize other criteria, such as ease of learning. However, languages vary greatly in their suitability for performing complex database operations. If such usage is part of the requirement for a system, this could become an important selection criterion.

INTERFACE PROPERTIES FRAMEWORK

This section describes 10 dimensions divided into two classes that can be used to describe DBMS interfaces (see Figure 12–2). Five of these are used to characterize an interface in terms of its basic approach to user/Database Management System (DBMS) communication. The other 5 refer to facilities for performing generic database functions. The following generic functions have been identified by Schneiderman based on previous work in the area of programming languages:

GENERIC FUNCTIONS

- Learning
- Composition
- Comprehension
- Debugging
- Modification

INTERFACE CHARACTERISTICS

- Embedded versus Self-contained
- User-Directed versus System Directed
- Natural versus Artificial
- Procedural versus Specification
- One-dimensional versus Two-dimensional

FIGURE 12–2 Interface properties framework.

1. *Learning.*   The first step in using any database language consists of learning its rules of syntax and semantics. Ease and speed of learning are obviously desirable, but these sometimes conflict with other objectives. For example, a particular language may be easy to learn because it is limited in its capability. A reasonable compromise might be to ask that the most commonly used features be easy to learn.

2. *Composition.*   Composition of a syntactically correct command is the second task that must be performed in using a language. It might seem that a language that is easy to learn will also be easy for composing queries, but this is not always the case. It may be quite difficult to compose useful commands in a language that is easy to learn because it includes only quite elementary capabilities.

3. *Comprehension.*   The third task is understanding a command composed by someone else. It is often necessary to read someone else's commands as part of the learning process as well as when a previously composed function must be modified. Ease of comprehension is not the same as ease of composition. It is generally easy to comprehend someone else's COBOL program, but not so easy actually to write one. The APL language, on the other hand, is easy to use, but figuring out what somebody else's APL program does can be a most challenging task!

4. *Debugging.*   Debugging of function syntax and semantics is the fourth task that must be performed. The functions may have been initially composed by oneself or by someone else. Debugging is obviously related to both composition and comprehension, but it goes beyond them. Techniques that have been developed for detecting syntax errors in computer programs can probably be used as a model for the equivalent task in database languages. However, it is much less clear what features can be built into a language to help the user determine that the semantics of a command are correct.

5. *Modification.*   The fifth task in this list is the modification of a previously working function prepared by oneself or another. It requires comprehending the existing function and then using composition skills to change it.

These five tasks are not always mutually compatible as illustrated by some examples based on familiar programming languages. Basic is easy to learn, but its limited capabilities make difficult the composition of some useful functions. On the other hand, COBOL is hard to learn because of the number of statement types and variations, but a COBOL program is relatively easy to comprehend. APL programs are easy for an experienced user to compose because of the variety and power of its operators. The exact same factors tend to make APL programs difficult to comprehend and debug. Database languages exhibit similar tradeoffs.

There is no uncertainty about how an ideal database interface would be characterized in terms of the preceding five dimensions. Obviously, it would be easy to learn, easy to use for composition, and so forth. Any deviations from this ideal found in actual interfaces are usually the result of limited knowledge or resources, and reflect a decision to enhance one function at the expense of others. The remaining five dimensions are somewhat different. They do not have one end of the scale that can definitely be said to be superior to the other. Rather, they represent different approaches to aspects of the user/DBMS communication problem. In these cases, the choice can often be made by reference to the requirements framework outlined previously. That is, certain requirements suggest the use of specific interface types. The five dimensions in this category are:

1. *Embedded Versus Self-contained.* An embedded language is, as the term suggests, part of a general-purpose programming language. A self-contained language is designed to be used on its own without having to write a conventional program. During one period in the early history of database management technology, an active debate existed between advocates of these two approaches. It is difficult today to understand the motivation for this debate because it is obvious that both capabilities are needed.

In terms of the Requirements Framework, it is obvious that embedded languages are designed for programmers, whereas self-contained ones are intended for nonprogramming usage. Programmers are usually considered to be relatively analytical, to have considerable formal training, and (usually) to be frequent users of the database. There may also be a slight emphasis on complex tasks because users with simple ones may tend to handle them directly.

Self-contained languages include query languages, report generators, and a relatively new class called application development facilities (or fourth generation languages). These allow complete application programs to be produced automatically from specifications entered by a nonprogrammer. Users of self-contained systems can range from clerks performing relatively routine tasks many times a day to high-level planners who use the database in bursts of activity a few times a year, usually for tasks that are different each time.

2. *User-Directed Versus System-Directed.* The user-directed versus system-directed dimension measures the way in which responsibility for guiding the interaction is divided between the DBMS and the user. A system-directed interface asks the user a sequence of questions to establish what is wanted. Some system-directed interfaces employ a questionnaire approach, but a better technique, especially when there are many alternatives to choose among, is the use of menus.

Menu-driven systems take a hierarchical approach to task specification. The system begins by presenting the user with a list of alternative primary functions. The user selects one and may then be shown a second menu that depends on what the first choice was and further refines the desired operation. This goes down as many levels as necessary until the request has been completely specified.

System-directed interfaces are, of course, directed toward nonprogramming user roles in the requirements framework and, in particular, toward infrequent users and/or those who have not received much training in the use of the system. Such users may often not be aware of the full range of capability of the system or of the circumstances in which each feature may be used. This approach is also well suited to users who do not understand the problem domain well. Many systems intended for use by the general public find menu-based interfaces effective.

User-directed interfaces rely on the user to take the initiative in solving his or her own problem. The system, in effect, says, "What do you want to do?", and the user has to know enough about both the contents of the database and the functions in the DBMS to respond.

The usual requirement for such an interface to work is that the user has either been well trained or uses the system often enough to remember how to instruct it. User-directed dialogs are much more economical in both computing and human time and energy. Experienced users tend to become impatient with system-directed interfaces that insist on taking them the long way around. On the other hand, inexperienced people are often at a complete loss when faced with a system that just sits there waiting for commands.

One solution is to offer both types of interfaces in the same system. A user can move from the system-directed to user-directed modes either by entering a command instructing the system to change modes or when the system recognizes that the user seems to know what he is doing. In either case, there must also be a way to escape back to the system-directed mode when necessary. Again, this could take place at the request of the user or it could occur automatically when the system senses that the user is having trouble.

A well-designed Help facility has an important role to play in any interactive system. In the context of a user-directed interface, the Help facility should allow the user to determine the current context and the command choices that may be given in that situation. Ideally, a sequence of increasingly detailed responses should be available. That is, on first asking for help, the user should receive a message describing the current context and indicating what the system is waiting for. If the user requests more help, the next message should list the most common possible responses. A third request should produce a complete list of valid responses together with a brief explanation of each; a fourth request should either expand the explanations or refer the user to a source of further assistance.

A Help facility is less essential in a system-directed environment because the system is already giving the user considerable information at each step about the available alternatives. However, it is still possible that a user will need assistance concerning the meaning of some of the choices or the consequences of picking a particular option.

3. *Procedural Versus Specification.*   The procedural versus specification dimension distinguishes between languages in which the user simply describes what is wanted and those in which he or she must also tell the DBMS how to do it. There are no immediately obvious connections between this property and any of the dimensions of the Requirements Framework, although individuals with an analytic cognitive style may prefer procedural languages. It might seem that procedural languages are specifically intended for programmers, whereas specification languages are ideally suited to nonprogrammers, but this is not the case. For example, the relational algebra is a procedural language that is intended for use by nonprogrammers, whereas a number of relational systems that use specification languages provide the same interface to both programming and nonprogramming users. There is also some evidence that specification languages are preferred for relatively simple tasks, whereas users find the procedural approach easier when faced with highly complex ones.

The issue of real significance with respect to the choice of a procedural or specification language is who is going to make the access path decisions. People who think users can make these decisions more efficiently than the system want the user to be able to make them. Those who think the system can make the decisions better prefer interfaces where the user cannot interfere. There would probably be general agreement that most users should not try to tell the DBMS how to do its job. If any users are to get involved in this level of detail, it should probably only be those having high levels of training and experience and needing to do rather sophisticated things. For all others, it should be unnecessary, perhaps even counterproductive.

Figure 12–3 shows two examples of the same query in a simple relational algebra. It might seem that this level of procedurality is not really getting too deep into the workings of the DBMS, but it is easy to verify that there will be an enormous difference in performance between the two.

The relationship between task complexity and language procedurality is an interesting one. Some research[5] has shown that users have difficulty with conventional specification languages when asked to construct extremely complicated queries. It appears that this is due to the need to form a mental image of exactly what characteristics the final answer to the query will have and to the fact that most people have little experience with some of the specifications that have to be used in a complex query. For example, it is easy for most people using most specification languages to express the query:

---

[5] Charles Welty & David W. Stemple, "Human Factors Comparison of a Procedural and a Nonprocedural Query Language," *ACM Transactions on Database Systems,* Vol. 6, No. 4 (December 1981), pp. 626–649.

QUERY: Find the titles of all books currently on
loan to Joan Reader.

Method I:

```
JOIN PERSON ON PERSON-ID WITH BORROWER ON
    BORROWER-ID GIVING TEMP1.
JOIN TEMP1 ON (LIB-NAME, BOR-NO) WITH VOLUME ON
    (LIB-NAME, BOR-NO) GIVING TEMP2.
JOIN TEMP2 ON CATALOG-NO WITH BOOKS ON
    CATALOG-NO GIVING TEMP3.
SELECT TEMP3 WHERE (FIRST-NAME = "JOAN") AND
    (LAST-NAME = "READER") GIVING TEMP4.
PROJECT TITLE FROM TEMP4 GIVING RESULT.
```

Method II:

```
SELECT PERSON WHERE (FIRST-NAME = "JOAN") AND
    (LAST-NAME = "READER") GIVING TEMP1.
PROJECT PERSON-ID FROM TEMP1 GIVING TEMP2.
JOIN TEMP2 ON PERSON-ID WITH BORROWER ON
    PERSON-ID GIVING TEMP3.
JOIN TEMP3 ON (LIB-NAME, BOR-NO) WITH VOLUME
    ON (LIB-NAME, BOR-NO) GIVING TEMP4.
PROJECT CATALOG-NO FROM TEMP4 GIVING TEMP5.
JOIN TEMP5 ON CATALOG-NO WITH BOOKS ON
    CATALOG-NO GIVING TEMP6.
PROJECT TITLE FROM TEMP6 GIVING RESULT.
```

FIGURE 12–3 Two examples of the relational algebra.

Find all the borrowers who have a copy of some book by Charles Dickens.
It is considerably more difficult to state the similar one:

Find all the borrowers who have a copy of *each* of Charles Dickens's books.

or:

Find the names of borrowers who are reading *only* books by Charles Dickens.

The evidence suggests that when faced with relatively complex queries, people
•do better with a language that is, at least, partly procedural. The explanation for
this is different, though, from the usual argument in favor of procedural languages. That is, it is not that the users want to get involved in the details of how

records should be manipulated, but they do seem to prefer dealing with complex queries in a step-by-step manner. This, for example, is the sense in which the relational algebra is a procedural language.

4. *One-Dimensional Versus Two-Dimensional.*   Most languages are one-dimensional, whether used for database access, other types of human-computer communication, or communication between people. A one-dimensional language is one that is expressed as a linear sequence of symbols. Ordinary English, for example, is a one-dimensional language. It is true that the page you are looking at is two-dimensional, but that is strictly a mechanical convenience. In terms of the structure of the language, the first character on each line follows directly the last character on the preceding line.

Most computer languages are also one-dimensional, if for no other reason than that they are based on one-dimensional natural languages. Most computer input/output devices are oriented toward one-dimensional messages as well. However, in ordinary usage, one-dimensional text is often supplemented by two-dimensional pictures, and there have been a few attempts to devise database languages that use pictures rather than text to express queries. Two such languages will be illustrated later in this chapter. One places pictures of relations on the screen in front of the user who then enters values and a few key words to express retrieval conditions and connections to other relations. The other, a more truly graphic language, uses symbols to represent relations, values, operators, and so on. It represents queries in diagrams that look rather like flowcharts, except that, being nonprocedural, there is no implied order among the various steps.

In general, two-dimensional languages tend also to be specification languages. Thus, all of the comments concerning preferences for specification languages would apply to this class also. Two-dimensional specification languages may be somewhat more suitable for complex queries than the one-dimensional kind. They permit the various parts of a query to be specified in any order, and they provide a more easily comprehended representation of the query as it is being constructed. It also seems clear that two-dimensional languages are intended for interactive use and, therefore, are not appropriate for programming user roles.

Graphical languages are appealing for both experienced users and novices. They seem well adapted to a variety of ways of thinking about a query and illustrate exactly what is going to be done before it is actually executed. They obviously require somewhat more complex interactive interfaces than systems using only one-dimensional languages, and they also demand the ability to move freely around on the user's screen—a function that is not extremely difficult to implement but that is not widely available on large systems.

The increasing use of microcomputers as terminals to large systems could have major implications for the use of graphical languages. Most micros have adequate graphical capability, and the processing required to compose a query can be done largely within the micro. When the user is satisfied that the query shown on the screen is complete, a compact representation of it can be transferred to the host system for processing.

5. *Natural Versus Artificial.*   The term "natural language" refers to language as it is spoken or written among people. Artificial languages are the other kind! It should be pointed out that some natural languages (e.g., the one used to draft legal documents) are not very natural.

There is a body of opinion that considers natural language the ultimate mode of communication between people and computers. Much work has been devoted to studying how computers can be made to understand English, for example, and some success has been achieved. However, a general-purpose system capable of understanding natural language is still a long way ahead of us, and as will be seen, it may not be nearly as appropriate for database interaction as one might expect.

In terms of the Requirements Framework, natural language seems ideally suited to users with little or no training. This may be illusory, though, because as will be discussed later, conversing with a computer in natural language is likely to be quite different from conversing with another human being. Natural language also appears to be most suited to situations where there is low frequency of use and low task complexity—or, to put it another way, natural language is *not* appropriate for frequent or complex usage. The rationale for the first of these statements is found in the "wordiness" of natural language compared to most artificial languages. Thus, frequent users would probably prefer to use more concise, specialized languages. It also appears that ambiguity and the sloppiness of everyday usage would make it difficult to express complex queries accurately in natural language. There is certainly no lack of evidence for this in other areas, such as the law, where precision of expression is important.

The main advantage of natural language for human/computer dialog is, of course, the fact that it is the language we are already accustomed to use for human/human dialogue. What could be more convenient than communicating with computers in the same language that we use for communicating with other people? One response to this is that the language of a dialog cannot be considered independently from the mechanism.[6] Natural language serves reasonably well for *spoken* communication with other people, but speech is not yet a common way of communicating with computers. As long as the keyboard remains the usual input medium, its relatively low speed and high-error rate must be considered important factors in evaluating languages. Natural languages are much less concise than the artificial languages usually used for communicating with com-

---

[6] This is one situation where interface characteristics other than language must be explicitly taken into account.

puters. Thus, queries expressed in natural language will require much more typing and, hence, also be susceptible to more errors.

Much effort has been expended in attempting to develop speech recognition systems, and some success has been achieved. Systems that will recognize a small set of spoken commands are widely available at low cost. However, recognition of long strings of arbitrary continuous text is a problem of a completely different scale. Progress is being made, but commercial availability of this technology is probably still a long way down the road.

Thus, the first problem with natural language is that it either has to be typed by the user (a tedious and error-prone activity) or it requires elaborate facilities (not yet available) for speech recognition. Once this obstacle has been overcome, there is still the problem of understanding precisely what the user wants. Natural languages are inherently ambiguous, and the meaning of a statement is frequently highly dependent on the context in which it is made. (As an elementary illustration, contrast the statements: "Call me George" and "Call me a cab.") Conversations between people work as well as they do largely because the participants have an extensive common background that is automatically invoked to aid in the interpretation of each other's statements. Even humans sometimes have considerable difficulty interpreting statements, ostensibly in the same language, made by people from a different cultural background.

Of course, computers do not have *any* cultural background in this sense. Before they can be expected to understand conversation at the same level that people do, ways will have to be found to represent such contextual information in computer-accessible form. Again, this is an area in which much research is being done but in which practical capabilities are some distance away. It should be noted that, even among people of common background, there is room for much variation in the interpretation of natural language. It is one of the things that provides job security for lawyers and judges!

Thus, although natural language might naively seem to be the best of all possible interfaces, it is not without serious defects in the highly constrained world of human/computer interaction. The mechanical interface poses the first obstacle, and the inherent ambiguity and complexity of natural language constitute the second. People might have to learn to express themselves quite precisely when dealing with computers, much as they would do if they were drafting legislation. It is possible that people could be taught to do this, but it would not be very "natural," and it might very well be more difficult than learning an appropriate artificial language.

This discussion began by emphasizing the drawbacks associated with using natural language for human/computer dialogs because, at first glance, natural language seems like such a good idea. What about the drawbacks of artificial languages though? The main one is, of course, the simple fact that they are

artificial. A person would have to make the investment in time and other resources to learn such a language before being able to use the computer facilities.
However, it is obvious that an artificial language invented for the specific purpose
of communicating with a computer will probably be well suited to that task. It
will contain all of the features needed and no others. Thus, once learned it would
be easy to use.

Are artificial languages difficult to learn? Because of the explosion in personal computer sales, vast numbers of people seem to be learning conventional
programming languages. In many cases, these are more complicated and not
nearly as well designed as languages for database access. It might also be noted
that, long before personal computers, most people had occasion to learn one or
more artificial languages. The language in which recipes are described looks like
ordinary English, but anyone who remembers their first attempt to make something out of a cookbook will realize that it is not. Ordinary terms have very
specific meanings and much important information is not stated explicitly at all
because the reader is expected to know it. Music and knitting are other examples
of precomputer milieus in which people have found it advantageous to learn a
language quite different from the one used in everyday discourse.

In each of these cases, the specialized language is used because, once learned,
it offers a more concise, less ambiguous way of expressing things. The advantage
gained is deemed to greatly outweigh the cost of learning the language, which
does not turn out to be excessive. This is precisely the case for artificial database
languages. They need not be too difficult to learn and, once the learning has been
accomplished, they make subsequent use of the database much easier than it
would be if the special constructs of the language were not available.

This is not to say that there is no place for natural language database interfaces. A number of experiments have shown that novice users of many kinds of
computerized systems prefer interfaces that are toward the natural language end
of the spectrum. This is not hard to understand. However, what is more interesting is that, as these users acquire experience and use the system more frequently, they come to prefer a language that allows them to express themselves
more tersely. Thus, it might be possible to characterize the market where natural
language would be preferred as consisting of untrained, infrequent users doing
simple things. As one moves away from this pole, the advantages of artificial,
specialized languages outweigh the initial cost of learning them.

Any system offering users the ability to express queries in natural language
must take steps to make sure that it properly understands the user's intent. In the
system that will be illustrated at the conclusion of this chapter, this is done by
engaging the user in a dialog. The system asks multiple-choice questions to
resolve ambiguities, requests any required information that may hve been
omitted, and, finally, restates the question in its own terms for verification by the
user.

HUMAN INTERMEDIARIES

When the direct user interface is not satisfactory to the intended users, one possible solution is to interpose a human intermediary as a buffer between the real user and the system. The user explains his or her requirement to the intermediary who goes off and wrestles with the computer, returning only when the answer is in hand. The use of intermediaries is a widely established, time-honored practice in business. For example, much of what a secretary does may be viewed as intermediation between an executive and such alien and hostile devices as the typewriter and the telephone.

In the computing field, intermediation is even more firmly entrenched, although it is starting to lose ground in the face of advancing technology. Professional programmers are, invariably, intermediaries. They instruct the computer how to solve a problem that is not their own but that has been given to them by someone else—the real user.

In the database environment, an APU is generally an intermediary. Nonprogramming users can also fall into this category when they are working as staff assistants or technical aides to the persons who really need the information.

There are both good and bad aspects to the use of intermediation for database processing. The most obvious bad aspect is the extra level through which the query and the response are passed. This extra level costs something in resources and time; more important, it provides one more opportunity for something to be misunderstood or miscommunicated. In addition, the process of interacting with a database helps to develop intuition about it as a byproduct of processing specific queries. When an intermediary is used, this intuition remains with the intermediary rather than with the person who is actually using the information.

On the other hand, intermediation may be a most attractive and effective mode of database usage for infrequent users or those who, for whatever reason, are not trained to use the database system themselves. The intermediaries will generally be well trained because this function is a major part of their job. They also tend to gain a lot of experience with the use of the database. Thus, they may become, in a sense, "professional" database users who are quite familiar with its contents and the techniques for manipulating it, and they can, therefore, complete tasks much more efficiently than a less experienced user. They can also provide an interface to the "real" user that uses natural language, graphics, and any other human-to-human communication techniques that may be helpful. Thus, the ready availability of intermediaries could be a substitute for expending resources on improving the DBMS's ability to deal with inexperienced users.

It is also possible to imagine the use of computer programs as intermediaries rather than human beings. The development of programs capable of functioning in this manner is one of the primary goals of the branch of Artificial Intelligence that deals with so-called *expert systems*. An expert system is a program that "understands" some body of knowledge or technique well enough that it can act as a consultant in much the same way that human beings develop specialized knowledge and assist others who have need of it.

An example of the use of intermediation can be found in the usual arrangements for interrogating the large bibliographic databases that have come into existence in recent years. The most common way to retrieve information from these systems is to discuss one's need with a librarian who has been trained in the use of the system and knows how to express the query in a way that will facilitate efficient retrieval. This usage mode is deemed appropriate because the databases are so large, and a poorly expressed query could be extremely expensive to process. In addition, most users of these systems do not use them too often, so, it is not reasonable to expect them to become expert in efficient query formulation. Finally, this particular intermediation function is close to the traditional role of a librarian in the precomputer environment. There has recently been some discussion of the possibility of building expert systems for this task.

LANGUAGE EXAMPLES

The first part of this chapter presented two frameworks for describing the user/DBMS interface. The first includes a number of user-related issues; the second characterizes the interfaces themselves. Where possible, connections between user characteristics and interface properties have also been identified. The remainder of the chapter will present examples of some commercial and experimental database interfaces. Chapters 4, 5, and 6 included conventional procedural language examples as part of the data model descriptions. Therefore, the languages illustrated in this section will all be specification languages and have been chosen on the basis of their importance and/or interest.

A sample database and query will be needed for the examples. The complete library system used earlier in the book is more complicated than necessary for this purpose. Most of the examples will use the simple subset of it shown in Figure 12–4 and the sample query:

> Find the names of all borrowers who are reading at least one book written by Charles Dickens.

Most of the work on interesting user interfaces has been done in the context of relational systems, so, most of the examples are based on that model. However, it

```
BORROWERS  {Borrower-No, Name}
    BOOKS  {Catalog-No, Author, Title}
    LOANS  {Catalog-No, Borrower-No, Date-Due}
```

FIGURE 12–4 Database for language examples.

should be remembered that a system may present to users an image of the database that is quite different from what is actually stored, and it may not always be possible to infer the underlying data model of a system from the characteristics of its user language.

Rendezvous

The first example will be the only one *not* based on the library database. It illustrates a DBMS interface called RENDEZVOUS that was developed by E. F. Codd of IBM Research.[7] In terms of the interface properties framework, RENDEZVOUS employs a one-dimensional natural language, is specification oriented, and is self contained. It is initially user-directed, but the system takes control when it needs to clarify user statements. There is no need to illustrate or discuss the RENDEZVOUS language because it is English. However, the most interesting aspect of this system is the approach taken to resolving ambiguities. This is illustrated in the example shown in Figure 12–5, which is based on a simple Suppliers-Parts database. A couple of explanatory comments are in order. First, the description of each attribute appearing in a RENDEZVOUS relation includes a specification of the domain (or abstract data type in our terminology) of which it is an instance. This information is used by the system to determine whether two attributes are instances of the same kind of thing. Second, as discussed earlier, any natural language system needs knowledge about the application environment to interpret many queries. An example of this occurs in Figure 12–5 at the point where the system asks for clarification of the term "Houston parts." It obviously realizes that Houston is the name of a place. (Compare this with an alternative query asking for a listing of red parts.) In RENDEZVOUS, this is handled in a quite simple way by including in the database description a listing of all the possible entries for domains that can take only a small number of values. A major area of research in artificial intelligence is concerned with generalized methods of representing knowledge in machine-processable form.

The only other comment to be made concerning the RENDEZVOUS example is the length of the clarification dialog following the user's original query. An infrequent user might find this acceptable rather than investing the time and effort to learn a more concise language, but it seems clear that anyone making frequent use of this database would prefer a less verbose approach. On the other hand, continued exposure to RENDEZVOUS's clarification dialogs might help users learn to be less ambiguous in the initial statement of a query.

---

[7] E. F. Codd, R. S. Arnold, J.-M. Cadiou, C. L. Chang, & N. Roussopoulos, "RENDEZVOUS Version 1: An Experimental English-Language Query Formulation System for Casual Users of Relational Data Bases," IBM Research Report RJ2144, January 1978.

SYSTEM: Please proceed

USER: Give me a list of the part numbers, quantities, and suppliers of Houston parts

SYSTEM: You are requesting (among other things) a listing of quantities of parts. Do you want:
          1. quantities on hand
          2. quantities on order
          3. quantities shipped?

USER: I want quantities on order

SYSTEM: Fine! Now, with regard to "Houston parts," do you mean:
          1. parts supplied by Houston suppliers
          2. parts supplied to Houston projects
          3. parts associated with Houston in some other way?

USER: I mean item 2

(Note: nothing prevents the user from responding in a manner that is incomprehensible to the system—for example, "le deuxième"—but if he or she does, the system tightens up the dialog by: "Please reply by means of one of the numerals 1 or 2 or 3.")

SYSTEM: Good! I need one more piece of information. In the listing of part numbers, quantity on order, and suppliers, how do you want suppliers to be identified:
          1. by number
          2. by name
          3. some other way?

USER: By name and by city

SYSTEM: O.K. This is what I understand your query to be: "Find all combinations of part number, quantity on order, supplier name, and supplier city *such that* the supplier supplied the part to a project located in Houston." Is this what you intended?

USER: Yes

SYSTEM: Do you want the listing to be ordered in any special way?

USER: Yes, by part number and then by supplier number

FIGURE 12-5 RENDEZVOUS example.

Structured Query Language (SQL)

Structured Query Language (SQL) is the current version of a language developed at IBM Research during the early 1970s and originally called SEQUEL (Structured English Query Language).[8] In terms of the properties framework, it is artificial, user-directed, specification-oriented, and one-dimensional. It can be *either* embedded or self-contained. In fact, one of SQL's more interesting characteristics is that it is specifically intended for both types of use.

The basic retrieval facility in SQL is the SELECT statement, which actually consists of three clauses in the general form:

```
SELECT . . .

FROM . . .

WHERE . . .
```

The SELECT clause specifies columns to be extracted from the relation specified in the FROM clause. The WHERE clause specifies the condition that must be met for tuples to be included in the result. In terms of the relational algebra described in Chapter 6, the SELECT statement is equivalent to a selection operation followed by a projection, although the selection criteria may be substantially more complex than is the case in the relational algebra. A simple SELECT statement can be illustrated by the query, "What are the titles of all books in the library by Charles Dickens?" This would be expressed in SQL as:

```
SELECT TITLE

FROM BOOKS

WHERE AUTHOR = 'Charles Dickens'
```

(It is not necessary to write a SELECT statement on three separate lines; that structure is used here to emphasize the three-part structure of the statement.)

There are numerous additional capabilities in SQL. However, the purpose of this section is not to present a comprehensive specification of the language, but merely to give a general feeling for its approach. The query that is being used for the examples in this section requires two additional SQL features. First, SELECT statements can be nested. The effect of this is that the result of one operation can be used in the WHERE clause of another. A second feature, often used in conjunction with nesting, is the IN keyword. This specifies set membership and can be

[8]D. D. Chamberlin, & R. F. Boyce, "SEQUEL: A Structured English Query Language," Proceedings of the ACM SIGMOD Workshop on Data Description, Access and Control, 1974, Association for Computing Machinery.

used to include tuples based on having an attribute value that is a member of some set of values. This capability is used twice in the sample query:

```
SELECT NAME
FROM BORROWER
WHERE BORROWER-NO IN
    SELECT BORROWER-NO
    FROM LOANS
    WHERE CATALOG-NO IN
        SELECT CATALOG-NO
        FROM BOOKS
        WHERE AUTHOR = 'Charles Dickens'
```

As this example shows, nesting of one SELECT inside another is SQL's mechanism for specifying the join of two relations. As is the case with other good specification languages, the SQL capabilities needed for most routine queries are easy to learn and remember.

SQL is the primary language for relational database systems developed by IBM. Because of that company's dominant position in the computer industry, its choice of a particular language often creates a de facto standard. Other relational DBMS's, such as ORACLE, also use SQL, as do some specialized database processors (see Chapter 15).

The version of SQL illustrated here is the self-contained one, intended for nonprogramming usage. There is also a version designed for embedded use in conventional programming languages. The main difference between the two versions arises from the fact that a SQL SELECT statement can produce a result consisting of a number of tuples, whereas conventional programming languages can only deal with one tuple at a time. This is handled by associating a *cursor* with a SELECT result that is used to mark an individual tuple. A loop in the applications program can be used to step through the SELECT result, retrieving and processing one tuple at a time.

Query by Example (QBE)

This is another language that has come out of IBM Research.[9] Originally intended strictly as an internal, experimental system, it was eventually released as a prod-

[9] See, for example, M. M. Zloof "Query-by-Example: A Data Base Language," *IBM Systems Journal*, Vol. 16, No. 4 (1977), pgs 324–343.

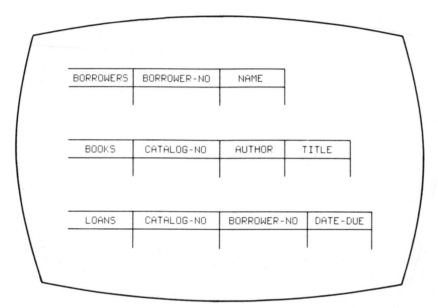

FIGURE 12–6 Query-by-example (QBE) 1.

uct in response to demand from outsiders who were intrigued by its unusual approach to database interaction. Query-by-Example (QBE) is an artificial, self-contained, user-directed specification language. Its uniqueness is associated with the fact that it takes a two-dimensional approach to query specification.

A user initiates a QBE query by instructing the system to display skeletons of relations that are to be manipulated. Commands and data values are then entered at appropriate places on these skeletons to specify the desired manipulations. This is best illustrated by following through the sample query. In Figure 12–6, the user has begun by asking QBE to display the BOOKS, BORROWERS, and LOANS relations. This is accomplished through a command that places a blank skeleton on the screen and then typing the desired relation name in the appropriate field. QBE responds by displaying the relation's column names, adjusting the size of the skeleton to conform. If the user did not know what relations were in the system, he or she could call up a blank skeleton and then, using the same commands that would be used to display any relation, look at one that is a directory of all available relations.

Because the user wants borrower names to be printed as the final result, a *P.* is entered in that column of the BORROWER relation (Figure 12–7). Similarly, the interest in only books by a particular author is signalled by entering "C. Dickens" in the Author column of the BOOKS relation.

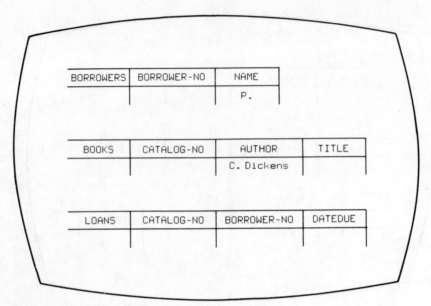

FIGURE 12–7 Query-by-example (QBE) 2.

What remains to be specified is that borrower names are to be printed only for those who currently have on loan a book by this author. It is clear that the connection between books and borrowers is made through the LOANS relation. In QBE, this is specified by entering on the relation skeletons "examples" of the desired connection. Examples consist of any text placed on the relation skeletons that is <u>underscored</u>. In Figure 12–8, the user has entered the Catalog-No, 123456, and the Borrower-No, 10. The fact that these are underscored tells the system that they are examples. It does not matter if these values actually exist in the database or not. However, the fact that the same example, in this case "123456", appears in the Catalog-No columns of both the BOOKS and LOANS relations tells QBE that only tuples from those relations with matching values of that attribute are of interest. This should be recognized as a JOIN operation. Similarly, the appearance of "10" in both LOANS and BORROWERS specifies another JOIN.

This example is now complete. It tells QBE, first, to find all the BOOKS tuples that have "Charles Dickens" in the Author field. (Because this value appears without underscoring, it is interpreted as an actual data value rather than as an example.) Then, QBE is instructed to find all of the LOANS tuples whose Catalog-No field corresponds to that in the BOOKS tuples already selected. Then,

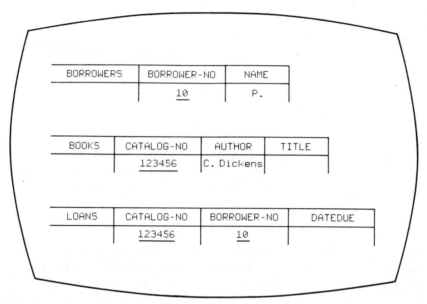

FIGURE 12–8 Query-by-example (QBE) 3.

the BORROWERS tuples whose Borrower-No matches that in any of the selected LOANS tuples are located, and finally the Name attribute of those tuples gets printed.

QBE seems to be most appealing to novice users because of its pictorial quality, the fact that it contains few rules that must be learned, and the ability to specify the various components of a query in any order. For example, in the preceding illustration, the user began by specifying what to print, then gave the main retrieval criterion, and, finally, the link between the two. The query shown is actually a relatively complicated one involving as it did interaction among three relations. Many of the queries that would arise in routine use are even simpler, and QBE will handle these with great ease. There are, however, more complicated ones that require use of additional capabilities and rules. Some research suggests that QBE can be divided into an "easy" part and a "hard" part. The easy part is quite easy to learn and use and is sufficient for a large fraction of real needs.

QBE is clearly a screen-oriented interface. When it was first developed, most interactive terminals were of the hardcopy variety. Terminals with screens were substantially more expensive. Thus, despite its inherent attractiveness, it did not achieve immediate wide usage. However, although QBE is a two-dimensional

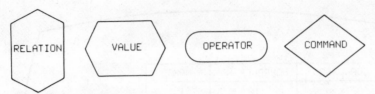

FIGURE 12–9 CUPID example 1.

language, it is not really pictorial. Full graphics capability is not required; merely the ability to draw vertical and horizontal lines and place text at arbitrary points on the screen. Subsequent advances in computer technology have made it possible to produce extremely low-cost terminals with these capabilities.

Cupid

The CUPID language falls into exactly the same framework categories as QBE, but it deserves attention because in addition to being two-dimensional, it actually does make use of the pictorial capabilities of the terminal. CUPID was developed for the INGRES relational DBMS at the University of California at

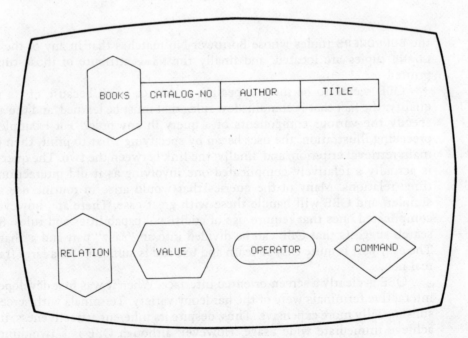

FIGURE 12–10 CUPID example 2.

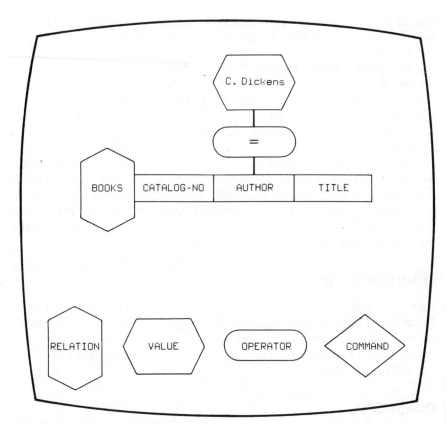

FIGURE 12–11 CUPID example 3.

Berkeley.[10] CUPID employs distinctive symbols for the basic components of a query, such as relation, value, operator, and command. These symbols might appear as a menu at the bottom of the user's screen (Figure 12–9). A query is constructed by selecting items from this menu, moving them to appropriate places on the screen to form the skeleton of a query, then inserting specific values.

The sample query could be started by selecting the RELATION symbol from the menu and placing it near the top of the screen. Typing BOOKS inside it causes it to be expanded with the full set of attribute names as shown in Figure 12–10. The fact that only books written by Charles Dickens are of interest might be the next thing to be specified. This is done by selecting the VALUE and OPERATOR symbols from the menu, placing them above the AUTHOR attribute and entering appropriate values (Figure 12–11). The remainder of the inquiry is built up in a

[10]N. McDonald & M. R. Stonebraker, "CUPID—The Friendly Query Language," Proceedings of the ACM Pacific Conference, San Francisco, April 1975, Association for Computing Machinery.

similar manner until the complete picture shown in Figure 12–12 has been produced. Note that as with QBE, the user is free to specify the parts of a query in any order.

CUPID represents a query in a form that looks very much like a flowchart, except, of course, that there is no implied order for the various steps. It obviously requires a terminal with fairly general graphical capability. Until quite recently, such terminals would have been quite expensive. However, most contemporary microcomputers have adequate graphical capability and resolution for this type of usage. Micros are often used as intelligent terminals for accessing large host systems. In such a configuration, all of the query formulation could be done within the micro as long as it had access to some of the basic data dictionary information. Completed queries could be passed to the host processor in a compact representation, such as that offered by SQL. The need for data dictionary information to be available in the micro to assist in query formulation raises some of the problems discussed in Chapter 14 on distributed systems.

TERMS TO UNDERSTAND

cognitive style	user-directed interfacers
parametric nonprogramming user (PNU)	specification language
generalized nonprogramming user (GNU)	natural language
applications programming user	intermediary
embedded language	

REVIEW QUESTIONS

1. Discuss the advantages and disadvantages of having languages for database manipulation that are Englishlike. What role do you think English will play in future database manipulation languages? Why?

2. Is there a single "ideal" Database Management System (DBMS) interface? If you think there is (or could be) describe it. If you believe that the idea is inherently unworkable, explain why.

3. Using the library database, show how you would determine the titles of books writted by C. Dickens that are overdue (a) Query-by-Example (QBE) and (b) CUPID.

4. What are the implications of having systems that allow end-users without technical training to access an organization's database directly?

5. In the late 1960s, a major debate took place between people who felt that Database Management Systems (DBMS's) should be self-contained—that is, have built-in query languages—and those who felt they should be embedded

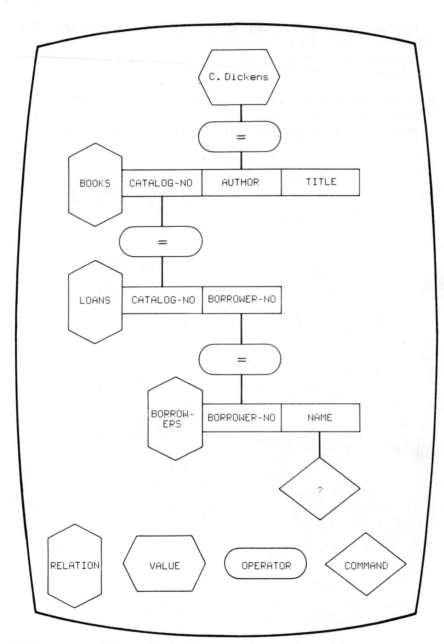

FIGURE 12–12 CUPID example 4.

in some conventional programming language. How do the DBMS requirements of a query language differ from those of an applications programmer? Is it possible to satisfy both sets of needs within the same system? Explain your answer.

6. It has usually been assumed that specification languages are easier for untrained users to master than procedural languages. Why? Is there any class of problem for which the procedural language is likely to be easier?

DATABASE CONTROL

Database control encompasses a number of areas concerned with ensuring that the content of a database is correct and that it is used only for authorized purposes. Most of the problems to be discussed in this chapter are not unique to a database environment, but the solutions tend to be quite different from those appropriate to traditional, file-oriented systems. In addition, there are some special problems that arise directly from the multi-usage nature of a database.

The first set of issues to be addressed are those dealing with maintaining the correctness of database contents. Controlling access to the database is discussed after that; then the problem of protecting individual privacy in a database environment is covered.

INTEGRITY

The term "integrity" is used to refer to the problem of ensuring the correctness of database contents. Values in a database can become invalid in several ways. Probably the most common cause is a data entry or update transaction in which some values are specified incorrectly. This can be the result of a program error; a mechanical user error, such as mistyping; or the user's misunderstanding of what is supposed to be entered. This aspect of the integrity problem is sometimes referred to as semantic integrity.

Data can also become invalid as the result of two or more data modification transactions that individually operate correctly but whose interaction produces invalid results. A ticket reservation system where two agents sell the same seat to different customers is a good illustration of this type of error. The term "concurrency control" is used to describe this problem and the techniques for dealing with it.

A third cause of integrity violations is hardware or software malfunctions. It is not always possible to detect malfunctions in time to prevent them from damaging the database. Thus, the emphasis has to be placed on undoing the damage they cause and returning the database to a valid state. The term "backup and recovery" is used to describe this process.

Each of these integrity problems will be discussed in turn. Before beginning, however, it is necessary formally to introduce the concept of a *transaction*. This term is quite familiar in the context of ordinary data processing and has a meaning that might be roughly stated as "unit of work". Paying a credit card bill and reserving a seat on an airplane are examples of transactions. A one-to-one correspondence does not usually exist between transactions and database operations because what appears to be a single transaction to the user of a system may require making a number of changes to the underlying database. From the point of view of the Database Management System (DBMS), a transaction can be defined as a sequence of operation that takes the database from one consistent valid state to another.

Consider the making of a loan payment by transferring funds from the individual's checking account. There are at least two database changes required: the debiting of the checking account for the amount of the payment and the crediting of a corresponding amount to the loan balance. If, for any reason, the first of these operations were to take place but not the second, the database would be left in an invalid state. The customer's money would be missing from his checking account, but the previous balance of the loan would still appear to be outstanding. In fact, some money would have disappeared from the system entirely!

Clearly, this sort of thing must not be allowed to happen. An elementary requirement for maintaining the integrity of a database is that either all of the operations associated with a transaction must complete successfully or those changes that have been made must be undone. Inplementing the transaction concept requires two general capabilities. First, the system must know where a transaction begins and ends. This is not, in general, something that it can figure out for itself. Individual database operations are not usually complete transactions. It might seem, as in the bank transfer example, that a matching pair of operations would qualify, but even this can not be guaranteed. Consider a request to deduct $100 from a customer's savings account, use $25 to pay a bill, and credit the remainder to his checking account. Three database operations, at least, are required.

The only reliable way to delimit a transaction is to have it done by the user (or, of course, the programmer, if it is a system where processing routines are defined in advance and the user merely supplies parameters). Only the user or programmer can know what set of database operations constitute a consistent whole. Unfortunately, the concept of a transaction is not supported in most commercial database systems. It is left to the application program or terminal user to ensure that database changes are reversed unless all of the related ones can be completed—a most unreliable approach. In those systems that do support the transaction concept, the usual technique is to have two additional statements in the data manipulation language: `Begin Transaction` and `End Transaction.` These are used to bracket all of the processing steps in either a program or an interactive terminal session that constitute a transaction. If the DBMS finds that it is unable to complete all of the processing between those limits, it is supposed to undo any changes that have been made.

This leads to the second requirement for implementing the transaction concept—the ability to undo database operations when necessary. Because most present-day computers operate serially, it is inevitable that operations that logically should occur simultaneously (such as the debit and credit in a bank transfer) will actually take place sequentially. To support the concept of a transaction, the

DBMS must be able to "remember" changes it has made until it knows for sure that the entire transaction will complete successfully. Changes made prior to that point are sometimes referred to as *uncommitted*. Changes are committed when the End Transaction statement is encountered.

In a single-user environment, all that is needed to implement the transaction concept is to retain the previous contents of changed fields until the change is committed. In a multi-user environment, things can be much more complicated. What happens if User A changes something in the database, User B then reads the changed value, and after that User A's transaction fails to complete and his change is undone? In essence, User B will have read a value that *never actually existed!* This problem associated with simultaneous usage is mentioned here only to tantalize. It will be discussed in detail in following section.

The importance of the transaction concept is that it specifies a unit of operations over which integrity is to be preserved. It is entirely possible that some database integrity conditions may be violated while a transaction is in progress—but when the transaction has completed, all integrity rules should hold.

Integrity rules may take a number of forms. One useful distinction separates those that relate to only a single data-item from those that describe a relationship that must hold between two or more data-items. One type of single-item integrity condition specifies the permitted structure for data values. This can be as simple as a rule stating that values for the data-item, Age, may contain a maximum of three characters that must all be numeric. A more complex structural constraint would specify that Canadian postal codes must be of the form: letter digit letter space digit letter digit. Social Security Numbers, telephone numbers, library catalog numbers, and even persons' names all have structure that can be expressed in an integrity constraint and used to ensure that obviously invalid data is excluded.

Of course, just having the right structure does not guarantee that a piece of data is actually correct. Another class of single-item integrity constraints deals with values. Age can be constrained to be greater than 0 and less than 150, for example. This would be an example of a range constraint, where minimum and/or maximum acceptable values are specified. Value constraints can also take the form of a list of specific legal values. Sex, for example, must be either "M" or "F." "Borrower numbers must be unique" would be another type of integrity constraint based on data values. Value constraints do not ensure that all data are entered correctly. However, they do detect entirely unreasonable values.

Some integrity rules refer to relationships that must exist between data-items. There are several classes of these rules. A constraint may relate two items within a single record: If rank is clerk, salary must be less than $25,000. There can also be constraints that apply to sets of records. For example, all of the people in a list of managers must also be in the list of employees.

It is possible to distinguish between constraints that must hold at all times (of which all the preceding illustrations are examples) and those that describe allowable *changes* in data contents. "New salary must be greater than old salary" is an example of a constraint on changes to the database. Note that to test this type of constraint, the DBMS must retain the original value until the transaction is complete.

Some constraints must be associated with particular operations. We might specify, for example, that no borrower record may be deleted from the library database if the person still has books on loan. Constraints can also be characterized as unconditional or conditional. "Salary must be less than $25,000 if rank is clerk" is a constraint on salary that is conditional on the value of rank. "Salary must be less than $80,000" is an unconditional constraint on salary.

Integrity constraints are specified as part of a database definition. In fact, the type and size specification given for each data item is a form of integrity constraint because values that violate these rules will not "fit" in the database. The availability of other integrity protecting mechanisms and the details of how to employ them depend on the database model and on the individual implementation. A few examples of data model dependent integrity constraints follow.

In the DBTG network model, the set insertion classes are a form of integrity constraint. They can be used, for example, to ensure that no VOLUME record in our library database is left unattached to some BOOK record. It is also possible to specify that all of the members of a set are to be deleted when the owner is deleted. However, a completely general capability to specify that other actions should occur whenever a certain one takes place is not provided.

The DBTG model also provides a CHECK clause as part of the data definition language. This can be applied at the data-item level:

(in a Volume record) Check is Copy-No > 0

at the record level (comparing two data-items within a Volume record):[1]

    Check is Date-Borrowed < Date-Due

and at the set level (comparing a data-item in the owner record to one in the member record):[2]

    Check is Borrower-No in Volume = Card-No in Borrower.

[1] For this test to make sense, it would have to be imagined that VOLUME records contain the date that a book is borrowed as well as the date on which it is due.

[2] This example assumes that VOLUME records contain a data-item, Borrower-No, which is not present in the version of this database developed in Chapter 5. In fact, this data-item would be redundant because the set relationship carries this information. However, its presence would allow this integrity check to be performed.

The CHECK clause can refer only to the particular data-item being checked in the first case, to any data-items within the record in the second case, and to any data-items within the owner or member records in the third.

Some of the most interesting work on integrity specification has taken place within the context of the relational database model. The Structured Query Language (SQL), which is supported by several relational DBMS's, employs integrity assertions and triggers that can be included in the database definition. An integrity assertion is merely a statement that is required to be true, for example:

```
ASSERT BR1 ON BRANCH : BRANCH.LIB-NAME IN (SELECT LIB-NAME FROM
LIBRARY)
```

This states that the Lib-name field in BRANCH tuples must have a value that corresponds to the value of the Lib-Name field in some LIBRARY tuple. This assertion does not specify when it is to be checked. It is left to the DBMS to decide. A logical interpretation would be that it should be checked whenever the Lib-Name field in either a LIBRARY or BRANCH tuple is changed, when a BRANCH tuple is added, and when a LIBRARY tuple is deleted. There is also nothing in the assertion to tell the DBMS what to do if the assertion is violated. Presumably, the operation will be aborted and the user notified via a message or status variable.

Another form of integrity assertion specifies that it is only to be checked at certain moments:

```
ASSERT V2 ON DELETION OF VOLUME : DATEDUE = NULL
```

This assertion states that a VOLUME tuple can only be deleted if the corresponding volume is not out on loan. Obviously, the constraint DATEDUE = NULL would not be expected to hold generally. This constraint will only be applied when a deletion is requested.

SQL also implements the concept of triggers. A trigger can be used to specify that some (user-supplied) procedure is to be executed whenever a certain operation is performed on a specified relation. This procedure can do anything the user wishes, including, for example, updating other relations to maintain consistency. SQL also contains data definition statements that can be used to prevent null values from being entered for specified fields and to ensure that the values of some field or combination of fields will be unique.

The relational DBMS, INGRES, specifies integrity constraints in a manner that is roughly similar to SQL. The interesting thing about INGRES is the way that these constraints are applied. A technique called *query modification* is used to ensure that no query ever gets executed that could possibly violate any of the integrity constraints! To illustrate, one constraint on the library database is obviously that copy numbers must be greater than 0. This would be expressed in INGRES as follows:

```
RANGE OF VOL IS VOLUME
DEFINE INTEGRITY ON VOL IS VOL.COPY-NO > 0
```

These statements cause INGRES to add a tuple to a system-maintained relation that holds all integrity constraints. Whenever an update operation is attempted, such as:

```
RANGE OF VOL IS VOLUME
REPLACE VOL (COPY-NO = COPY-NO - 5)
WHERE VOL.CALL-NO = '12345'
```

INGRES will search the integrity relation and append any constraints that apply to the referenced relations before beginning to process the query. In this case, the query would be turned into:

```
RANGE OF VOL IS VOLUME
REPLACE VOL (COPY-NO = COPY-NO - 5)
WHERE VOL.CALL-NO = '12345'
AND COPY-NO - 5 > 0
```

Processing from this point will proceed exactly as if the user had entered the query in this latter form. Obviously, any VOLUME tuple whose initial COPY-No value is less than 6 will fail the selection criteria and will therefore not be updated. There will be no error messages because, in fact, no error has occurred! The update will simply be restricted to those tuples for which it can be performed without violating the integrity constraints. This seems to be a particularly elegant way of dealing with integrity and is also economical in terms of the DBMS features required to support it.

CONCURRENCY

The preceding section has discussed techniques for making sure that individual transactions do not introduce invalid data into a database. If the DBMS requires that each transaction be completed before another can begin, then database integrity is assured. However, such a restriction would drastically reduce the system's throughput. It is usually assumed that many users will have access to a database at the same time. Unless steps are taken to control multiple simultaneous access, it is entirely possible that several transactions, each one of which is individually correct, will result in leaving the database in an incorrect state. A general discussion of preserving database integrity while permitting multiple concurrent use is beyond the scope of this book. However, the remainder of this section presents a simplified overview of the problem and of some techniques that can be used to solve it.

There are two things that can be noted at the very beginning. First, only transactions that alter the database are cause for concern. Multiple simultaneous retrievals cannot cause any possible difficulty. On the other hand, a transaction that only reads the database can obtain invalid results if another transaction is updating the database at the same time. Throughout this discussion, updating will include the insertion and deletion of records as well as changing values in existing ones.

The second general observation is that an obvious solution to the concurrency problem is to never allow more than one transaction to proceed at a time. This is known as a *serial* solution and is usually ruled out for reasons of performance. However, it is possible to prove that simultaneous accesses *that obey certain rules* are logically equivalent to serial solutions and are, therefore, acceptable. Such solutions are called serializable, even though they actually allow more than one transaction to be in execution at the same time. It is presumably possible that some nonserializable strategies will also preserve database validity. However, serializability is obviously a sufficient condition, and it is relatively easy to determine whether a particular strategy is serializable. Thus, serializability has become the usual criterion for evaluating concurrency mechanisms.

The most serious problem that can arise from uncontrolled simultaneous access to a database is the so-called *lost update*. This is illustrated by the sequence of events in Figure 13–1. Suppose that a database contains inventory data and is used in an order processing application. User A receives an order for 10 widgets at time T1. He queries the database to determine if the quantity on hand is sufficient to fill the order; if it is, he reduces the quantity value by 10. User B receives a similar order for 15 units at T2. Each user will read the same inventory figure, subtract the quantity ordered, and then store the new value in the database. If events happen in the order shown in Figure 13–1, User A's update will have been lost, resulting in an incorrect inventory figure. A similar difficulty will arise if User A's update is completed before User B reads the inventory value, but A's transaction is aborted for some reason as in Figure 13–2. Then the DBMS will restore the database to the state it was in before User A began, and all trace of B's update will have disappeared.

A second type of concurrency problem, less serious than the lost update, is the so-called *dirty read* or *phantom read*. This occurs when a user reads information that was not committed and that, because of a subsequent reversal of the transaction that stored the information, turns out never to have really been there at all! An example of a phantom read is shown in Figure 13–3. User A records an

TIME	ACTION	DATABASE QUANTITY ON HAND
		18
T1	User *A* reads quantity 18 from database.	
T2	User *B* reads quantity 18 from database.	
T3	User *A* accepts order for 10 widgets, subtracts this from retrieved quantity and updates database.	8
T4	User *B* accepts order for 15 widgets, subtracts this from retrieved quantity and updates database.	3

FIGURE 13–1 Lost update problem.

update to some inventory record. *B* reads that value and determines that there is not enough on hand to fill his order. If *A*'s transaction is subsequently undone, *B*'s decision will have been incorrect, and there will no longer be anything in the database that explains why it was made.

The third, and least serious, type of concurrency problem is the *inconsistent read*. This can occur in several ways. One is illustrated by the airline reservation case where a customer calls up to inquire about a proposed trip. The agent queries the database and retrieves information about all of the suitable flights on which space is currently available. The customer thinks it over for a few moments and makes a choice. When the agent attempts to reserve a seat on the requested flight, he finds that space is no longer available.

As another example of an inconsistent read, consider the cases where User *A* is summing the balances in a list of 10 accounts. After *A* has read the balance in account 4, User *B* transfers some money from this account to account 9. Meanwhile, *A* continues to retrieve balances and add them up. When *A* gets to account 9, the updated balance will be read. The net effect is that the amount transferred will have been counted twice.

TIME	ACTION	DATABASE QUANTITY ON HAND
		180
T1	A reads quantity 180 from database.	
T2	A accepts order for 10 widgets, subtracts this from retrieved quantity and updates database.	170
T3	B reads quantity 170 from database.	
T4	B accepts order for 15 widgets, subtracts this from retrieved quantity and updates database.	155
T5	A's customer cancels order. A returns database quantity to its original value.	180

FIGURE 13–2 Another lost update problem.

Serializability Through Locking

As previously mentioned, these problems can all be avoided by making sure that the database operations requested by the various transactions are carried out in an order that is equivalent to some serial execution of the transactions. The usual approach to ensuring this is to have transactions lock portions of the database as they need them to prevent other transactions from proceeding.

An alternative to locking is to timestamp each update so that other transactions can see if the data they are working with is the most current. This chapter will concentrate on locking approaches because that is the technique most often implemented in current DBMS's. There is some indication that timestamping may be more appropriate in distributed database systems and will be discussed in the next chapter.

The big question surrounding all locking mechanisms is what to lock and when. Obviously, the larger the unit that is locked and the longer the lock is held,

TIME	ACTION	DATABASE QUANTITY ON HAND
		18
T1	A processes an order for 10 widgets and updates database.	8
T2	B receives an order for 15 widgets, retrieves quantity, 8, from database and rejects order.	
T3	A's transaction is aborted and database is restored to original value.	18

FIGURE 13-3 Phantom read example.

the more likely it becomes that other transactions will be forced to wait. This degrades the overall throughput of the system. On the other hand, locking small units for shorter periods of time increases the amount of processing overhead required for lock management. It also increases the prospect of two or more transactions getting into a deadlock situation in which each has locked something but cannot proceed until it gets access to something else that is locked by one of the other transactions.

As will be seen, the objective of allowing as much concurrent activity as possible while avoiding integrity violations is facilitated by having two kinds of locks. An exclusive lock on some data object can be granted to only one user at a time. While an exclusive lock is in effect, no other user is permitted to do anything to the locked data. The lost update problem can be completely eliminated by requiring a user to obtain an exclusive lock on the data to be altered before changing it.

Consider Figure 13-4, which reexamines the example of Figure 13-1 but with exclusive locking. User A knows that he may wish to change the data, so, an exclusive lock is requested at the beginning of the transaction. Then, when B attempts to retrieve the same data, he is locked out until A is finished. (Exactly when locks are released will be discussed a bit later.) When B is finally allowed to proceed, the data retrieved will reflect A's updates, so, no problem arises.

TIME	ACTION	DATABASE QUANTITY ON HAND
		18
T1	User A LOCKS database and reads quantity, 18.	
T2	User B attempts to read locked value and is suspended.	
T3	User A updates and UNLOCKS database.	8
	User B is allowed to proceed.	

FIGURE 13–4 Elimination of lost updates.

Shared Locks

When a transaction intends to alter a database, it is essential that other transactions be prevented from even retrieving the affected data until the updates are committed. The ability to ensure this is what is provided by an exclusive lock. However, as the preceding example made clear, this has a severe impact on the amount of concurrent usage that can take place. A higher degree of concurrency without any increase in risk can be achieved by utilizing a second, less restrictive type of lock. For example, a transaction containing only retrieval operations may want to prevent other transactions from concurrently modifying the data to avoid phantom or inconsistent reads. However, it can have no objection to any amount of simultaneous retrieval. This objective is accomplished using *shared locks*. A shared lock on a data object can be granted to any number of users at the same time. Its effect is to prevent the object from being exclusively locked by anyone.

If both types of locks are supported, a strategy is available that minimizes the number and duration of exclusive locks. This involves always using shared locks for retrievals and upgrading to an exclusive lock if and when it becomes necessary to modify the retrieved data object. Note that this makes it unnecessary to know whether or not an object will be modified at the time it is first retrieved. What is involved in upgrading a lock? It is really no different than any other request for an exclusive lock. Because a shared lock on the object is already held, it is impossible for anyone else to have an exclusive lock on it. If, in addition, there are no other shared locks, the lock is simply upgraded to exclusive. If there are other shared locks on the same object, the request must wait until all of them are released. If one of these other users also attempts an upgrade while the first transaction is already waiting, a deadlock occurs. "Deadlock" is the term used to describe the situation that arises when, for example, transaction A is waiting for transaction B to do something, and transaction B is simultaneously waiting for some action by transaction A.[3] Neither one will ever be able to proceed unless the deadlock is detected and resolved. Techniques for accomplishing this are discussed later in this chapter.

Proper use of exclusive and shared locks is sufficient to prevent all of the concurrency-related integrity violations discussed so far. A transaction that intends to modify the database can ensure that its update will not be lost by requesting an exclusive lock on the affected data object and waiting until the lock has been granted before proceeding. A transaction that only needs to read data and wants to be protected against phantom or inconsistent reads need only obtain a shared lock before commencing. This will not interfere with anyone else who also wants only to read the data. However, any request for an exclusive lock (for updating purposes) will be refused while the shared lock is held.

The concurrency issue as discussed so far does not present any insuperable problems. However, there are cases that have not yet been considered. For example, Figure 13–5 shows another way in which a phantom read can take place. User A wishes to transfer $25 from account 10 to account 20. He begins by retrieving the record for account 10 with an exclusive lock. The $25 is subtracted and this account record is stored back into the database. Because A is now finished with account 10, the lock on this account is released. User A now goes on to retrieve the record for account 20 with the intention of adding $25 to its balance. In the meantime, User B wants to retrieve the balance in account 10; because there is currently no lock on that record, the retrieval is allowed. Now, suppose that for some reason, A's attempt to update account 20 fails. Perhaps an access control restriction is violated. Perhaps User A got the wrong account number and there is not any account 20. Perhaps there is some failure in the application program. In any of these cases, User A's transaction must be aborted, and to preserve the integrity of the database, the $25 must be returned to account 10. User B has still been the victim of a phantom read despite the use of locks.

The problem in this example is that User A released the lock on account 10 *too soon*. Although A had no further intention of altering this record, A could not be certain that the change already made was going to stick, that is, the change to account 10 could not be committed until it had been determined that the change to account 20 could be committed also. In this case, the update to account 10 does not constitute a complete transaction. Because the transaction involves a transfer of funds between two accounts, both of them must be successfully up-

---

[3] In this particular case, both transactions hold shared locks on some data object and neither can proceed until the other one releases its lock.

TIME	ACTION	DATABASE BALANCE ACCOUNT 10
		$100
T1	A LOCKS account 10, reads balance of $100.	
T2	A subtracts $25 from balance, then updates and UN-LOCKS account 10.	$ 75
	A then LOCKS and reads account 20.	
T3	B LOCKS account 10, reads balance of $75, then UN-LOCKS account 10.	
T4	A is unable to complete update of account 20, so update of account 10 balance is undone.	$100

FIGURE 13–5 Another phantom read.

dated or both must be returned to their original states. One way to avoid this type of difficulty is simply to retain all locks until the end of the complete transaction, at which time all of them can be released.

This is a perfectly feasible approach and has the advantage that the release of locks need not be explicitly dealt with by the user or applications programmer but can occur automatically as part of the End Transaction processing. Of course, holding locks longer than necessary reduces the degree of concurrency that can be achieved.

Two-Phase Locking

In view of the apparent complexity of this problem, it may be somewhat surprising that there is a simple set of rules for acquiring and releasing locks that avoids holding any lock longer than necessary. The prescription is as follows:

1. Each data object must be locked before it is used. (A shared lock for retrieval; an exclusive one for update)
2. No lock may be acquired after *any* lock has been released.

It will be noted that the second part of this rule would have prevented the problem illustrated in Figure 13–5. Because User *A* would not have been allowed to acquire the needed lock on account 20 once the lock on account 10 had been released, *A* would have had to leave the first one locked until the second had been successfully accessed.

This rule is referred to as the *two-phase lock protocol*. It implies that transactions have an early phase in which they acquire locks but do not release any and a second phase in which locks are released but no new ones are acquired. The terms "growing" and "shrinking" are often applied to the two phases, for obvious reasons.

In practice, it is usual to postpone the release of exclusive locks until the point at which the transaction is ready to commit (or rollback, as the case may be). In the example of Figure 13–5, this means that the lock on account 10 will be held, not just until the lock on account 20 has been acquired, but until it is certain that the updating of account 20 can be completed. If this stricter rule were not followed, and User *A*'s transaction did not complete successfully, it is possible that other, possibly committed, transactions might also have to be rolled back as a result of having read the changes made by User *A*, which were later reversed. Thus, holding all exclusive locks until the commit point, although not absolutely necessary, greatly simplifies the process of maintaining database integrity in a concurrent usage environment.

Ideally, users and applications programmers should not have to worry about requesting and releasing locks. This is true not only because it complicates their work, but also because the integrity of the concurrency management process should not depend on users always doing everything correctly. Thus, explicit commands for acquiring and releasing locks are frequently not included in data manipulation languages. Instead, the basic Data Manipulation Language commands will automatically issue lock management requests at the appropriate times. For example, retrieval commands normally request a shared lock. If an update is then attempted on something that has already been retrieved, the lock status is upgraded to exclusive. Locks are released when the transaction terminates. Some systems also offer explicit locking commands that may sometimes allow greater efficiency than would be possible using the normal rules.

The unit that is locked is usually the record (or segment or tuple). Locking smaller units, such as individual fields, seems to cost more than it is worth. Locking larger units—entire relations or files—has too severe an impact on concurrency for general use. However, it is obviously always safe to lock more than

TIME	ACTION
T1	*A* LOCKS record 10.
T2	*B* LOCKS record 20.
T3	*A* attempts to lock record 20 and is suspended.
T4	*B* attempts to lock record 10 and is suspended.
	!DEADLOCK!

FIGURE 13–6 A deadlock situation.

is really needed, and it may sometimes be more efficient to trade a number of locks on small units for a single lock on a larger object.

Deadlocks

There is still one important aspect of concurrency to be dealt with. Consider the sequence of operations in Figure 13–6. Users *A* and *B* acquire locks on record 10 and 20 respectively. User *A* then discovers that he or she needs record 20 but finds it locked. User *A*'s transaction is put into a waiting state until the lock on record 20 is released. Meanwhile, User *B*'s transaction decides that it needs to do something to record 10, which, of course, is still locked by User *A*. Both transactions are now blocked, and each is waiting for the other to complete. Obviously, this situation will go on forever unless something is done to break the deadlock.

Deadlocks have been studied in detail in other contexts, for example, the allocation of resources to jobs by an operating system. However, in these cases, the number of units to be allocated—tape drives, printers, and so on—is usually quite small, and the complete resource requirements of a job can normally be determined *before* the job begins execution. In the database context, the number of logical objects to be allocated is enormous, and it often happens that the full set of objects required by a transaction cannot be determined in advance. Under these conditions, the techniques used by operating systems to avoid deadlocks are not appropriate. It seems, therefore, that database deadlocks cannot be avoided, and that DBMS's must be prepared to detect and unravel them.

The detection of deadlocks is not difficult, but it is slightly more complicated than might first appear. In addition to worrying about cases where *A* is waiting for *B* and *B* for *A*, it is also necessary to be able to recognize cases where *A* is waiting for *B* who is waiting for *C* who is waiting for *D* who is waiting for *A*, and so on. Actually, a study of locking done on System R indicated that deadlocks involving more than two transactions are extremely rare.[4] Deadlocks can be detected by constructing a graph that shows who is waiting for whom. Such a graph has a node for each current transaction and an arc from node i to node j if transaction i is waiting on transaction j for something. A cycle in this graph (i.e., a path that returns to its starting point) indicates a deadlock, and good algorithms exist for finding cycles in a graph. The test for deadlocks can be performed each time a transaction requests a lock and is refused. However, because deadlocks appear to be rare, this is probably unwarranted. Alternatively, the check can be performed on some periodic basis. Observing that a transaction has not completed after some reasonable amount of time may also be used to trigger the deadlock detection process.

Once a deadlock has been detected, it must be broken by aborting one of the deadlocked transactions, undoing any changes it has already made, and releasing its locks. The aborted transaction should then be reinitiated. This whole process ought to be invisible to users, except perhaps for a degradation in response. It should be noted that choosing the transaction to abort to break a deadlock is not a trivial problem. It may be that one is much more central to the bottleneck than another. It would also be desirable to avoid the possibility that a transaction might get aborted and restarted, only to again encounter the same deadlock. This might argue either for giving precedence to the transaction that has been waiting the longest or for choosing the "victim" at random so that the same one would not always get picked.

BACKUP AND RECOVERY

If all of the precautions already described are taken, a database should be secure against human error or bugs in applications programs. However, there is still the possibility of damage as the result of a failure in the hardware or operating system or, indeed, the DBMS itself. Thus, a facility for reconstructing a valid, consistent version of a database following a failure is absolutely essential.

A good recovery system should be as automatic as possible to reduce the probability of additional error being introduced through human lapses during the recovery process. Because all or part of a database is probably unavailable to users during recovery, it is desirable to have it take as little time as possible.

A complete recovery system provides two types of facilities. The first is a set of functions that are always active and whose job is to prepare for the possibility that an emergency recovery may have to be made. Essentially, these functions are responsible for retaining enough information about the database and transactions

---

[4]J. N. Gray, "Experience with the System R Lock Manager," IBM San Jose Research Laboratory, Spring 1980.

so that a valid copy of the database can be reconstructed. The second group of facilities are those responsible for actually performing the reconstruction following any malfunction.

Recovery Preparation Facilities

One recovery preparation function is the maintenance of a copy of database contents offline, and preferably at a different physical location. Keeping the copy offline protects it against damage caused by a system malfunction. Having it at a separate location helps to ensure that any natural disaster, such as fire or flood, that damages the main database will not also affect the copy. Maintaining a backup copy of information is not a new idea and does not apply only to a database environment. However, making a copy of a database is somewhat more complicated than the equivalent function in a traditional file-based system.

In the latter case, the natural unit for saving and recovery is the individual file. Files are not often extremely large and are usually not in constant use. Thus, it should not be difficult to find time to make a backup copy without disrupting normal usage. Neither of these conditions is met in the case of a database. The integrated nature of a database means that it is difficult to identify small pieces that can be backed up independently. In general, it may also be difficult to ensure that ongoing transactions will not alter a portion while it is being copied unless the entire database is taken out of service for the duration of the save operation. This latter alternative is rapidly becoming unfeasible because of the length of time the data would be unavailable. If the copy is made incrementally without taking the database out of service, then it is not a consistent snapshot of the complete contents at an instant in time, but something more like a motion picture that shows one part as it was at one moment and another part as it was some time later. Obviously, recovering a database from this type of copy is much more complicated than simply recopying it from the backup to the primary storage devices.

To help make sense out of this type of "rolling" copy, as well as to meet a number of other needs, the other part of recovery preparation consists of keeping a record of all transactions against the database. (For recovery purposes, it is sufficient to record only those transactions that result in some change to the database. However, as will be seen later in this chapter, there are reasons to keep track of pure retrieval activities as well, and the same mechanism can be used for both.)

The transaction log records the date and time of each operation, and identifies the data and the user. In the case of an operation that will modify the contents of the database, both *before* and *after* images should be recorded. It is obviously essential that the transaction log itself be protected against loss. Steps that could be taken to protect the log include the use of dedicated storage devices and recording two copies to guard against failure on a logging device. Magnetic tape is generally preferred to disk because it is less likely that a hardware or software failure will result in destroying log entries. However, if it is desired that the recovery process be as automatic as possible, the log should reside on a direct access device. In this case, it may be possible to modify existing devices to eliminate overwriting of existing log entries. New storage technologies just becoming commercially available have exceptionally high capacity and speed, using write-once media, such as photographic film. These would be ideally suited to logging applications.

One problem with any logging system is making sure that the log and the database remain synchronized. That is, each change that appears in the database must appear in the log and vice versa. Because of the serial nature of contemporary computers, it is inevitable that either the log or the database will be written first.[5] If the change is recorded first in the database but a failure occurs before the corresponding log entry is made, there would be no way to undo the change. Thus, the alternative of making the log entry *before* changing the database is clearly to be preferred. If this strategy is followed and a failure occurs after the log entry but before the database change, there is enough information available to restore the database to a known consistent state. When the recovery routine processes this log entry, it will be able to recognize that the database matches the *before* image rather than the *after* one, and it will be immediately clear what happened. Either the database will be changed to match the *after* image in the log or the transaction will be backed out and restarted.

There is another technique for handling updates that helps to maintain consistency by not actually making any changes at all to the database on a real-time basis. Such changes are simply saved in a so-called *differential file*. From time to time, the main database and the differential file are merged to produce a new version of the database. The previous version of the database, which is out of date, but still internally consistent, becomes the backup.

Of course, this technique creates certain problems for information retrieval. It is necessary to search the differential file first, in reverse order, to find the most recent value of the desired data. Only if no entry is found there is the value in the main database used. The additional searching makes retrieval more complex and expensive, particularly in a database that is being updated frequently. However, in a situation where the database contents do not change very rapidly, this can be

---

[5] This problem is complicated by the fact that database updates are normally made to a *copy* of the information residing in an in-memory buffer rather than directly to the disk. Buffers are written to secondary storage at unpredictable times determined by the operating system. Thus, a system failure after a buffer had been updated but before it had been copied to disk would result in a situation where the operation would appear to the DBMS to have been completed successfully, when in fact, it had not. Some systems partially alleviate this problem by dumping the buffers to disk when updates are committed.

an attractive approach. It has the additional advantage of reducing the time required to perform an update in systems that employ complicated index structures to speed retrieval.

One example of a database system that uses differential files is SPIRES, developed at Stanford University primarily for bibliographic data. Bibliographic databases are often large and usually relatively static. Most updates are additions rather than modifications of existing data. Inverted lists, which are relatively expensive and time consuming to update online, are employed to speed retrieval. Thus, SPIRES was designed to record updates in a differential file that is automatically searched as part of all retrieval operations. The actual update of the main database is performed on command from the database administrator, presumably at a time when the database is not in use and when processing time is available.

A similar approach is used by INGRES but with a markedly different effect. As a general purpose DBMS, INGRES cannot be sure that its databases will experience the low update rate characteristic of the SPIRES environment. INGRES uses differential files to store database changes during a transaction, but it automatically merges them with the main database when the transaction is complete.

Database Reconstruction Techniques

There are two main techniques for processing a transaction log to recover from a malfunction that has compromised the integrity of the database. If the failure was one that did not affect the integrity of secondary storage, then the only possible problem is that there may be some transactions that were stopped in the middle. The uncommitted modifications to the database associated with these transactions must be backed out and the transactions themselves restarted. Undoing the results of partially completed transactions is accomplished by processing the log backwards and restoring the appropriate *before* images. This is called *backward recovery*.

For malfunctions that have actually damaged or destroyed part of the database contents, it is necessary to begin the reconstruction process with the most recent complete copy of the database. This copy will be internally consistent but, of course, out of date. It is brought up to date by processing the log in a forward direction to redo all of the database changes made since the time the copy was made. This procedure is called *forward recovery*.

The efficiency of both of these techniques can be improved considerably compared to a simple brute force approach. Consider the case of forward recovery. It may be that a particular database record has been changed many times between the last save and the failure. If the log is processed in the most obvious way, recovery will involve repeating each of these changes individually when all that is really needed is to find out what the last valid state of the record was. Recovery can be greatly facilitated by periodically consolidating all log entries that apply to a given record as well as by sorting the log according to physical data addresses.

AUTHORIZATION

The authorization problem in database management is concerned with specifying who has what type of access to what information. This problem arises in non-database environments as well, and is closely related to the problem of controlling access to things other than information. For example, controlling use of the computer, itself, or of particular programs poses many of the same problems.

The overall access control problem may be divided into three parts. One is the specification of a set of rules stating what access is permitted. Another is the provision of adequate enforcement mechanisms to ensure that the rules will be obeyed. The third is the identification of the data objects, users, programs, and so on, that are involved so that the enforcement mechanism knows which rules to apply. This section will focus primarily on how the first of these tasks is accomplished in a database environment. The second depends heavily on hardware and operating system features that are beyond the scope of this book. Aspects of the third issue will be discussed at appropriate points.

Authorization Rules

An authorization rule consists of four parts: subject, object, action, and conditions. It is interpreted as specifying what *actions* the *subject* is allowed to perform on the *object* under the specified *conditions*. A fifth consideration in this process is the *authorizer*, the person empowered to specify authorization rules. Each of these will be discussed in turn.

There are two general approaches to assigning responsibility for specifying authorization rules. In most traditional systems, the person who creates a data object is considered its *owner* and has complete control over it, including the right to specify what access others should have to it. The intuitive justification for this approach is obvious. However, in a modern database environment where information is widely shared, it may not be possible to determine who the owner of a data object is. In such a case, it may be more reasonable to grant authorization power over all of the data to the Information Resource Manager or Database Administrator. Some organizations have a Security Administrator specifically to handle this function.

One problem associated with separating ownership and authorization is the question of responsibility. The author knows of a situation where a group of about 10 clerks are all involved in maintaining a particular collection of financial information. A single terminal is located in the office where these clerks work. The first one to arrive in the morning signs on the terminal and it is left signed on all day so that clerks can just walk up to it and enter transactions with a minimum of effort. The clerks and their manager like this system because it is so easy and convenient. The Data Administrator, on the other hand, is quite concerned about the fact that, if a fraudulent act were to be committed, it would be impossible to tell which of the clerks was responsible. In fact, the possibility could not be ruled out that someone else had entered the office during the lunch hour and used the terminal when none of the regular staff was present. The Data Administrator wants to give each clerk his or her own password and require that clerks identify themselves to the system as part of each transaction. The department manager resists this strongly because of the extra work involved. If responsibility for this data was clearly assigned to the manager, he would probably have a different view of the appropriate balance between convenience and security!

Combining authorization responsibility with ownership seems to make sense wherever ownership can be clearly identified. One potential disadvantage, though, is that it will probably be harder to achieve consistent adherence to authorization rules. Individuals down on the firing line will be tempted to bend the rules for the sake of short-run convenience.

An interesting question in this context deals with whether there is, or should be, anyone in an organization who has access to *all* of the data. With decentralized authorization, this would not, in general, happen, whereas it seems to be unavoidable if authorization is handled by a central administrator. However, as will be seen, authorization to retrieve data can be easily separated from authorization to define authorization rules. That is, although the central administrator would have authority to make or change all of the access rules, he or she would not automatically have access to all of the data. Of course, power to change the rules allows the administrator to grant himself or herself access to any desired data. The way to control such abuse is to have all authorization actions logged automatically and checked by someone who is independent of the authorization function—the internal auditors for example. This would not prevent an unscrupulous Security Administrator from making improper use of his or her authority, but the independent, external review should be a powerful deterrent.

The *subject* of an access rule may be a person, a program, a terminal, or any combination of these. Access is usually thought of as being granted to an individual. To facilitate this, most systems assign a unique ID to each user and require this to be entered along with a password that is supposed to be kept secret. This is not the appropriate place to discuss user identification procedures at length. However, a few comments may help to expose the dimensions of the issue. First, an individual can be identified on the basis of something he or she *is*, *has*, or *knows*. The most common technique, passwords, is an example of something the individual knows. Something the user has might be a special key to unlock the terminal or a machine-readable badge. Fingerprints or voiceprints are examples of something a user is that could be used for identification.

Although the password approach is the easiest and least costly to implement, it also offers, by far, the poorest reliability. People are notorious for giving out their passwords for the sake of convenience. Furthermore, if users are allowed to choose their own passwords, they usually pick something that is easy to guess—the name of a family member for example. If the system assigns passwords, users often write them down somewhere as an aid to memory, despite strict injunctions not to do so. Most systems continue to rely on passwords, despite their known limitations, presumably because the reduced security is outweighed by the extra cost of a better method.

Sometimes it is necessary to grant access to something other than an individual person. All of the clerks in the example mentioned above have the same job, so, it should be possible to specify that they are members of a single group and then grant appropriate authorization to the group. This is especially convenient when a new clerk is added to the group or an old one leaves. Instead of having to specify the authorization details on an individual basis, the person is either added to or subtracted from the group, and the access authorization changes automatically.

There are also cases where there is no concern about who has access to certain information but only with controlling the actions they are allowed to perform or, perhaps, with charging them for using the information. The easiest way to accomplish this would be to grant access to a specific computer program rather than to people. Any user wishing access to this information would have to invoke the authorized program, which could perform any desired procedure prior to granting the access.

Another factor that may be considered in defining a subject for authorization purposes is the location from which the request is coming. The most often quoted instance of this would be a military system that, when asked to retrieve secret data, may want to make sure not only that the requestor is authorized for such data, but also that he or she is using a terminal in an appropriately secure location. As it becomes more and more common for computers to be connected to common carrier communications systems, it will become increasingly useful to know where a request is coming from to decide whether or not it is valid.

Specification of a particular program or terminal as part of identifying the subject of an authorization rule may be taken as examples of the more general ability to attach *conditions*. Day of the week or time of day might be other equally relevant factors. For example, authorization rules in a banking system might not only specify that a certain request must come from a terminal in a branch manager's office, but also that it must be during normal banking hours.

The *object* of an authorization rule in a database system is, of course, data. However, being able to grant or prohibit access only to an entire database would usually be much too blunt a tool to be of practical value. Most traditional systems implement access control at the level of a file. This would correspond roughly to a relation in a relational database, a logical database record in a hierarchical one, or a record type in a DBTG system. In many cases, even this is not sufficient, and the ability to specify authorization down to the level of an individual field or data-item is required. Such schemes are not particularly difficult to design or implement, but as the unit of authorization gets smaller, the overhead associated with checking access and the work required to specify the rules both increase. If an authorization system is too hard or too expensive to use, there is a great risk that it will simply be circumvented.

One way to describe objects for authorization purposes is to use values of certain attributes. A simple form of this specifies an upper or lower bound for some value. For example, bank tellers may be allowed to enter withdrawals for less than $10,000 without a supervisor's approval. Another type of value-based object description would be to grant a manager the right of retrieval of all employee records where the employee's department matched the manager's department.

A generalization of value-based object descriptions is to use *views* as the units of authorization. A view is a virtual data object that does not actually exist but that can be derived from the underlying real database. Systems that support views usually offer quite powerful facilities for describing how a view is derived. In a relational system, for example, the view definition language should be very much like the query language. Anything that can be expressed as a retrieval request should be definable as a view. This may require joining several base relations together as well as deleting certain columns or rows. In the DBTG model, a subschema is equivalent to a view. Subschema definitions can contain records made up of pieces from different physical records, and some set relationships may be omitted, but there is no basis for including or excluding data based on values.

Using the view mechanism for authorization is quite elegant because it avoids the need for a separate facility. One possible drawback is that it is not always possible to update a view. This is not a comment on the limitations that may be present in some specific implementation. Rather, it is a basic property of the view concept that the transformation from the underlying database to a view is unidirectional. For example, consider a physical relation in a personnel system that contained the fields Name, Department, and Salary, among others. With a good view mechanism, it would be possible to define a view based on this relation that contained the fields Department and Total Salary. It is easy to see how this view is derived from the underlying base relation. It is also easy to see that updating this view is impossible! If a transaction attempted to add $10,000 to the Total Salary of some department, the system would have no way to know how to reflect this in the underlying database that records the salaries of individuals. Does the increase all go to one person? Should it be allocated in equal dollar amounts to all the employees in the specified department or perhaps in equal percentage increments? Each of these is a possible interpretation of the transaction, but a choice among them made by the DBMS would have to be purely arbitrary, and this can not be acceptable.

The view concept is probably the most convenient general method of defining objects for authorization purposes. The user should not be able to tell that his or her view of the database is not the real thing—a useful feature of any access control mechanism. The one difficulty that must be dealt with is that, as the preceding illustration shows, views are often not updatable.

The fourth component of an authorization rule is the *action*. The exact set of actions that must be dealt with depends on the database model and on the level of aggregation, but there are three basic functions that must be accommodated: retrieval, update, and control. The retrieval function is the least powerful. It gives the subject only the right to read values from the database. Update access allows the holder to modify the contents of the database. This includes adding new records and deleting old ones. We would normally think of update access as including retrieval access, but this need not be the case. It is not unusual to find situation where a user is allowed to add additional information, but not to read or change what is already there. This can be accomplished by distinguishing insertion as a separate function from update.

The third basic action is control. This includes the ability to modify database definitions and authorization rules.

The discussion of authorization may be summarized by recalling that an authorization rule is a statement of the actions that may be performed by some subject on some data object under a given set of conditions. These rules must be stored by the DBMS for reference on all requests for service. The mechanism for specifying authorization rules is usually similar to that for integrity constraints, although there are some additional requirements that do not arise in the case of integrity measures.

For example, there are cases where no individual data can be released, but certain types of statistical inquiries are permitted. The best-known example of this is census data. An authorization system in this case must be able to distinguish statistical access from normal retrieval and must also be able to determine when an apparently permissible request will result in an information leak.

One strategy that could be adopted in such a case would be to refuse to answer any query where the answer would be based on fewer than some minimum number of data values. For example, the inquiry, "What is the average salary of chief executive officers in the computer industry under the age of 35?" might not be answered if less than, say, 10 people were in this category.

Two warnings must be attached to this type of protection. First, the refusal to answer, in itself, gives certain information. In this case, it places an upper limit on the number of people in the category. This may actually be what the inquirer wanted to know! Second, it is easy to show how sequences of individually legitimate statistical inquiries can result in the release of information that would not be provided if requested directly. To illustrate, suppose that you are a female statistics professor in some university and are curious about the salary of the only other female professor in your department. If you have access to a personnel database that allows only statistical inquiries, you could enter the following two queries:

What is the average salary of male statistics professors?
(As long as there are more than the minimum number in this category, an answer will be provided, and does not, in itself, compromise anyone's individual salary.)

What is the average salary of all statistics professors?
(If the first question was answered, this one surely will be as well because it involves a sample that has two additional members.)

Obviously, knowing the numbers of people in the two groups and your own salary, you can easily compute that of your lone female colleague.

It might seem that the answer to this is to have the authorization mechanism remember your past inquiries and use that information in deciding whether a new one might result in a security violation. This can, in fact, work under some circumstances, although the processing can become extremely complicated. However, it is virtually impossible to imagine how such a system could be expected to uncover cases of collusion where two or more users each enter one seemingly innocuous query and then pool their results.

There is another situation in which authorization control can be more complicated than enforcing integrity constraints. For example, suppose that our objective is not to release the salary of any individual employee. This does not mean that no access can be given to salaries. We can still provide views of the personal database that included salary information as long as it could not be associated with anything that could be used to identify individuals. To enforce this type of rule, the system must know which fields can be used for identification purposes.

PRIVACY

The increasing use of computers in business and government over the past two decades has been accompanied by a corresponding increase in concern about the potential for using them to violate the privacy of individuals. One factor contributing to this concern is the possibility that computers will be used to collect together information that was previously widely dispersed and that they will allow the making of otherwise impossible connections between data from different sources. As a result of public concern over these issues, a number of proposals have been made for legislation to control the collection and use of personal information. A number of countries actually have passed such laws, and more may be expected to follow in the future if public concern with this issue remains high.

A complete discussion of the computer/privacy issue would be inappropriate in a database text. However, it is relevant to consider the impact of database technology on the public concern for privacy as well as the implications of existing and proposed privacy legislation for users of database systems.

The reader will certainly have recognized that the concerns listed at the beginning of this section relate directly to database usage. In the precomputer era, a high degree of privacy existed, despite the fact that massive amounts of personal information were collected by various public and private agencies. The protection resulted from the high cost and difficulty of processing these large manual files. It was particularly difficult to relate information in one system to that in another because of likely differences in filing systems and in methods of identifying individuals. Another contributing factor was the relatively high error rate in these files that made it even more difficult to determine which records from different systems referred to the same person.

Early computer-based systems had an impact on some of these problems, particularly the cost and time required to search a file. Erroneous data and interfile linkage problems remained and were (perhaps) even compounded by the difficulties of harnessing the new computer technology. Ironically, one factor that contributed to public concern about computerized storage and handling of personal information was the flood of highly publicized announcements for ambitious new systems, most of which turned out to be beyond the technical capabilities of the time.

Our society is now at the point where DBMS's are starting to become a common feature of data processing operations. Those who have been involved in the implementation of database systems know that, here too, more has generally been promised and advertised than has been delivered. Nevertheless, in principle, database technology could actually provide the sophisticated searching and linking capabilities that would make privacy violation a practical problem.

Beginning in the late 1960s, a number of laws were passed regulating the collecting and use of personal data. At present—in the mid 1980s—the coverage of these laws is still quite spotty. In some countries, only governmental systems are regulated; in others, only private ones. Some laws apply only to certain industries. Whether the coverage of these laws expands in the future will depend on the extent of public demand, which itself will be greatly influenced by how the technology is used. In any case, despite the wide variation in coverage, there is a high degree of consensus concerning the content of laws to protect privacy. Thus, it is not difficult to forecast what the impact on database users will be, even in areas that are not currently regulated.

A number of studies conducted in several countries have generally agreed on the objectives of privacy legislation. One concise statement of these objectives is that produced by a committee under the auspices of the U.S. Department of Health, Education, and Welfare:[6]

1. There must be no personal data record-keeping systems whose very existence is secret.
2. There must be a way for an individual to find out what information about him is in a record and how it is used.
3. There must be a way for an individual to prevent information about him that was obtained for one purpose from being used or made available for other purposes without his consent.
4. There must be a way for an individual to correct or amend a record of identifiable information about him.
5. Any organization creating, maintaining, using, or disseminating records of identifiable personal data must assure the reliability of the data for their intended use and must take precautions to prevent misuse of the data.

There are a number ways in which the first principle could be implemented, but none of them seem to relate to the use of database technology at all. (For those who do not follow the privacy issue, the significance of Principle No. 1 is that individuals must know that a recordkeeping system exists before they can possibly invoke any other rights with respect to it.)

Principle No. 2 implies that the operators of a personal data system (PDS) must be able to retrieve all of the information relating to an individual on request. Legislation implementing this principle usually specifies that it must be complied with even if the normal mode of retrieving the data is *not* based on personal identifier. Furthermore, the individual is not required to supply any particular identifying number, such as a Social Security Number, to invoke this provision. In addition, there is usually a low limit, often zero, on the fee that can be charged for this retrieval. The clear implication for organizations operating PDS's is that they must include a provision for locating all of the data on an individual on the basis of routine identifying information, such as name and address. Furthermore, this retrieval should be reasonably efficient and economical because it will not be possible to pass on the full cost to the inquirer.

The second part of Principle No. 2 gives individuals the right to find out what their information has been used for. It would appear that this could be met by a straightforward extension of the transaction log. The requirement for supporting

---

[6] *Records, Computers, and the Rights of Citizens*, Report of the Secretary's Advisory Committee on Automated Personal Data Systems, Willis H. Ware, Chairman, U.S. Department of Health, Education and Welfare, DHEW Publication No. (OS)73–94, July 1973, pgs xx, xxi.

database recovery can be met by a log that only includes transactions that modify the database. Logging for privacy law purposes would obviously have to include retrieval transactions as well. This might seem to be a major difference that would greatly increase the cost of the logging function. However, some preliminary research on the cost of implementing privacy laws suggests that logging has only a minor impact.[7]

In any case, it appears that logging of all transaction is needed to maintain database security. This need arises because although a good access authorization mechanism can prevent unauthorized individuals from obtaining information from the database, it can not tell when an authorized person is making an inquiry for an improper purpose. There have been a number of cases reported where trusted employees have used their access privileges to retrieve information for others. This may be done for profit or simply because the employee was sympathetic to the other person's desire for the information. In any case, such activity is virtually impossible to prevent through normal access control measures. However, logging *all* database transactions and periodically examining the log for unusual activity may result in the detection of improper use. If employees know that such checks are performed, they may be deterred from improper actions.

Principle No. 3 implies that information identifying permitted uses will have to be contained in a PDS. Most permitted uses will apply to all of the records of a particular type and, thus, would only need to be stored once. However, it is to be expected that some subjects might approve a certain use, whereas others would not. Thus, there must be a mechanism for storing some usage authorization information at the level of the individual record.

The main impact of Principle No. 4 is not directly apparent from its statement alone, but it becomes evident when one examines the way this principle is expressed in legislation. If the operator of a PDS declines to modify a record to comply with the wishes of the data subject, the subject typically has the right to append a rebuttal to the record. In addition, the rebuttal must be included with all subsequent disseminations of the record. There is usually a limit of (perhaps) 500 words on the subject's rebuttal statement. The demand placed on the database is that it must be possible to store these rebuttals and link them to the main record in such a way that they will always be retrieved together.

Principle No. 5 is an omnibus provision that includes a number of general security, integrity, and fairness provisions. Its legislative implementations usually include the following. First, whenever an error is corrected in somebody's record, past recipients of the erroneous information may have to be notified. This may also apply to past recipients of disputed information, even if the PDS operator does not consider the data to have been in error. Thus, a log of past

[7] R. C. Goldstein, *The Cost of Privacy*, Honeywell Information Systems, Inc., 1975.

recipients must be maintained for some length of time, typically at least two years. Personal data is also required to be maintained in a state of completeness, accuracy, relevance, and timeliness sufficient to ensure that decision based on it will be fair to the data subject. Deciding exactly what the standards for accuracy, timeliness, and so forth, will probably be a job for the Information Resource Manager. He or she can be aided by DBMS features in enforcing whatever standards are decided on. This could be done, for example, by using times when the system is lightly loaded to check randomly selected records against the standards. Another approach would be to include these checks as part of the retrieval function. This would ensure that no record was released that did not meet the standards, but might also mean that responding to a request might have to be delayed while the validity of the data was rechecked.

These are the main provisions of current and proposed privacy legislation most likely to affect database systems. It can be seen that there are some specific capabilities required by this legislation that are not usually included in existing systems. It appears, however, that complying with such legislation would be easier in an organization using a database management package than in one relying on conventional files.[8] There are two reasons for this. First, the DBMS is the logical place to install many of the special privacy-protecting features. If they are not incorporated into the DBMS they will have to be included in each application program, which would almost certainly be a more expensive and less reliable alternative. Second, under certain circumstances, for example when data is going to be transferred from one organization to another, it is necessary to be able to certify that the systems are in compliance with the privacy legislation. This would most likely be accomplished through an audit procedure, which if done properly, would require detailed examination of the data-handling programs. DBMS vendors would probably find it worthwhile, for marketing reasons, to get their systems certified as complying with the regulations. Then, certifying a database that used one of these "approved" DBMS's would be much simpler and cheaper than certifying one that employed custom software.

TERMS TO UNDERSTAND

integrity	deadlock
transaction	two-phase locking
concurrency	backup
serializability	transaction log
lost update	differential file

---

[8] Goldstein, *op. cit.*

phantom read	backward recovery
inconsistent read	forward recovery
exclusive lock	authorization
timestamp	security
shared lock	privacy

REVIEW QUESTIONS

1. It is often asserted that a system should respond in the same manner to a query where (a) the information does not exist and (b) the information exists but the user is not authorized to retrieve it. Explain the point of such a policy. Give an example where violation of it could be harmful to an organization.

2. Given an example of the use of triggers within the context of the library example.

3. The deadlock problem may be dealt with by detecting the occurrence of a deadlock and untangling it or by avoiding deadlocks completely. What are the advantages and disadvantages of each of these approaches? Outline basic strategies for implementing each of them.

4. Describe interactions between two database users that can lead to a lost update, a phantom read, an inconsistent read.

5. Compare the security of data under control of a Database Management System (DBMS) with data in conventional computer files and with noncomputerized paper files.

6. If a system offers exclusive locks, what is gained by also having shared locks?

7. There are six bad things that can happen to data as shown in the matrix below. Give an example of each and recommend a suitable technical or administrative safeguard for preventing it.

	Destruction	Improper Disclosure	Improper Modification
Intentional			
Accidental			

8. What are the implications of depending on the user (or programmer) to signal the beginning and end of each transaction? Is there any possibility of eliminating this dependence through more advanced hardware or software?

9. Describe a situation where a user would prefer to *not* have his or her database reflect changes made by other concurrent users. Describe a situation where a user might not care whether or not other users' changes affected "his" or "her" database.

10. What are the strengths and weaknesses of using query modification to implement integrity and authorization controls?

11. Why are both *before* and *after* images usually stored on a transaction log?

12. What can be done to prevent (or at least detect) improper actions by individuals who are authorized users of a database?

CHAPTER 14

DISTRIBUTED DATABASES

Although the basic principles of database management have been with us since at least the late 1960s, many aspects of the topic are still not fully understood. One of the least understood areas, and one that is coming into increasing prominence, is the concept of distributed database. At first glance, this term might seem self-contradictory. The database approach is founded on the notion that all of an organization's data should be managed as a single coherent whole. What, then, is a distributed database? The traditional view of database seems to imply not only centralized management of data, but also centralized collection, maintenance, and dissemination of data using a large, centralized computer system. This is compatible with the conventional wisdom that large systems provide more cost effective computing than small systems.[1] However, users have often found centralized data processing departments not adequately responsive to their needs. As a result, pressure has been created to decentralize data processing despite the economic argument in the other direction.

Fortunately, at exactly the same time that this movement was developing, a fundamental change in computer technology was occurring. This development, which was of course the large-scale integrated circuit or chip, drastically altered the economics of computing. Instead of the economies of scale that existed in the past, the new technology brings the hardware cost of computing almost to zero as long as the performance required per unit is within the capabilities of one or a few chips. Of course, year by year, the capabilities of microprocessors have grown at a rapid rate so that today quite significant computing power can be provided at a cost that is hardly more than that of a good secretarial typewriter.

There have also been major advances in communications capability based on satellites and, more recently, fiber optics. This might seem to work against the trend to distributed computing because it makes a central system more accessible to remote users. However, computing capabilities and costs have improved even more rapidly. The net result is that there is a growing incentive to move computing out to where the users are.

It is now perfectly feasible, considering only factors relating to hardware, to distribute computing power all over an organization to handle local tasks (hopefully) in a highly responsive way. However, when organizations try to implement these systems, they quickly discover that there is more to the problem than merely finding small, cheap computers. Individual business functions do not operate in a vacuum. There is frequent need for the computers serving users in one location or business function to be able to exchange information with those in other parts of the company. The technical problems of getting multiple, dispersed computers to communicate with each other are being addressed through the rapidly developing field of computer networking. Information exchange also

---

[1] For readers unfamiliar with this argument, Grosch's Law states that the power of a computer rises as the square of its cost. Originally based on casual observation by Herb Grosch, it was carefully tested and confirmed by several empirical studies covering the 1960s and 1970s.

implies some overall coherent organization and management of data, and that is the subject of this chapter.

In principle, the information requirements of a distributed computing system could be met by storing the entire database on a single, centralized computer that would be accessible to all of the remote computing sites via communications lines. However, there are some serious shortcomings to this approach. First, it does nothing to alleviate user dissatisfaction with centralized systems. Second, every database transaction requires communication between the originating site and the central one. Communication speeds in a typical computer network are far slower than those associated with accessing local secondary storage.[2] Finally, this configuration is still vulnerable to a total service interruption as a result of a failure at the central site.

To see how these problems would be solved in the context of a distributed database, consider the example of a large Canadian bank. A Canadian bank is specified because the banking regulations in Canada differ from those in the United States in a way that is quite significant for data processing functions. All Canadian banks are chartered by the federal government and are allowed to do business anywhere in the country. This has led to a concentration of banking activity in the hands of about half a dozen extremely large institutions. A typical bank has 1000 or more branches covering a 4000-mile geographic expanse.

The idea of banks that operate nationwide is attractive in some ways because it allows a customer to travel anywhere in the country and conduct personal or business banking transactions without the complications of dealing with a new bank. Transactions of this type are obviously the exception however. Most activity at any branch is associated with local accounts.

A bank that wanted to use the conventional database approach for its customer accounts would probably set up a large computer center somewhere in the middle of the country and connect it to terminals in all of the branches. This is, of course, the way most U.S. banks function, and it works for them because of the small geographic area that is spanned and (in most cases) the relatively small number of branches. However, it is evident that this approach would be unfeasible for a Canadian bank because of the huge communications costs and delays as well as the risk of having *all* transaction processing interrupted by a failure at the central site.[3]

---

[2] Modern disk systems offer transfer rates in the range of 1 to 3 million bytes per second. By contrast, the ARPANET network on which much distributed computing research has been performed, provides a bandwidth of approximately 25,000 bytes per second.

[3] As a matter of interest, before computer networking and distributed database technology became available, most Canadian banks handled data processing in a *decentralized* fashion. That is, a number of computing centers were established, each one serving branches in a particular region of the country. Although, of course, data was exchanged among them in batch mode, there was no ability to refer to a database on one of the other systems in real time. As a result, customers usually were unable to access their accounts at distant branches.

In a distributed approach, local computing facilities would be established across the country. One of these centers might serve a single large urban branch or a group of smaller branches in a local area. The records for the customers served by those branches would be kept at that site. This should relieve much of the concern about data being outside the user's control. For the vast majority of transactions, the entire processing cycle would be completed locally. This solves the response-time problem. However, when an out-of-town customer appears, the local computer can still complete the transaction by communicating with the computing site where the information is stored.

Should one of these local processing centers go out of service for any reason, its database will become temporarily unavailable, but the rest of the system will continue to function normally. In fact, in applications where service interruptions are considered intolerable, a distributed system could be configured that would provide for the storage of every account record at a minimum of two sites. Through such techniques, the probability of any account being totally inaccessible can be as small as desired.

Following this rather informal introduction to distributed databases, the next section will offer a somewhat more structured definition and assessment of advantages and disadvantages. This will be followed by a discussion of issues involved in partitioning a database, some consideration of how to process queries against a distributed database, and, finally, some comments on how the database control problems discussed in previous chapters are different in a distributed environment.

CONCEPTS AND RATIONALE

Distributed database is a variation on the original concept that is intended to increase efficiency in environments where the demand for data is dispersed. Because it is purely an efficiency-related idea, it affects only the internal level of the ANSI/SPARC[4] framework. The conceptual and external levels are unchanged. One implication of this is that a user sitting at a terminal should be unaware of whether the database is distributed or centralized, except for possible cost and response-time differences. In particular, user procedures for manipulating the database should not depend on where the data is located. This concept is sometimes referred to as *location transparency*. Another basic principle, *replication transparency*, states that if there is any duplication of data within the system, all work required to keep the various copies consistent should be invisible to the user.

The main advantages claimed for the distributed database approach should be obvious from the introductory example. Storing data where it is most often

[4]ANSI/SPARC: see footnote 1, Chapter 7, p. 131.

used provides rapid, low-cost processing of most transactions. In addition, having the ability to access remote data when needed means that the conceptual advantages of a single integrated database are maintained. Finally, the distributed database approach can greatly reduce the danger of being unable to access data when it is needed.

Data accessibility is a combination of two factors. *Reliability* refers to the likelihood that the system itself, will be available for use. It is self-evident that a centralized system is completely vulnerable to a single failure. A distributed system, on the other hand, can continue to function, even though some components may be unavailable. Of course, the level of service provided will be reduced. *Availability* is a similar concept, except that it applies to data rather than to the system. To the extent that a distributed database employs replication, data can be available even when some sites are out of service.

Distributed systems are also considered to provide a viable solution to capacity and growth problems. Some organizations have database applications that are simply too large for even the most powerful current computers. There is no alternative to somehow breaking such a large database into pieces; unless this is done most carefully, many of the advantages of the integrated database approach will be lost. The distributed database approach offers a methodology for accomplishing this physical separation while retaining logical integration. Similarly, once an organization has developed a distributed database design, growth can be accommodated by adding additional nodes. This should be easier and less disruptive than completely replacing an existing installation with a new, more powerful one.

Finally, one of the chief arguments raised in favor of distributed *computing* is the claim that it is more responsive than traditional, centralized systems to individual user needs because it is under local control. This argument may be less applicable to distributed *database*. Although it is true that data is stored throughout the system, it is still necessary to think of all these individual pieces as part of a single database for management and control purposes.

The main disadvantage of distributed database is simply its complexity, and this often translates into high cost. Many of the problems involved in designing and operating a distributed database are still unsolved—at a theoretical as well as a practical level. Distributed database must be regarded as still highly experimental. No commercially available Database Management Systems (DBMS's) offer all of the distributed database facilities described in this chapter.

PARTITIONING THE DATABASE

The first important question in distributing a database is deciding what information should be stored at each location. At one extreme, the complete database is stored at each site; at the other extreme, no data is stored at more than one location. In general, there are two approaches to partitioning a database. They are commonly described by using the terms *horizontal partitioning* and *vertical partitioning*, which have particular relevance to the relational database model. With horizontal partitioning, each site uses the same database definition but has only some of the data. With vertical partitioning, it is the database definition, itself, that is divided up among the sites. These concepts will be made clear in the following section.

The main consideration in choosing a particular partitioning of a database is cost minimization, where the total relevant cost includes components associated with processing, storage accessing, and communications. Reliability is a second criterion and takes into account the enhanced availability associated with replicating data as well as the additional work required to maintain consistency.

In a conventional database system, there is a rough rule of thumb that says that disk accessing is the dominant cost and performance factor. Database designs usually strive to minimize the number of disk accesses required to process a query. In a distributed database, accessing a local disk is orders of magnitude faster than transmitting information from one site to another. Thus, it appears, that minimizing the need for data communications is the dominent performance consideration.

It might seem that communication is minimized (in fact, reduced to zero) by simply duplicating the entire database at each site. Any desired information will always be available at the local site, so, no communication is required. However, update operations will require a large amount of communication because each change will have to be propagated to all sites. In addition, great care will have to be taken to synchronize activities so that two transactions running at different sites and updating their own copies do not damage the integrity of the database.

Some idea of the complexity of distributed database management can be gained from a consideration of how integrity-preserving updates might be accomplished in a system with some replication of data. The site initiating an update transaction would notify each other site holding a copy of the information of its intention. This would probably be done by "broadcasting" a message to *all* sites unless there was a mechanism for efficiently determining which ones will actually be affected. The initiating site would then wait for replies from all of the others indicating that it was possible to update their copies. (This is, essentially, a generalization of the locking process described in Chapter 13.) Then, the change itself would be broadcast; again, the initiating site would have to wait for confirmation from all others that the update had been received and processed successfully. If any site was unable to accept the update—for example, because its computer was out of service—the other sites would have to recognize this. Information about the update would have to be saved until the malfunctioning site could accept it, and care would have to be taken to ensure that, when the site was back in service, it processed all pending updates before using or disseminating any information. Even without going into the technical details, it should be clear that the procedures needed to ensure consistency in a system with replicated data is both complex and costly.

The preceding discussion may appear to argue that duplication of an entire database at multiple sites should never be considered. However, there are cases where this could be the best approach. The decision depends on the frequency of updates relative to retrievals. An often-mentioned example of a large database that is extensively duplicated in full is the telephone directory. As far as a normal subscriber is concerned, this is updated only once a year, and it is accomplished by giving each user a complete new copy.

The opposite extreme would be a distributed database with no duplication at all. This, of course, eliminates any concern about coordinating updates between sites and also minimizes the total amount of storage required. However, these benefits are gained at the expense of having frequently to access remote sites in the course of processing a query. Given the relatively low speed of intersite communications compared to local secondary storage accessing, this could place a severe limitation on system throughput. It also means that any failure at a site eliminates all access to whatever data was stored there.

The best solution is probably a compromise between these extremes. An analysis of the specific needs of each site should be used to determine what data to store there. Widely used data may be replicated many times, whereas other information may be stored only once. If all the costs, including those for processing, storage, communications, and availability, can be quantified, mathematical optimization methods might be used to determine the optimal allocation of data to the available sites. An important reservation concerning such techniques is that the results will be valid only to the extent that the assumptions on which the optimization method is based are valid. In addition, it is usually necessary to simplify real problems to make them mathematically tractable, and there is a danger that such simplifications will obscure critical aspects. An optimal solution is not necessarily of much value if it is for a problem that differs in important ways from the one at hand. Finally, usage patterns are not static. As they change, a database design that was initially optimal may become less satisfactory.

The database distribution problem is sufficiently complex that, even when a reasonable optimization model can be constructed, only an approximate solution can usually be obtained. Even worse, the solution procedure may require many hours of computation on a large computer. However, because database design is something that is presumably done only rarely, it may not be unreasonable to invest a considerable amount of time and money to determine the best possible design.

Database Model Implications

Characteristics of the most common database models have been discussed at length in previous chapters. Aside from whatever their various general virtues and weaknesses may be, there are additional factors that enter into their suitability for use in a distributed system. Most research on distributed databases has been done using the relational model. However, vendors of commercial systems that use other models have also introduced some distributed capabilities.

THE RELATIONAL DATABASE MODEL

In the context of the relational model, horizontal partitioning may be described as taking a relation and dividing it horizontally. Each resulting subdivision retains all of the original columns, but only some of the rows. More generally, horizontal partitioning applies the same database definition to all sites and merely partitions the data. This method can be applied to any database model. It is best suited to applications where the sites are geographically dispersed but functionally homogeneous.

Vertical partitioning, on the other hand, takes a relation and divides it vertically, giving each site certain columns. This corresponds to a partitioning of the database design and works best when different sites perform different functions. In practice, horizontal and vertical partitioning techniques can both be used in the same system.

The absence of permanent links between relations make it relatively easy to partition a relational database. Each relation can be examined independently and the appropriate horizontal and/or vertical subset assigned to each site. There do not seem to be any particular problems raised by vertical partitioning of normalized relations as long as the usage requirements of each site have been correctly assessed. If they have not, much costly, additional communication may be required.

Examples of horizontal and vertical partitioning of the relational library database are shown in Figures 14–1 and 14–2. The horizontal partitioning might be most suitable for a decentralized administrative structure. Each library has its own database, which contains all of the attributes of the original but only those tuples pertaining to that library. Because the database definition is the same for all sites, Figure 14–1 demonstrates horizontal partitioning of just the BORROWER relation. Note that the Lib-Name attribute can have only one value at any given site, and may, therefore, appear to be superfluous. However, this attribute can not be eliminated from the logical database design because it is needed to identify tuples properly in the context of the complete database. If it were removed, the result would be some number of *separate* one-library databases rather than a single distributed database for all of them. On the other hand, this does not mean that the library name would actually have to be stored as part of every tuple in which it appears as an attribute. This illustrates the difference between the conceptual and internal views of the database. The value of the Lib-Name attribute might be stored just once at each site and attached to all relevant tuples as needed.

BORROWER relation for the university library

Lib-Name	Borrower-No	Borrower-ID
Univ.	228	123-45-6789
Univ.	432	604-22-8656
Univ.	634	261-03-9511
Univ.	929	216-32-1265

BORROWER relation for the municipal library

Lib-Name	Borrower-No	Borrower-ID
Municipal	261	604-22-8656
Municipal	395	270-49-1419
Municipal	610	216-32-1265

BORROWER relation for the regional library

Lib-Name	Borrower-No	Borrower-ID
Regional	112	216-32-1265
Regional	212	265-12-3612
Regional	216	617-27-0419
Regional	604	604-22-8656

FIGURE 14-1 Horizontal partitioning of BORROWER relation.

Circulation department database

LIBRARY {Lib-Name, Br-Name, Catalog-No, Copy-No, Borrower-No, Date-Due}

Inquiries desk database

BOOK {Catalog-No, Title, Author, Publisher}

Administration database

BORROWER {Lib-Name, Borrower-No, Borrower-ID}

PERSON {Person-ID, First-Name, Middle Names, Last-Name, Address}

BRANCH {Lib-Name, Br-Name, Br-Address}

FIGURE 14-2 Vertical relational library partitioning.

It is easiest to imagine vertical partitioning being used where the library system was functionally organized and each function had its own computer. Assume that the functional divisions are Circulation, Inquiries, and Administration. The Circulation function would be primarily concerned with the VOLUME relation, but would have access to BORROWER and BOOK to decode card numbers and catalog numbers. The Inquiries function would use the BOOK relation most, but would need the VOLUME relation to determine where a particular book could be found. The other relations would be most closely associated with the Administrative function. The vertical partitioning in Figure 14–2 assumes that there will be no replication of relations between sites. Each user group would store the relation(s) most closely associated with its work. Based on an analysis of the volumes of various types of transactions, a copy of the VOLUME relation on the Inquiries system might be justified.

It seems likely that the best overall solution to the library distribution problem would involve a combination of approaches. VOLUME would be horizontally partitioned among the branches; BOOK would be duplicated at each site; and the other relations would be kept at the central administrative office.

THE NETWORK DATABASE MODEL

Applying horizontal partitioning to a network database would consist of giving each site a subschema that matched the original schema in structure (see Figures 5–1 and 5–3) but that assigned individual records to sites in accordance with usage information. Each branch that has a copy of a certain book will have a BOOK record for it. Each of these BOOK records will own a COPIES set, which includes as members *all* of the volumes that are copies of that book. In other words, such a set may have members scattered across many sites. If each COPIES set included only the members at a single site, the result would be separate, independent databases rather than a single distributed one. Nevertheless, it is easy to imagine that set linkages between sites could be a cause of considerable inefficiency.

Vertical partitioning would assign specific record-types to each location. Figure 14–3 gives an example of how a network library database might be partitioned among Administration, Inquiries, and Circulation functions. In the absence of extensive replication, only the simplest database designs could avoid having sets spanning multiple locations. An important distinction between the network and relational models is that, in the latter case, the intersite links are constructed when needed—usually by moving all or part of one relation to another location. In the network model, these links must be maintained at all times.

As always, the network model expects the user or programmer to make detailed decisions about access paths and, therefore, to be familiar with the details of what is stored where.

Circulation database

VOLUME records

Inquiries database

BOOK records

Administration database

LIBRARY records
BRANCH records
BORROWER records

FIGURE 14–3 Vertical partitioning of a network.

THE HIERARCHICAL DATABASE MODEL

As with the other models, horizontal partitioning of a hierarchical database would give each site a local version of the complete database *structure*. Actual data segments would be distributed to the various locations. Because the only explicit links in a hierarchy are of the parent-child variety, this is essentially equivalent to having separate independent databases at each location. Vertical partitioning would be accomplished by allocating specific segments or database record-types to each site. For the sake of efficiency, this would probably be done in such a way that there was no need to maintain parent-child links between sites. Figure 14–4 shows a possible vertical partitioning of the library database along functional lines. LIBRARY, BRANCH, and BORROWER segments would be kept in the Administrative database. The Inquiries function would certainly have BOOK segments and would also need a VOLUME segment that gave the location and status of each volume. Circulation would be primarily concerned with LOAN segments but would need to have Borrower-No included. The identity of a book or borrower could be determined, when needed, by passing the appropriate identifying number to one of the other sites.

Because there are no explicit connections between portions of a distributed hierarchical database, some of the complexities of distributed databases disappear. So, too, do some of the advantages. The Multiple Systems Coupling of IBM's IMS feature allows a program running on one system to invoke the execution of a program at another site that will access that site's IMS database. There is no connection between the two databases however. This feature will be described in more detail in the section on query processing.

Administration database

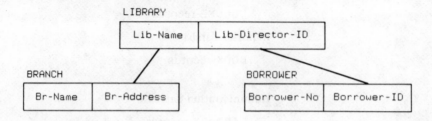

Inquiries database

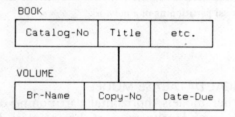

Circulation database

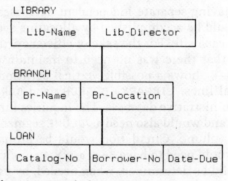

FIGURE 14–4 Vertical partitioning of a hierarchy.

MULTIPLE DATABASE MODELS

Up to this point, it has been tacitly assumed that all of the sites in a distributed system are running the same DBMS. An interesting question revolves around whether this is necessary; if not, whether it is possible that the DBMS's running at different sites could be so different as to implement different database models. The answer to this question really depends on how strict a definition of a distributed database is used. It is certainly possible to have queries refer to databases using different DBMS's and even different data models. The only requirement is a standard protocol for exchanging commands and data among the systems. However, it seems clear that the user or program originating the query in such an environment will have to be responsible for the ultimate coordination of the portions of the solution coming from each DBMS. This violates the principle of location transparency, which asserts that a distributed database should look just like a conventional one at the user level.

For example, in the last section of this chapter, the special problems of keeping track of what is in a distributed database will be discussed. The primary mechanism for doing this is a generalization of the standard data dictionary. It is not too hard to conceive of a local data dictionary containing information about, say, some relations and a network. However, it does not seem possible to hide from the user the fact that these are two distinct things. They could not be viewed as aspects of a single database. The *distribution* aspects could perfectly well be hidden though. Thus, the user would probably have to be aware that some of the information used was in relational form and that other information was in a network, but he or she would not have to know *where* any of this information was.

There is an increasing number of organizations that, having acquired one DBMS and used it to develop some applications, discover that they really need a different one. In principle, the "old" applications could be converted to the new DBMS, but this does not seem to happen too often in practice. The reasons are partly the complexity of making such a change and partly the reluctance to divert resources to modify something that is working satisfactorily. Perhaps the major problem with such a situation is that the organization now has two (or more) independent databases rather than a single integrated one. The portion of distributed database technology concerned with integrating different DBMS's might be applicable to solving this problem, even in organizations where geographic or functional distribution were not required.

Distributed databases where all of the partitions are managed using the same DBMS are said to be *homogeneous*; those where different DBMS's are used are *heterogeneous*.

QUERY PROCESSING

Determining the structure and content of a distributed database is a complex problem but, presumably, one that does not have to be solved too often. It is, therefore, not unreasonable (as previously suggested) to employ elaborate, expensive, and time-consuming techniques to obtain good solutions. The problem of how to process a query in such an environment is also complex, with numerous alternatives to be considered. However, this problem occurs constantly, perhaps many thousands of times per day. Often, a user is actually sitting at a terminal waiting for a response. Thus, it is not feasible to employ sophisticated optimization techniques to determine the most efficient approach to processing each query.

There are a few rough rules of thumb that can be employed to avoid the worst query-handling strategies. For example, the objective of minimizing data communication is always valid. Thus, the first step in processing a query should be to do anything that can be done at a single site, which will reduce the amount of data that must be moved somewhere else. In a relational system, this usually means that selections and projections should be done before any transmission. It may mean that a join should be postponed until after the data has been moved, even when both relations to be joined are initially at the same site![5]

Although it is usually assumed that the communications delays in a distributed system will result in slower response than if all data were available locally, this need not always be the case. Because a distributed system inevitably contains more than one computer, it is sometimes possible to increase overall performance by taking advantage of multiprocessing. That is, a sophisticated strategy may be able to identify cases where two or more sites can perform, in parallel, operations that are needed for the final answer and, then, combine their results more rapidly than a single computer could do the work, even if it had quick access to all the data!

An excellent illustration of the importance of a good query processing strategy has been provided by Gavish and Segev.[6] They developed and tested some heuristics for determining query processing strategies. The analysis shows that there are large differences in performance between reasonable-appearing alternatives and that appropriate heuristics can achieve performance that is quite close to the theoretical optimum.

CONTROL IMPLICATIONS

All of the control problems associated with a conventional, centralized database exists also in a distributed environment. The solutions to them discussed in Chapter 13 often have to be altered or expanded to cover the additional complexity of a distributed database. In addition, the distributed environment poses some unique control problems of its own. The remainder of this chapter will sketch the impact of database distribution on three major control areas: data dictionary

---

[5] The result of a join operation will usually be larger—possibly much larger—than the combined sizes of the relations that are being joined. Thus, it makes sense to transmit the individual relations and join them at the destination.

[6] B. Gavish & A. Segev. *Query Optimization of Horizontally Partitioned Distributed Data Bases,* Working Paper, Graduate School of Management, University of Rochester, 1982.

management, concurrency, and the enforcement of integrity and authorization rules.

Data Dictionary Management

One problem unique to the distributed environment concerns the storage of data dictionary information. In a traditional, nondistributed database system, the most significant question is whether the data dictionary should be integrated with the actual database or managed separately. However, there is no uncertainty about *where* it will be stored. Clearly, it will be within the same computer system as the actual data.

In a distributed environment, the problem of how to distribute data dictionary information is similar to the one of determining the appropriate distribution of the database itself. It seems clear that the portions of the data dictionary that describe data objects in detail should be stored at the same site as the objects being described. However, there are several reasonable alternatives for dealing with the directory portion, which is used to find out what information is in the database and (in a distributed system) where it is stored. Among the most obvious possibilities:

- The directory can be kept at a single master site.
- Each site can have a copy of the complete directory.
- The directory can be divided up among the sites in some way.

The first alternative corresponds to adopting a centralized approach to directory management and would seem to wipe out most of the benefits of distributing the database. Each query would have to communicate with the site where the directory was located, even when the required data was available locally! Needless to say, if the directory site was out of service, all ability to process queries would be lost.

The second approach, storing a copy of the complete directory at each site, offers the simplest and most efficient support for inquiries because the information needed to devise a query-handling strategy is available at each location where a query can originate. However, as in any other case of data replication, updates must be coordinated and propagated to all sites—a complicated business.

Because there are significant problems associated both with a centralized directory and a fully replicated one, it is appropriate to consider intermediate alternatives. One obvious possibility would be to partition the directory horizontally and store at each site the entries for data located there. Access to local data would be controlled through the local directory in a straightforward manner. However, when a query involved nonlocal data, the originating site would not have any way of knowing where to go for it—or even if it were available anywhere in the system. A message would have to be broadcast to all other sites in an attempt to locate the needed information. It is easy to see that this could lead to lengthy delays in query processing as well as to congestion in the communications network. This difficulty could be alleviated by supplementing the local (partial) directories with a complete one at a single, master site. Instead of an all-sites broadcast to locate nonlocal data, a single message would be directed to the central directory location. However, as with any centralized approach, this one is dependent on the availability of that central system. If it were out of service, only queries that could be processed locally could proceed. It also seems possible that heavy communications traffic to the central directory could create a major performance bottleneck.

The preceding paragraphs have described a number of reasonable-sounding approaches to the directory distribution problem and identified weaknesses in all of them. The discussion will conclude by summarizing the strategies adopted by two actual distributed database systems: R* from IBM Research and Computer Corporation of America's System for Distributed Databases, SDD–1. Both of these systems are based on the relational database model.

SDD–1 adopts the elegant strategy of treating the directory just like any other data and deciding where to store it on the basis of the same usage criteria used to distribute the database itself. Information about all relations is stored in a Catalog relation. The catalog can be partitioned and/or replicated in exactly the same way as any other relation.

It could be argued that the SDD–1 approach is *too* general. For instance, it is possible that the catalog entry for a relation could wind up at a site different from that of the relation itself, leading to needless inefficiency. In addition, with unconstrained partitioning of the catalog permitted, there is no way to know which other site will have the catalog entries for a desired data object. In SDD–1, this problem is solved by having a sort-of index that tells where the catalog entry for any particular object can be found. The index is replicated at each site, exposing the system to the possibility of having to propagate an index update to all sites whenever a catalog entry is moved from one location to another. Presumably this does not happen too often.

A somewhat different solution has been adopted for R*, the distributed version of System R. Each site maintains a catalog containing entries for all data objects that are currently stored at that site and for all of those that were *originally* created there, even though they may have subsequently been moved elsewhere. By convention, R* assigns a unique name to each data object when it is created, and that name remains unchanged as long as the object is in the system. (Users normally refer to objects using more convenient, local names that are not required to be unique.) The unique name includes a specification of the site at which the object originally existed.

Each site maintains a synonym table for each user at that site. The synonym table gives the unique, systemwide name corresponding to each data object that the user knows about. Thus, even though users reference data in terms of local names, the system always knows the unique name of each object that is referenced.

When a reference is made, R* first checks to see if the complete catalog entry is available locally. If it is not, then the birth site, as indicated in the unique name, is queried. The data object may no longer be at that site, but even if it is not, a directory entry will be maintained for it there that will (among other things) identify its current location. This is something like the alternative discussed earlier of having local directories in combination with a centralized one, except that the latter is now distributed around the entire system to reduce congestion and the impact of a malfunction.

Concurrency

Another area in which a distributed database presents unique control problems is the coordination of concurrent updates. The locking techniques described in Chapter 13 are equally applicable to a distributed environment. However, to the extent that data is replicated, locking involves taking coordinated action at all of the affected sites. Many messages must be transmitted back and forth to accomplish this and (as has been mentioned before) communications tend to be the most expensive and time-consuming aspect of distributed query processing. Much of this communication for the purpose of coordinating updates could be avoided by using a single site to keep track of all of the locks. The reader is invited to consider the problems created by this approach.

As discussed earlier in this chapter, any concurrency control system that relies on locking is susceptible to deadlocks. Although the detection and resolution of deadlocks present no insuperable problems in a conventional database system, in a distributed environment, a deadlock can arise *between sites* that is not detectable by the deadlock resolution mechanism at any one of them. Again, this can be solved by keeping track of all the waits at a central location, but as has been stressed before, any use of a central master site in a distributed system carries with it problems of communications traffic and reliability.

The alternative to locking for control of concurrent accesses is timestamping. Imagine a mailroom clerk, part of whose job is to pass each incoming envelope through a timeclock so that it is stamped with the date and time of arrival. This information is useful for several purposes. One is that it makes it possible to determine the order of receipt of a collection of messages. Timestamping in a distributed computer system serves much the same function. Because a large organization may have more than one point where mail is received, the timestamp should specify where the event occurred, as well as the date and time. Similarly, two transactions in a distributed computer system could originate at the same moment in time at different locations. Thus, in this case also, the timestamp must consist of two parts—time and site-ID. The time is simply the value of the system clock[7] at that particular site. There is no requirement that all of the systems have their clocks synchronized.

The working of a timestamp-based concurrency system will not be discussed in any detail. In rough outline, each data-object carries the timestamp of the transaction that last read it and the one that last updated it. Updates are not actually performed unless and until the transaction completes successfully. Whenever a transaction attempts to read or update a data object, it can tell by looking at the timestamps on that object if it is in potential conflict with another transaction. When a conflict is detected, one of the transactions is aborted and restarted, which means, of course, that it receives a new timestamp. There are several variations on this general method that differ in the amount of overhead required and the amount of concurrency allowed. A particularly interesting feature of timestamping methods is that deadlocks, including particularly intersite deadlocks, are impossible. For this reason, many people feel that timestamping is a more appropriate concurrency managing technique for distributed systems than locking. The question will not be completely resolved until there is some actual experience with operational systems.

Integrity and Authorization

The last issue to be mentioned in this section will be the impact of distributing a database on the enforcement of semantic integrity constraints and authorization rules. Horizontal partitioning complicates the problem of enforcing global integrity constraints, such as the requirement that all tuples in a relation have unique keys. A site that wished to add a tuple would have to make sure not only that its key was unique at its site but that it did not duplicate the key of any tuple in another partition of that relation. The most practical way to do this seems to be to attach an originating-site identification code to the key for each relation. If each site keeps track of tuples it has created, it can determine whether or not a new key is unique without having to check all of the other locations. Similarly, proper enforcement of certain authorization rules may require knowledge of what information a user has retrieved from other sites.

---

[7] Essentially all modern computers include a calendar-clock built into the hardware. Assuming that it is properly set when the system is turned on, it continues to function exactly like its manual equivalent, allowing the computer to determine the correct date and time at any moment. Just as people are not always careful to set their watches precisely, the clocks on two computers may not agree exactly with each other. This causes no difficulty in the present case because the main purpose of the timestamp is simply uniquely to *identify* each transaction. If it is important to find out the detailed sequencing of a stream of transactions, the computers can coordinate their local clocks.

TERMS TO UNDERSTAND

centralized database
decentralized database
distributed database
horizontal partitioning

vertical partitioning
heterogeneous distributed Database
location transparency
replication transparency

REVIEW QUESTIONS

1. Consider a manufacturing company with three factories, each responsible for a single product line, and five warehouses, each of which handles all products for a specified geographic area. Describe how the database might be organized for this company following the centralized, decentralized, and distributed approaches.

2. What is the difference between *reliability* and *availability* in the context of a database system?

3. What economic and noneconomic factors have led to the growth in interest in distributed databases?

4. State criteria that might be used to evaluate alternative database distribution proposals. Is it possible for one design to satisfy all of your criteria simultaneously? (If it is, you have not identified all the relevant criteria!)

5. Design a distributed database for the library example. Use the relational model to keep things simple. Assume that some portion of the database will be located at each branch, some at the headquarters of each library, and some at a centralized inquiry-handling location. First, decide what should be kept at each site. Then, make some reasonable assumptions about the volume of data at each location and attempt to estimate the cost of a few alternative query processing strategies. Assume that the two major cost factors are processing (which is proportional to the amount of data handled) and communication (which is proportional to the number of characters that must be moved from one site to another).

6. What new problems associated with concurrency control arise with distributed database systems?

7. List some of the problems that can arise when a single site is used to keep track of all the locks in a distributed database system.

8. What are the advantages of having a heterogeneous distributed database system? What difficulties might one encounter?

9. What are the possible ways one could distribute the data dictionary in a distributed database system? How would you decide which method to use?

C H A P T E R 1 5

DATABASE COMPUTERS

Nearly all contemporary computers are descended, in an architectural sense,[1] from machines designed in the late 1940s when the primary application was large numerical calculations. It has long been realized that this architecture is not well suited to the demands of modern business data processing systems that emphasize interactive multiple-access computing and relatively simple computation on large amounts of data as opposed to the heavy computational demands of scientific computing.

Conventional architectures seem particularly badly designed for database processing and this fact is sometimes blamed for the poor performance exhibited by most current Database Management Systems (DBMS's). Nevertheless, a revolutionary change in computer architecture is unlikely because of the enormous investment in hardware, software, and experience based on the existing approach. One possible solution to this dilemma would be to continue to use conventional computers but to supplement them with additional hardware that has been optimized for, and dedicated to, the database management function.

There is an excellent precedent for this approach in the way most modern terminal-based systems handle communications functions—another example of a requirement that was almost nonexistent when the traditional computer architectures were being developed but that has subsequently become quite important. Communications handling is not a difficult task, but one that can seriously disrupt applications processing if the same hardware is required to do both. Lines have to be monitored, characters checked for validity and assembled into messages, and so on. All of these activities have to be performed on a timely basis or information must be lost. Thus, the processor must interrupt its other work whenever the communications function demands attention.

Because the communications task is so simple and yet so demanding, most modern systems split it off from routine processing and give it to a specialized computer: a front-end communications processor, that does only this task (Figure 15–1). It handles all of the detailed work of managing terminal communications and only interrupts the main computer when it has a complete message ready to be acted on. The term "front-end" is applied to these computers because they appear logically in front of the main computer.

A number of years ago, database researchers wondered if similar benefits might be obtained utilizing a back-end computer to handle database manage-

---

[1]It is difficult to explain at a nontechnical level exactly what is meant by the "architecture" of a computer. Basically, it is an abstraction of the hardware design. The detailed function of each instruction is specified, as are the numbers and capabilities of the various modules that comprise the system, such as temporary storage registers, arithmetic units, and input/output channels and their interconnections. With current technology, one could speak of a "logical" and "physical" architecture, much as one speaks of logical and physical database design. For example, all of the models of a computer series, such as the IBM System/370 have the same logical architecture, although the implementation of that architecture in hardware varies dramatically from the top to the bottom of the line.

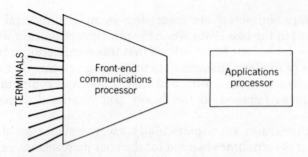

FIGURE 15–1 Front-end communications processor.

ment. The analogy seemed valid. Database processing is, of course, a heavily input-output oriented task. As such, it is limited by disk accessing speeds, and yet it requires bursts of attention on demand. It was hypothesized that a small, dedicated computer handling this work would release a more than proportionate fraction of the main processor's capacity. Figure 15–2 shows how such a configuration would look.

There are actually two ways in which the use of a back-end database processor can be beneficial. The first is the elimination of contention for the main processor between applications and the DBMS. The second is the possibility that the processor dedicated to the DBMS might be specialized for this role. The term "back-end processor" can be used for *any* processor dedicated to the database function. If, in addition, that processor employs a specialized architecture, the term "database machine" is often used.

This chapter discusses the use of systems incorporating a separate computer for the database function. The term *"database computer" (DBC)* will be used to refer to either a processor specialized for database functions or a conventional computer dedicated to database processing. Later in the chapter, the specialized hardware systems will be called *database machines* or *database processors*. The

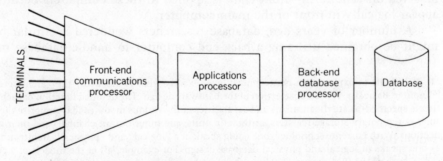

FIGURE 15–2 Back-end database processor.

next section will discuss the implications of dedicating a processor to the database function, regardless of its architecture. Then, the role of specialized hardware will be considered. The final section of the chapter will summarize experience to date with back-end systems.

IMPLICATIONS OF DATABASE COMPUTER USE

The good points and bad points of DBC's will be discussed together because most of the strengths have a corresponding weakness and vice versa. The topics to be covered are:

- Performance
- Cost
- Complexity and Reliability
- Security
- Modularity

Performance

A DBC impacts the overall performance of a system in several ways. The simple fact that the total processing capability resides in two units instead of one opens up the possibility of achieving some parallelism. That is, the host central processor can go on to other things while the DBC is performing a database operation. This division of labor also eliminates the overhead required for switching a single processor between functions. If, as a result of specialization, the DBC can handle database operations more efficiently than they could be done on the main computer, there is an additional benefit.

On the other hand, every database operation incurs additional overhead when a DBC is used because of the need to transfer requests and responses between the two machines. In fact, experience with some early systems suggests that the communications link between the two processors is likely to be the most serious performance bottleneck.

One response to this is to minimize the required amount of communication through the use of relatively high-level, specification-type database languages. A query is passed to the DBC using a language, such as SQL. The DBC then processes the entire query independently and only communicates again with the host when the final result is available. With a procedural language that manipulates records (or segments) one at a time, the volume of communications traffic would be much greater. Thus, the effective use of a DBC tends to deprive users of the detailed control over DBMS operation that is often advocated by supporters of the network database model.

Another performance-related benefit that can be associated with use of a DBC is the possibility of opening up additional growth paths for organizations with heavily loaded main computers. When a data processing system nears its maximum capacity, the usual solution is to replace the processor with a more powerful model or to add additional primary memory. This is not feasible for many database users because they have already reached the expansion limits of current hardware offerings. Even when expansion or upgrading is technically possible, it may not be cost effective. One often pays a significant premium for additional capacity at the top end of the performance spectrum.

The only recourse in such cases may be to establish a complete second system and transfer some applications to it. This, itself, can be expensive and disruptive because it implies dividing the database into two separate pieces. Unless this can be done in such a way that the separate components are quite independent, the organization is essentially creating a distributed database with all of the complications discussed in the previous chapter. Such extreme measures may be avoided through the use of a DBC. Because DBMS's are known to be big consumers of both memory and processing power, transferring this function to a DBC will usually significantly increase the resources available on the main system for applications processing.

Cost

Cost reduction is probably the most significant advantage of the DBC approach. A dedicated DBC should cost much less than the main processor upgrade needed to provide an equivalent increment in performance. This advantage will be partially offset by the cost of the interprocessor communications channel and perhaps by the need to have more resources in the system than would be needed in a single processor configuration.

This latter point requires some explanation. In a conventional system, a certain amount of processing—primary memory, secondary memory, and so on—is available. It can be allocated and reallocated among currently executing tasks on a highly dynamic basis. In a back-end configuration, each processor will have its own facilities, and these will probably not be easily transferable to the other. If one processor is dedicted to applications and another to the DBMS, then excess processing capacity on one cannot be used to help relieve bottlenecks on the other. The same observation is obviously true for primary memory and less obviously for secondary memory. It might seem that disk units could be simply unplugged from one processor and connected to the other. However, this would be feasible only if there was no information at all stored on the disk to be transferred and only if the two systems used the same type of disks. Because of the large capacity of modern disk units, one could have a great deal of excess capacity without having an entire unit free for transfer. The second requirement is also unlikely to be met. It is often proposed that minicomputers are suitable for the DBC task, and they tend to interface with disk units in quite a different way from large mainframes.

Thus, the host system and DBC will each have to have available enough resources to meet their own maximum requirements, even though there may be idle resources on the other system. On balance, though, it appears that the ability to replace a relatively expensive processor upgrade (if available) with a much less expensive DBC is the dominant cost factor.

Complexity and Reliability

Conventional engineering wisdom suggests that additional complexity implies reduced reliability because there are more things that can go wrong. A back-end database system is more complex than a system using a single computer, in that it has more hardware in a somewhat more elaborate configuration. However, theories that describe conventional machinery may not apply directly to systems of linked computers.

It is often possible for a computer to detect the fact that it is beginning to malfunction, depending on the nature of the problem and the amount of built-in error checking. In a system of two or more tightly interconnected computers, it is possible for each to monitor the performance of the other(s). Thus, a presumably healthy computer is used to help determine that another is failing, a technique that should be more effective than relying on the malfunctioning computer to detect its own problem unassisted. Small computers, such as those that may be used as DBC's, may also be inherently more reliable than large ones because they have fewer components. In other words, a more complex hardware configuration has a higher probability of failure, but the existence of multiple, independent processors increases the likelihood that problems will be detected before serious damage is done.

There are also complexity considerations with respect to software. On the positive side, experiments with back-end processors have shown that database management software intended for use on a dedicated DBC is much smaller and simpler than a DBMS that runs as one task among many in a general-purpose system. The back-end DBMS takes less time to write and debug and is consequently cheaper. On the other hand, additional software is needed to manage the interprocessor communication in a back-end configuration.

Security

One of the most attractive features of the DBC approach is the opportunity it offers for enhancing the relatively weak security controls in most current operat-

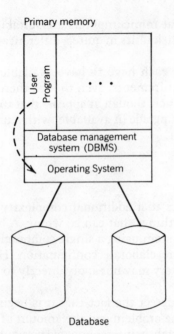

Primary memory

User Program

Database management system (DBMS)

Operating System

Database

FIGURE 15–3 An end run around Database Management System (DBMS) security.

ing systems. Database security is, of course, important, and DBMS's tend to pay it quite a bit of attention. However, DBMS security controls may be irrelevant if it is possible for a user to circumvent them and directly access files through the operating system (Figure 15–3). With a back-end configuration, there is complete physical separation between users and the database. User programs do not run on the DBC, so, they have no opportunity to evade DBMS controls and access data directly. Similarly, the only database data that exists on the host system (where it *can* be accessed by user programs) is data that has been sent there by the DBMS running in the DBC. Each request for data must pass through the communication channel and be checked by the DBC authorization function before it is acted on (Figure 15–4). There is no way to evade this process.

The other side of the DBC security argument is that it provides a visible, single focal point for attacking the system. If the DBC authorization function can not be evaded, penetration efforts can concentrate on trying to fool it. All that a user has to do to get something out of the database is convince the DBC security module that he or she is authorized to have it. This is a strategy that is equally relevant to penetrating a conventional DBMS, so, it does not represent a new risk.

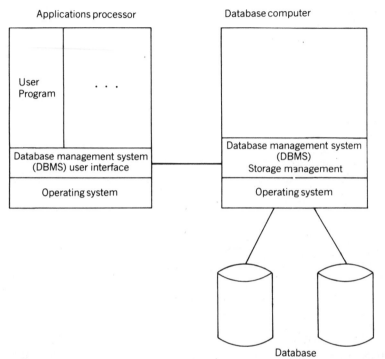

Applications processor   Database computer

User
Program   . . .

Database management system
(DBMS) user interface

Operating system

Database management system
(DBMS)
Storage management

Operating system

Database

FIGURE 15–4 Security with a back-end configuration.

Modularity

The final topic in this general discussion of the back-end DBC approach deals with the modularity that it implies. There are now two processors performing portions of the work that formerly was done by a single processor. Providing a dedicated processor for the database management function greatly simplifies the problem of sharing databases among applications running in several hosts. This functional separation also makes it possible to consider specialized hardware for database management.

Many organizations today, either by accident or choice, operate multiple and perhaps incompatible computer systems. This may occur because no single system is available with sufficient capacity. It may also result from a firm acquiring one type of computer initially and later deciding to move to another type of computer. In such a situation, the firm may wish to leave existing applications that are performing adequately on the old system. In the predatabase era, having a set of incompatible computers was not necessarily a cause for concern because

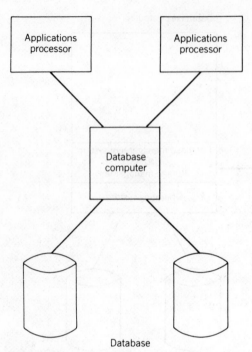

FIGURE 15–5 Database computer (DBC) serving multiple hosts.

there was rarely a need for intimate intersystem linkage. However, if the need arises to have incompatible systems access a common database, something has to be done to reconcile differences in character codes, word sizes, and other basic characteristics.

The traditional approach to this problem would be to leave the DBMS on one of the applications-processing-systems. Requests from applications running on one of the other systems would have to be relayed to the one responsible for the database, and it would bear a disproportionate share of the communications and compatibility burdens. Large mainframe computers are usually not a cost effective way to handle these functions. Even when all of the applications-processing-computers are of the same type, a program will likely have to access the database differently if it is running on the same computer as the DBMS or on one of the others.

The modularity provided by a DBC provides an easy answer to this (Figure 15–5). There is little conceptual difference between a DBC serving a single host and one serving multiple hosts. The main additional requirement is to keep track of the source of each transaction so that the reply can be routed appropriately.

Readers familiar with computer networking concepts will recognize that what
has just been described is, essentially, a database server—a specialized node on a
network whose function is to provide database services for all of the other nodes.

The other advantage of modularity is the ability it offers to specialize each
component of a system for its particular task. Just as the processors used for front-
end communications handling are designed to be particularly efficient for that
task, it should be possible to design computers for the back-end role that are
especially efficient for database processing.

In the early days of relational database management, the poor performance of
these systems was often explained by referring to the unsuitability of existing
computers for the type of processing that is important in relational systems.
However, more recent systems demonstrate that if a relational system uses the
sophisticated memory management techniques commonly used by network and
hierarchical systems, it can achieve comparable performance. (It may be noted
that the technical and economic feasibility of large primary memories has also
played a significant role.) The comparatively satisfactory performance of some
modern relational DBMS's has been used as justification for claiming that there is
no need for specialized database hardware.

Although it is nice to know that the relational model can be used without
incurring a performance penalty, it is more interesting to ask whether the performance of any database system can be improved *beyond current levels* through
the use of specialized hardware. Much theoretical and experimental work has
been done on the design of database machines. Most designs employ high degrees
of parallelism to achieve significant performance improvements. This seems attractive because database manipulation usually involves performing relatively
simple operations on large numbers of data objects. Details of some specific
database machines are presented in the following section.

BACK-END SYSTEM ARCHITECTURE

Figure 15–6 shows how primary memory might be allocated in a typical conventional system where the applications and DBMS reside in the same computer. For
comparison with the back-end alternative, the sequence of steps required to
process a query is briefly reviewed:

1. An application program calls on the DBMS using data manipulation language
   commands.
2. The DBMS consults schema and subschema tables, decides if the request is
   legitimate, and, if so, what actual disk records are needed to satisfy it.
3. A request for this data is passed to the operating system, which copies the
   information from disk to the DBMS buffers.

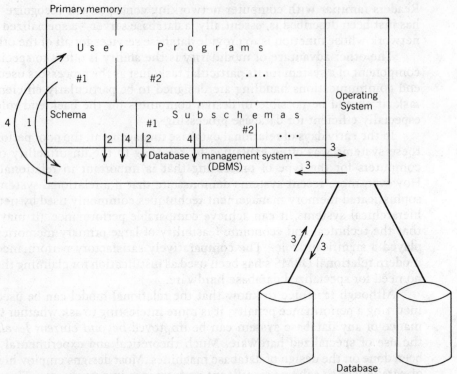

FIGURE 15–6 Query handling in a conventional Database Management System (DBMS).

4. The DBMS reformats this information, again referring to the schema and subschema, and eventually moves the final result into the application program's work area.

   If the database computer in a back-end configuration is of conventional design and a minimally modified conventional DBMS is used, the corresponding steps are (Figure 15–7):

1. The application program delivers its request to a host interface (HINT) module.

2. HINT transforms the request into a form suitable for transmission over the communications link to the back-end. This function is probably extremely trivial. A special module is defined for it only to allow the use of a back-end configuration to be completely transparent to the application.

3. The query is transmitted to the DBC where it is received by the back-end interface (BINT) module. This module passes the query to a task running in the DBC on behalf of the particular applications program.

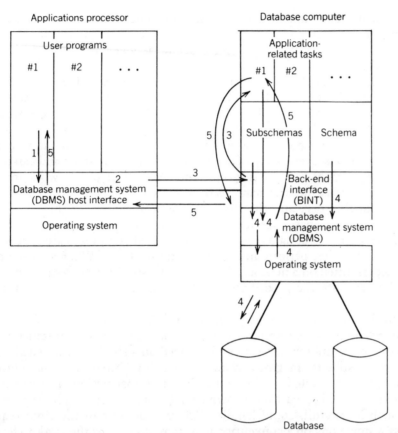

FIGURE 15–7 Query processing in a back-end configuration.

4. This DBC task now passes the request to the back-end DBMS, which processes it in the usual manner, referring to schema and subschema information and employing the back-end operating system for actual disk accessing.

5. The results are passed by the DBMS back to the DBC task and then to the application program through the intermediation of the BINT and HINT modules.

   The DBC task acts as a surrogate for the application program in the database processor. The HINT and BINT exist to facilitate the passing of requests and responses between these two. If the DBMS is specially designed for a network environment, it may already include the functions described here for the BINT and DBC tasks.

   The operating system needed in the DBC is much simpler than those in general use today. It never runs user-supplied programs, so, it does not have to defend itself against undebugged or malicious code. Because the only application running in the back-end is the DBMS, it is also unnecessary for the operating system (OS) to provide the complete set of services associated with general-purpose OS's.

A number of back-end database systems have been built using conventional hardware for the DBC and, sometimes, even using an only slightly modified version of a conventional DBMS. However, perhaps the most interesting feature of using a backend DBC is the opportunity it offers to apply specialized hardware to enhance database processing performance. The typical general purpose computer of today has a repertoire of several hundred instructions and can perform a wide range of tasks with reasonable efficiency. Most of the work involved in processing database queries requires only a few basic operations. The main characteristic of this task and the thing that is responsible for the relatively poor performance of database systems is the need to do these simple things to exceedingly large numbers of data objects. Conventional computers are sequential machines. That is, they perform instructions one at a time.[2] When a given procedure must be performed on a number of data-objects, some type of looping mechanism is used to execute the procedure repeatedly until all of the data has been processed.

This is not the only way that computers could be built. It is perfectly feasible to design machines that will process many objects of data simultaneously. Now that a complete microprocessor can be placed on a single integrated circuit chip, it is quite feasible to imagine a system containing 1000 or more such processors. In one approach, each would execute the same instructions in a synchronized manner but would operate on its own data. Such a system, applied to a repetitive task, such as payroll, could handle 1000 transactions in the time required to process a single one on a conventional system. As long as the work to be done on each entity is independent of the others, this is extremely simple. Such a system can also function when there is some dependence between transactions, although its efficiency will generally decrease.

ASSOCIATIVE MEMORIES

The inspiration for most specialized database machines is a technical curiosity called *associative memory*. Conventional computer memories, both primary and secondary, locate data by address. Given an address, the value of the data stored at that location can be quickly obtained. An associative memory, on the other hand, is composed of cells, each of which holds one record. There is no particular

---

[2] To be absolutely accurate, it should be pointed out that many modern computers make use of some parallelism to improve performance. However, database processing appears to involve a much higher degree of parallelism than is present in any conventional computer.

significance attached to the location or address of a cell. Records are retrieved by specifying a value or range of values for one or more fields. The memory examines all of its cells in parallel and flags those meeting the specified criteria. These might then be copied to conventional memory for processing or, alternatively, used again in a succeeding operation.

This can be illustrated by considering the following database transaction:

```
Give a 10% raise to all employees working in Department X who
currently earn less than $15,000.
```

If all employee records were in an associative memory, the first step would be a test in each cell to see if the specified department and salary conditions were met. A "Selected" bit would be turned on in each cell that qualified. The next operation would replace the salary field in a cell by 1.1 times its current value. However, this operation would be executed only by those cells whose "Selected" bit was on.

Consider what is required to handle this task. First, each cell is fully independent of all others. The processing required for the selection is simple: an exact match on one field and a between-limits match on the other. The second step applies only to the selected cells. The others will be idle during this operation.[3] In each selected cell, the salary field will be read out, altered, and restored.

A hardware implementation of a cell requires just enough memory to hold a single record and a processor capable of evaluating conditions and performing basic arithmetic operations. The processor need not be particularly fast because the system relies on processing many data objects at once to achieve high overall throughput. The obstacle to wide use of associative memories has always been that a practical implementation requires a quite large number of cells. Ideally, there should be one for every record in the database—perhaps millions! If there are not enough cells to handle all records at once, the logic of associative-memory use becomes much more complicated. At the very least, it means that every operation must be performed in several stages. More significantly, if the database is too large to fit into the associative memory at once, portions of it must be copied in from disk or other backup storage and partial results retained somehow.

Because of these problems, up to now associative memories have been used only in applications where the amount of data is quite small. Virtual memory management is an example of such an application.

Recent advances in microelectronics should have a major impact on the practicality of associative memories. Single chips are currently available that implement processors of more than adequate power for a cell. Commercially available memory chips currently offer up to 256K bits. Because even 64K bits

---

[3] This, of course, reduces somewhat the overall efficiency of the associative memory.

would be quite generous for a cell memory, a one-chip associative cell containing both processor and memory seems technologically feasible. The one-chip cell should greatly increase the maximum practical size of associative memories. However, because a true associative memory would require a cell for each record, much greater technological progress would be needed before associative memories could be applied to general database management tasks. Currently only magnetic disks offer the combination of high storage density and low cost needed for these applications.

ASSOCIATIVE DISKS

Recognizing this problem, some researchers have concentrated on applying associative techniques to disk-based data. This can be done, for example, by attaching a microprocessor to each head of a disk unit. The criteria relevant to each query are tested by the microprocessor as the data is read from the disk. Records that qualify are copied to primary memory for further processing; the rest are ignored.

Varying levels of cost and performance can be achieved as a function of the number of processors employed in these so-called *associative disks*. One extreme is represented by a head-per-track disk system. This allows the entire database to be read, and, hence, processed, in a single disk revolution, using a number of processors in parallel equal to the number of tracks occupied by the data being processed.

A significantly less expensive system could be constructed by having only a single head (and processor) for each disk *surface*. Of course, in this case, there would be far less parallelism. The inevitable performance degradation could be minimized by allocating data to disks so that a relation, for example, was spread across a number of surfaces. The least expensive associative disk alternative would employ conventional storage devices and position a single processor between the disk controller and the host computer's data channel. In this case, the database processor can apply various filters to the information coming off the disk and discard data that is not relevant.

Performance

An interesting restriction on associative disk systems is the need for the processor to be able to keep up with the flow of data. Because disks are synchronous devices, they cannot be slowed down or stopped while the processor catches up! It has been estimated by Date that current conventional DBMS's execute about 10 instructions per byte of data in the evaluation of selection expressions.[4] Typi-

---

[4] C. J. Date, *An Introduction to Database Systems, Volume II*, Addison Wesley, 1983, p. 353.

cal current disk systems transfer data at the rate of 1.2 million bytes per second. This implies the need for an extremely powerful processor, particularly by the standards of current single-chip systems. In practice, it would probably be necessary to use a relatively slow disk to keep within the capabilities of the processor.

The effectiveness of any of these mechanisms depends on the amount of parallelism available in the database processor and the amount that is inherent in the task. A pure associative memory has a cell for each record so that all are processed in a single cycle. An associative disk system can be thought of as having fewer cells than records—but with larger cell memories. More than one record will be stored in a single cell and the records within a cell will be read and processed sequentially. An IBM 3350 disk stores about 19,000 bytes per track.[5] If such technology were used in a head (and processor) per track system, the cell memory size would be 19,000 bytes. Assuming a nominal record size of 200 bytes for purposes of illustration, a single cell will be capable of holding up to 85 records. A database operation, such as a selection, that can be evaluated on a record-by-record basis could be completed in the time required for one revolution of the disk—16.7 milliseconds. If interrecord comparisons are required (as for a join) the times become much longer.

Having a head and processor for each track represents the high cost, high performance end of the associative disk spectrum. A less expensive alternative would employ a disk device with one head (and processor) per surface. Again, using 3350 specifications, this would give a maximum cell size of 555 tracks or slightly over 10 million bytes, enough to store about 50,000 records of 200 characters. The time to read (and process) an entire surface would be about 10 seconds, and this would be the maximum time to process a query that did not require interrecord comparisons. However, only an exceedingly large application would use the full capacity of a surface in this way. Recalling the general characteristics of disk devices, it is clear that even a head-per-surface system could process a query in a single revolution if all the data resided on a single cylinder. Cylinder capacity of an IBM 3350 is about 570,000 bytes or 2850 records of 200 characters. For larger collections of data than this, additional cylinders would be used. Because cylinders would have to be processed sequentially, the capacity and processing time would increase in direct proportion to the number of cylinders.

Task Parallelism

The amount of parallelism in the task is also a significant factor in assessing the value of these systems. In terms of this criterion, the salary-incrementing ex-

[5] The IBM 3350 is a very widely used disk system as of the mid 1980s. However, other commercially available disk technology offers significantly improved size and speed.

ample given earlier is ideal because each record can be dealt with individually. A similar (but much less satisfactory) query would be:

```
What is the total amount paid to all employees in Department X
who earn less than $15,000?
```

The selection could, again, be performed in parallel. However, computing the sum would require retrieving the value from each selected cell in sequence and adding them up in the old-fashioned way.

A similar problem arises with respect to any operation that requires a relational join. A join would be performed by taking tuples of one of the relations one at a time. For each of these, the value of its join attribute would be used in a global selection to find all of the tuples of the other relation that had matching values.

These examples show that the full parallelism available in the hardware is not always usable in practice, making the advantage of specialized hardware less dramatic than might be anticipated. In addition, more conventional systems have ways of compensating for their slower processing speed. For example, instead of scanning an entire relation looking for tuples that match a given criterion, an index can be used to directly determine the specific tuples to be retrieved.

Some studies have shown that under a wide range of conditions, a conventional system with appropriate indices can have performance that approaches what can be achieved with specialized hardware.[6] For example, a conventional system can do quite well on a complex retrieval if all the right indices exist. After all, an index is merely a tool for determining the address(es) where a particular data value can be found. A full associative memory or a processor-per-track associative disk does not need indices because it locates data *directly* on the basis of its value. A tremendous amount of unnecessary processing is done, but it does not cost anything.

The extra storage occupied by indices in a conventional system can be a significant cost and performance factor. It is sometimes overlooked that associative devices need to store a lot of additional information as part of every record. In particular, descriptors, such as record-type and field names need to be carried with every record so that the processor can tell how to interpret the data it is reading just on the basis of information contained within the cell.

The further away a particular technology is from offering full associative processing, the more inefficient it becomes to scan large portions of the database looking for specific values. Indices or other equivalent tools become important again. For example, with an associative, moving-head disk having a processor per surface, an index can be used to determine the cylinder where the desired infor-

[6]C. J. Date, *An Introduction To Database Systems, Volume II,* Addison Wesley, 1983, p. 359 and footnote 3.

mation is located. Once the read/write heads have been positioned, this type of device can process all the data within a cylinder at the same rate as the head-per-track alternative.

CURRENT EXPERIENCE

Probably the first working back-end database system was XDMS (eXperimental Data Management System) developed at Bell Laboratories in the middle 1970s.[7] A Univac 1108 was employed as the host system. The database processor, a relatively obscure Digital Scientific META–4 minicomputer was selected specifically because it had user-alterable microprogramming. The Bell Laboratories' research team thought that it would probably be helpful to implement some new instructions in the back-end designed specifically for database processing. As it happened, this topic was never investigated, and the META–4 was used in its standard form. A working DBTG system was constructed for the META–4 and used to manage a real database over a period of several months.

Several useful conclusions emerged from this project. First, it worked! The back-end configuration was perfectly feasible. Second, back-end DBMS's are relatively simple. The META–4 DBTG system (which included most but not all DBTG features) was developed with less than six man-years of effort and occupied only about 30K bytes. These measurements are quite small compared with typical mainframe computer DBMS's. Third, it *is* possible to increase the application-handling capacity of a host system by offloading the database function. The XDMS interface in the host used only about 4.5K of 36-bit words, far fewer than the DMS–1100 DBMS it replaced.

The main shortcoming of the XDMS configuration was the slow, 2000-bits-per-second link between the two processors. Typical DBTG commands required transmission of about 250 bytes. This added 1 second to the time required for every operation. Because the DBTG data manipulation language is highly procedural, many commands are required to complete a database transaction. In a commercial implementation of such a design, one would expect to see a channel-to-channel communications facility that might easily be four orders of magnitude faster.

It is unfortunate that the XDMS project was not extended to investigate the value of adding new instructions to the META–4. It seems intuitively plausible that specialized database instructions could be valuable. Thus, some recent evidence to the contrary is of particular significance.[8] A study was done to examine the possibility of improving the performance of the INGRES relational DBMS.

[7] R. E. Canaday et al., "A Back-End Computer for Data Base Management," *Communications of the ACM*, Vol. 17, No. 10 (October 1974), pp. 575–582.

[8] Michael Stonebraker et al., "Performance Enhancements to a Relational Database System", *ACM Transactions on Database Systems*, Vol. 8, No. 2 (June 1983), pp. 167–185.

One of the options considered was the addition of new, microprogrammed instructions. To estimate the value of this, measurements were made to determine how much time was spent in each of the modules comprising INGRES. The results were (perhaps) surprising. Approximately 32% of execution time was spent in two routines that check to see if tuples meet the conditions of selection expressions. No other single module accounted for more than about 4% of execution time. Thus, even if the two relatively high-usage modules could be reduced to zero execution time, the impact on overall system performance would be quite modest. The authors attributed this result to the fact that the hardware, a Digital VAX, was of relatively modern design and, therefore, possessed a good instruction set.

It should be noted, though, that these experiments do not consider alterations to the basic architecture of INGRES. The usual objective of using a specialized database processor is to reduce the total time for a transaction, not necessarily the number of instructions that will be executed. Because INGRES uses reasonably conventional disk files for storing its data, the processing required to manage the disk system probably dominates the time to evaluate queries, especially for those queries that involve a great deal of data. As has been noted, many of the database machine proposals discussed here actually execute vast numbers of unnecessary instructions in the process of handling many pieces of data in parallel.

Another approach to constructing a back-end system is to take an existing commercial DBMS and modify it to work as a back-end. The advantage of this approach is that a potential market already exists among users of that DBMS in its conventional version. The (ADABAS) Database Machine, for example, consists of a special version of the ADABAS software bundled in with a 370-compatible processor, a stripped-down operating system, and a communications package that allows a host to use multiple back-ends as well as a back-end to serve multiple hosts. Back-end versions of other popular DBMS's have also been produced. The database computer is usually either a minicomputer, such as the Digital Equipment Corporation's PDP-11 or a small 370-compatible processor.

Computers designed specifically for database processing have also recently begun to appear. Perhaps the best known database processor is the Intelligent Database Machine (IDM) developed by Britton Lee, Inc. The IDM implements the relational model and, in fact, can accept queries in SQL. Online databases as large as 10 billion bytes can be processed on a system that costs less than $80,000. A number of studies have been performed comparing the performance of a VAX computer running the INGRES DBMS to the same computer employing the IDM. The database processor provides faster response on database manipulation tasks and also makes it possible, by reducing demands on the host computer, for a higher level of multiprogramming to be sustained without performance degradation.

TERMS TO UNDERSTAND

computer architecture
front-end communications processor
back-end processor
database computer (DBC)

end run (authorization violation)
associative memory
associative disk

REVIEW QUESTIONS

1. What is the motivation for using a back-end database computer?

2. Why are conventional computers not ideally suited to database processing?

3. What are the implications of database computer usage for distributed systems?

4. Would the use of a database computer have any impact on the selection of a user interface or data model?

5. How are the problems of data security and integrity affected by: (a) the acquisition of a DBMS, (b) the acquisition of a backend DBMS, (c) the establishment of a database administration function?

6. Outline how a join operation would be performed using an associative memory. What can you say about the time required for such an operation as compared to the time required using a conventional processor?

PHYSICAL DATA REPRE-SENTATION

Database Management Systems (DBMS's) often organize data in ways that are quite different from what appears to the user. One reason for this is that databases are usually intended to be used by different people for different purposes. It is unlikely that the same view of the data will be appropriate for all these different applications. Second, it is probable that the storage structure that offers the greatest processing efficiency is not exactly what is wanted for *any* application! Thus, it is necessary for a DBMS to be able to present data to users in various ways that may be quite different from each other and from how it is actually stored.

One of the great virtues of the database approach is that each user sees the data in a form that suits his or her needs. There is rarely any reason for users to be aware of the particular strategies used by a DBMS for storing and manipulating data. However, some understanding of such issues could be helpful to someone faced with evaluating DBMS's and may be of interest to anyone who is curious about how database systems work. This Appendix describes some of the techniques that are available for organizing and manipulating data in a computer.

Such a discussion must begin with a consideration of what data looks like down at this physical level. That is, what exactly are the things that are to be stored? The smallest unit of data is, of course, the *bit*, which can assume only two values, 0 or 1. Combinations of bits are used to represent more complicated values. For example, in most modern computers, an 8-bit unit of storage, called a *byte*, is used to store each character. In large computers, four contiguous bytes are often said to constitute a *word*. This amount of storage, 32 bits, is sufficient to represent numbers of the size and precision encountered in most work. Thus, internal registers and data paths are often designed to handle 32 bits at a time. In small systems, the registers and data paths may be narrower—commonly 16 bits. In this case, the computer would be described as having a word size of 16 bits and, of course, two words would be required to represent a number that would fit in a single word of the larger size.

The next larger unit of storage is the *page*. This is the unit in which data is transferred between primary and secondary storage devices. In most current large computers, the page size is 1024 words or 4096 bytes. In small computers, it is usually smaller.

Bits, bytes, words, and pages are units of physical storage. The user is more aware of a somewhat different hierarchy whose smallest unit is the *field*. A field is the block of storage used to hold the value of an attribute. There is no uniform fixed size to a field. Years Experience would probably be two digits, whereas Place of Birth might well be 30 characters. In fact, such a field could actually vary in size according to the data being stored, with Dayton, Ohio, taking up much less space than San Francisco, California.

The collection of fields holding all the attribute values for a particular entity occurrence is usually called a *record*. In the nondatabase environment, the term *file* is used for the collection of all the records for entities of the same type. To illustrate, an inventory file is a collection of inventory records, one for each item in the inventory. A record consists of a set of fields, all of which refer to a particular inventory item. Each field holds the value of one attribute of that item. In terms of the model introduced in Chapter 2, the file corresponds to an entity-type, the individual inventory items are entity occurrences, and the actual records are physical representations.

When information is being organized for storage in a computer system, a field is nearly always assigned to a set of contiguous bytes. The fields comprising a record are usually stored contiguously, but not always, and much more complicated techniques are often used to relate the records that make up a file. The rest of this Appendix will describe some of the common data structuring techniques and evaluate them in terms of their storage utilization and their performance with respect to retrieval and update. Retrieval operations are those that simply require locating stored information. Update implies that the data will be altered in some way, for example, by inserting or deleting records or by changing the contents of existing records. It will be observed that there is often a trade-off between storage space and processing time. That is, extra storage space can be used to reduce the processing required to access data or, conversely, space can be saved at a cost in additional processing time. However, it should be noted that storage requirements affect processing time because of the slow access to data on disk compared to internal computer processing speeds. In practice, it appears that the number of disk access required for an operation is the key determinant of the time required to perform it.

A similar trade-off frequently exists between the time required to retrieve information and that required to alter it—structures that are efficient for one of these operations often being relatively inefficient for the other. Thus, the choice of storage structure in a particular situation will depend on a number of inter-related factors:

• The amount of data to be stored
• the importance of efficient sequential processing
• the need for rapid direct access to arbitrary records
• the relative frequencies of retrieval and update operations

SEQUENCE

The simplest data structure of all is the *sequence* where items of data just follow one after another. This is the structure that is nearly always used for storing the fields that comprise a record. A particular field is usually located by knowing where it starts relative to the beginning of the storage block for the record. In

Name   Emp No. Sex Yrs-Srvc   Job-Title

| LEE, ALLEN | 2929 | M | 8 | PROGRAMMER | | | | · · · |

| LEE, ALLEN | # | 2929 | # | M | # | 8 | # | PROGRAMMER | # | · · · |

FIGURE A–1 A record is a sequence of fields.

some cases, where the existence of a field is optional, or where it may vary in size, other techniques are used. For example, the fields may appear in a fixed order with a special character used to separate them. Figure A–1 depicts a fixed-format personnel record, and an alternative approach that reduces storage requirements at some additional cost in processing time to locate a particular field.

The sequence can also be used to organize the records within a file. In this case, the records for various entity-occurrences simply follow one after the other as in Figure A–2. To process such a file, one has to start at the beginning and proceed *sequentially* from record to record. One advantage of the sequential file organization is that it is economical in its use of storage space because nothing but the actual data must be stored. Sequential files are also considered efficient if all or a sufficiently large fraction, of the records in a file are to be processed in a single run.[1] It is obvious that if only a single record is to be accessed and if it happens to be near the end of the file, sequential processing will be exceedingly expensive and time consuming.

Needless to say, the *order* in which records appear in a sequential file is absolutely critical in determining its efficiency for a particular task. Thus, the notion of *sorting* goes hand in hand with using sequential files. Typically, a file will be sorted according to the value of the primary key, but to make some queries reasonable to process, it may first be necessary to construct a new copy of a file sorted in some other sequence. For example, a personnel file would probably be sorted by its primary key, Employee Number. However, for a Labor Distribution report, a version would be needed sorted first by Department, and within a department, by Project.

The time to retrieve a single record depends on where the record is in the file. A record located close to the beginning will be found quickly. Finding one near the end will require reading almost the entire file. On average, the time to retrieve a record is the time required to read half of the file. Because sequential files

[1] The figure of 10% is often quoted in this context. That is, if a processing run is going to affect 10% or more of the records in a file, it is more economical to process the entire file sequentially than to access directly only the needed records.

BURGESS, LINDA		
0618	F	12
ANALYST		
ELLIS, ANNE		
8195	F	5
PROGRAMMER		
FRANKLIN, GREG		
1894	M	7
PROGRAMMER		
KEEN, NANCY		
2827	F	3
SECRETARY		
LEE, ALICE		
0120	F	2
SALESMAN		
LEE, ALLEN		
2929	M	8
PROGRAMMER		
PRICE, DAN		
4064	M	7
PROGRAMMER		
WILD, GREG		
2442	M	3
ANALYST		
WILLIAMS, DAVID		
2570	M	15
ANALYST		

FIGURE A–2 A sequential personnel file.

are often used where quite large amounts of data are involved, this could be a long time indeed. However, as previously noted, a single pass through the file can retrieve and process as many records as desired at little additional cost in time. Thus, the sequential organization is especially well suited to batch processing applications.

Modification of a sequential file is relatively expensive. Because the records must be kept in proper order, insertion of a new one requires making a hole at the appropriate place in the file. To accomplish this, all of the records below the insertion point must be moved down. The reader is invited to construct an algorithm for this that will work on a storage device that permits direct access. How would it work on magnetic tape that allows *only* sequential access?

Logical deletion of a record in a sequence can be accomplished simply by marking the record in some way to show that it is no longer valid. Of course, the record is still there so it is still taking up space. To reclaim the space, all of the records after the deleted one would have to be moved up. (Try to devise an algorithm for doing this on magnetic tape.)

As a practical matter, both insertion and deletion of records in a sequential file are normally accomplished by writing a complete new copy of the entire file. If this were done to insert or delete a single record, the cost could be enormous. However, the same amount of work allows the insertion and/or deletion of any number of records. This is another example of why sequential files are usually processed in a batch mode.

It might seem that alteration of a record in a sequential file could be accomplished by simply locating the record and writing the new values into the same space. Unfortunately this does not work. It obviously will not work if the new values require more space than the old ones. It also does not work even if no more space is required because of the way in which magnetic tape is read and written. Thus, *any* update to a sequential file requires rewriting the entire file. One important *advantage* of this is that the old copy remains intact as a record of what the file looked like before the modification as a backup in case the new copy should be unusable for any reason.

Sequential files can be the preferred choice where large amounts of data must be stored and where either a large fraction of the records are processed at the same time or where the file is processed infrequently. It also has the virtue of simplicity compared to most of the other file structuring alternatives.

The use of sequential files may also be dictated by limitations of the storage hardware. Early computers made extensive use of magnetic tape as a file storage medium and tape is an inherently sequential medium. In the middle 1960s, storage devices not restricted to sequential access started to become more widely available, but because of their greater cost and complexity, they tended to be used only when sequential access was clearly unfeasible. As this technology matured, the difficulties were largely overcome and storage devices, such as magnetic disks that are not restricted to sequential access may actually be less expensive today than the sequential devices. Nevertheless, the sequential file continues to be widely used, even on hardware that permits more sophisticated organizations, because it is logically appropriate for many applications.

LIST

The *list* structure, sometimes referred to as a *linked list*, is logically equivalent to a sequence in the sense that the records in a file appear in a particular order. However, instead of having the records actually stored in that order, they may be scattered at random throughout the available storage space. The information about which record follows which is represented by a set of pointers linking the records together. A *pointer* is an extra field in a record that specifies the location of another record. Thus, the (logically) first record in the file contains a pointer field giving the address of the second record. The corresponding field in the second record gives the address of the third, and so on. Of course, this only makes sense if the file is stored on a device permitting direct access to any location. A list structure could not usefully be constructed on magnetic tape. The pointer field of the last record in the list contains a null value to indicate that there is no following record. In this appendix, an asterisk is used in the diagrams to represent the null value. The list structure is illustrated in Figure A–3.

A list structure requires somewhat more storage than the equivalent sequence because the pointer field must be added to each record in addition to the fields that contain actual data. However, the storage required for pointers is normally a tiny fraction of that used for the data.

Retrieval is also normally slower and more expensive. Getting from one record to its immediate successor in a sequential file on magnetic tape is quite fast. However, with a list structure, for example, on magnetic disk storage, a separate disk access is required for each record. With current technology, disk accessing is frequently the bottleneck in file processing applications.

The advantages of the list structure become apparent when updating operations are considered. First, records may be inserted or deleted in a list much more easily than in a sequence. Insertion is accomplished merely by creating the new record at any convenient location on the storage device, then altering pointers to show where the new record belongs. Similarly, deletion of a record requires merely replacing the pointer field of the record before the one to be removed with the value of the pointer field in the discarded record. Figures A–4 and A–5 illustrate inserting and deleting records in a list.

With disk storage, it is possible to alter data in place as long as the new value fits in the same space as the old. Thus, modifications of this type are exceptionally fast and economical. If the new record does not fit into the old space, then it is stored somewhere else and the pointers adjusted appropriately. Of course, if the

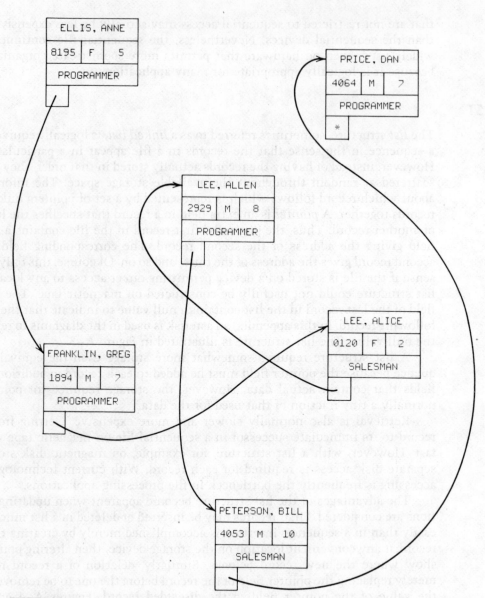

FIGURE A–3 A list structured file.

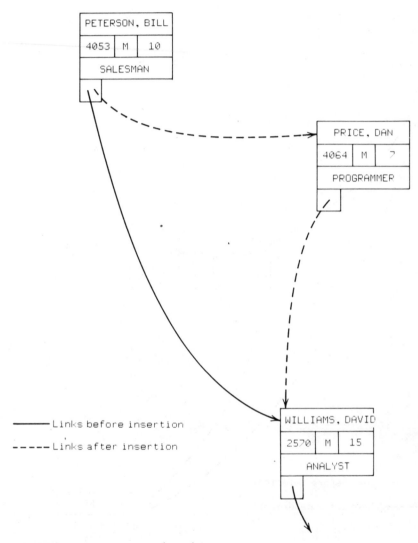

FIGURE A-4 Inserting a record in a list.

update involves changing the value of the primary key, then the pointers also have to be changed to reflect the record's new position in the list.

It may appear that list structures are rather careless in their use of storage space. Deletion, for example, appears to leave the space occupied by the deleted record forever inaccessible. This, of course, would not be allowed in practice. Rather, another list would be maintained of all the currently unused spaces in a

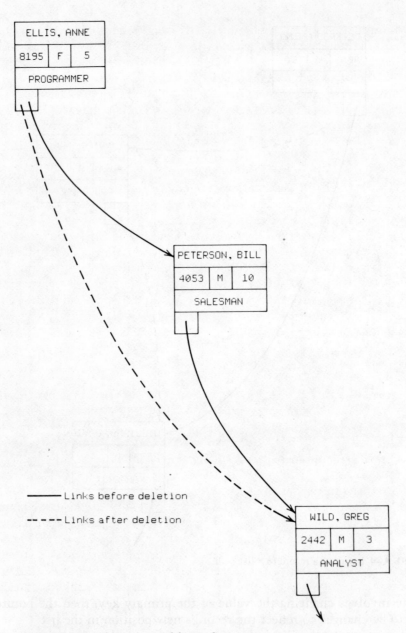

FIGURE A–5 Deleting a record from a list.

particular file or physical storage device. This list might be ordered on the size of the spaces. When a record is deleted, its space is inserted on this so-called *free list*. Whenever space is needed for a new record, the free list is searched to see if there is a fragment of storage available of the appropriate size.

List structures are especially useful if it is often necessary to process a file in a sequence other than that of the primary key. With a sequential file, this would require making a new copy sorted on another key. List structures, on the other hand, effectively allow us to have a file sorted simultaneously into as many orders as we wish. All that is required is a pointer field in each record for each sequence that is to be maintained. Such a structure is called a *multiply-threaded list* in contrast to the simple variety, which is a *single-threaded list*. Figure A–6 illustrates an employee file sorted simultaneously on Employee Name and Employee Number that uses two pointer chains.

One set of pointers in a list structure can also be used to keep track of the record that *precedes* each one as well as for the more routine function of locating the *following* record. If a record has been reached by a scan starting at the head of the list, it is always possible to "remember" the address of the previous one. However, if a list entry has been reached by some method other than such a scan, an easy way to locate the previous record can be valuable indeed, for example, if the record is going to be deleted.

RINGS

An interesting variation on the list structure is obtained by replacing the null pointer in the last record with a pointer back to the first record in the list. Such a variation is called a *ring* for obvious reasons and is illustrated in Figure A–7. The main significance of a ring structure is that it does not have a beginning or end. This effectively means that *any* record can be used as the beginning of a sequential scan that will efficiently cover all records in the structure and terminate when it returns to its starting point.

As an example of the application of a ring structure, consider a transaction processing program that must always keep track of the most recent five transactions. This could be easily accomplished using a ring of five storage areas, each large enough to hold one transaction record. The first transaction is stored in the first area, the second in the next, and so on. When the fifth transaction is stored, all locations are full. Because of the ring property, the sixth transaction will replace the first, and in the same manner, each subsequent one will replace the one that has been stored for the longest time.

The ring property is especially useful in conjunction with multiply-threaded list structures. For example, consider an order-entry system where each order record is on a list associated with the customer that placed the order and on another list associated with the item that is being ordered. Suppose that a particu-

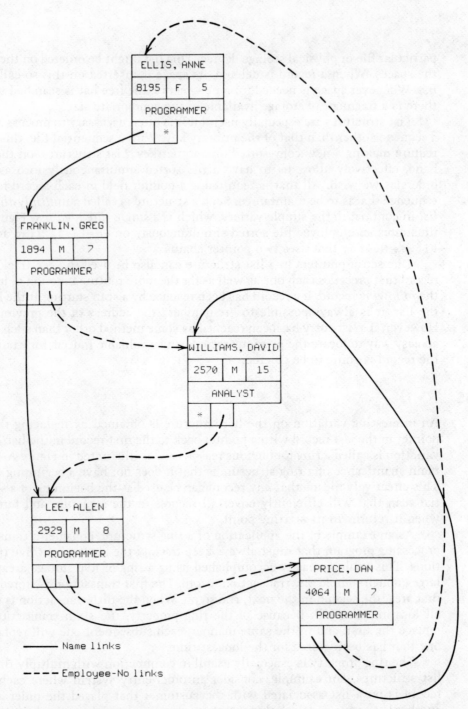

FIGURE A–6 Multiple pointer chains in a list structure.

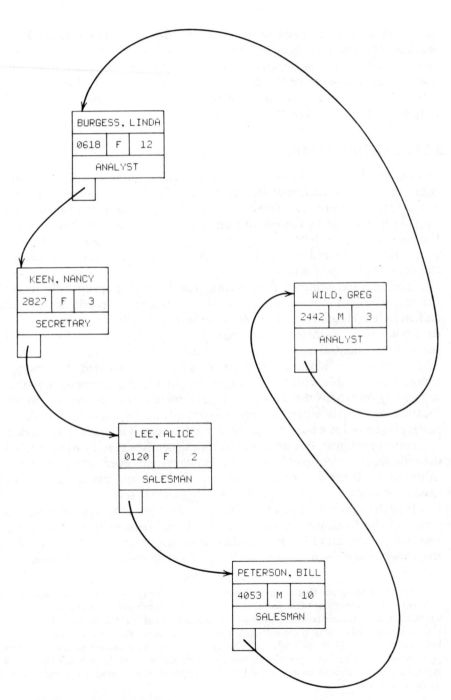

FIGURE A–7 A ring structure.

lar record has been reached by traversing the *item* list and we then want to know what other items have been ordered by this customer. This requires scanning all of the other entries on the *customer* list. In general, the record from which this scan begins would not be the first one on the customer list. However, with a ring structure, the scan can just begin at the record that is at hand, and it will terminate when that record is encountered again.

INDEXED SEQUENTIAL STRUCTURE

In many real-world data processing applications, there are files that are sometimes processed sequentially but which must be directly accessed at other times. For example, updates to a personnel record may be expected to occur relatively irregularly, suggesting the use of some sort of direct-access approach to keeping the file current. On the other hand, printing of paychecks is a batch task requiring access to every record in the file. This is precisely the situation where a sequential organization performs best.

The *indexed sequential* structure was developed specifically to deal with this situation. An indexed sequential file consists of two portions—the data itself and an index (Figure A–8). Both must be stored on a direct-access device, but the data portion is organized sequentially based on the primary key so that tasks requiring sequential access can be accommodated with reasonable efficiency.[2] The index is used when a particular record must be located. The index may be thought of as a table with two columns. The first lists a number of possible values of the key on which the data records are ordered; the second column gives the location in the file where the record having that key may be found. Finding a particular record is a two-step process. First, a search is made in the index for the key value of interest. If it is found, the index specifies exactly where to look in the data file for the corresponding record. However, not every key value need appear in the index. If the desired one is not there, the index entries that bracket it are used as starting and ending points for a sequential search.

It is clear that there is a trade-off here. Putting more key values in the index increases the likelihood of finding a match and reduces the need for sequential searching in the data file. On the other hand, nothing has yet been said about how the index, itself, is organized and processed. If index is kept small, any of a

---

[2] It is worth pointing out that sequential processing on a disk-type device is unlikely to ever be as efficient as on tape because of the fact that the disk rotates continuously. It does not stop at the end of a read so as to be properly positioned when the computer is ready to read the next block. Thus, when it is time to continue reading, there will usually be, at minimum, a short delay while the disk rotates to bring the desired block to the read head. This can be avoided by measures such as allocating enough primary storage to hold two disk blocks. Initially, both will be filled. Then, while the second is being processed, there is time to locate the third block and bring it into the storage area previously occupied by the first block.

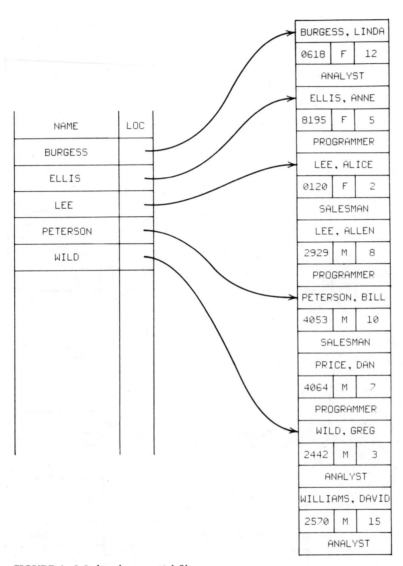

FIGURE A–8 Indexed sequential file.

number of simple techniques will be adequate. However, as the index grows, more and more time will be spent finding the appropriate entries. Eventually, it might be necessary to consider having an index to the index! For very large files, such multilevel indices are quite common. Multilevel indices are often coordinated with the physical storage units (Figure A–9). That is, the lowest level might include all the records on a particular cylinder. The level above that would be used to get to the correct cylinder.

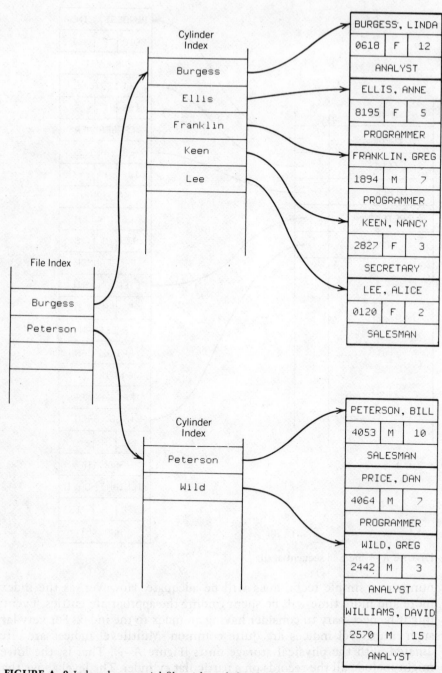

FIGURE A–9 Indexed sequential file with multilevel index.

The storage requirement for an indexed sequential structure consists of two parts: space for the actual data and space for the index. It is usual to allocate more space to the data area than is actually needed to allow for efficient insertions (discussed below).

Retrieval using this structure tends to be quite efficient. As already discussed, the index is searched to find the approximate position of the desired record, and then a (usually short) sequential search is used to locate it precisely. If the index fits entirely in primary memory, extremely efficient techniques such as binary searching can be used for the index scan. If the index itself must reside on disk, then the tree structures discussed later in this Appendix would probably be recommended for organizing the index.

Because the data part of an indexed sequential file is stored sequentially, it might seem that all of the disadvantages of sequential files with respect to update operations would still apply. However, because a direct access storage device is being used, it is possible to reduce greatly the magnitude of these problems. In the first place, when an indexed sequential file is initially created, some empty space is left in each disk block. When a new record is to be inserted, the index is used to find the block where that record should go. If there is enough unused space remaining there, the new record is added and the block rewritten on the disk. On the otherhand, if the block is already full, the new record is written in an *overflow* area somewhere else on the disk and the address of that area is placed in the appropriate index entry. On retrieval operations, if the desired record is not found in its expected place in the sequential part of the data file, the corresponding overflow area is searched.

This approach works because even though the records are organized sequentially, they are on a storage device that is not restricted to sequential access. Of course, as time goes on and more and more records have to be stored in overflow areas, the overall performance of the file deteriorates. Whenever the level of deterioration becomes unacceptable, the file can be rewritten with all of the overflow records inserted in their proper places.

DICTIONARY LOOKUP

Dictionary lookup may be thought of as a variation of the indexed sequential structure where every value of the primary key appears in the index and no attempt is made to keep the actual data records in sequence. The storage requirement is simply the space needed for all of the data plus that for an index that will contain a unique entry for each record (because primary keys are defined to be unique).

Retrieval requires a search of the index and then a direct access to the data record and is, therefore, quite fast. Updating is also comparatively efficient. A change to any field other than the primary key can be made without any fuss, unless it makes the record too large for its original space. Then, the index entry has to be changed to point to the new location. If the primary key value, itself, is to be changed, then the index also needs to be updated. In practice, this is a relatively rare occurrence. Dictionary lookup is the basis for the inverted structure discussed in the next section.

INVERTED STRUCTURES

The inverted structure is a generalization of the dictionary lookup approach. It uses a similar index concept, but instead of having an index only for the attribute designated as the primary key, it can have indices for any attributes that are frequently used as the basis for retrievals. If an index exists for a particular attribute, the structure is said to be inverted with respect to that attribute. In an extreme case, it is possible that there might be an index for *every* attribute in the record. In this case, the structure is described as *fully inverted*. Figure A–10 shows part of a personnel file inverted on sex and job-title.

Each index lists all of the values of an attribute that occur in the file. Attached to each such value is a list of the addresses of all the records having that value. The term "inverted" is used for this structure because of the way in which data is accessed. With most other structures, one first locates a record and can then obtain the values for any of its attributes. In this case, the attribute value is the starting point, and it directs the user to the record location.

The storage requirement is, of course, the space needed for the data plus that which is required for all of the indices. Because there is no attempt at maintaining sequence, it is not necessary to leave unused space in the data area as is done with the indexed sequential approach. However, because each value of an attribute selected for inversion must appear in the index for that attribute, the index space can become quite large. A rough rule of thumb states that if a file is inverted on all of its attributes, the index space will approximately equal the data space! As will be seen momentarily, storage space can sometimes be reduced by referring to attribute values in the indices rather than actually repeating them in the data records.

This structure is especially well suited to fast retrieval, even using quite complex search criteria. Many queries can be answered directly from the indices, without ever looking at the actual file. For example, "How many employees are women?" can be answered simply by looking up Female in the Sex index and counting the number of record addresses listed there. "Are there any women who are programmers?" can be handled by comparing the address list retrieved above with the one attached to Programmer in the index for Job-Title. Only employees who meet both criteria will have the address of their record on both lists. Because the indices are normally far smaller than the actual data file, they can be processed much more quickly.

This excellent retrieval performance must be weighed against a complex and

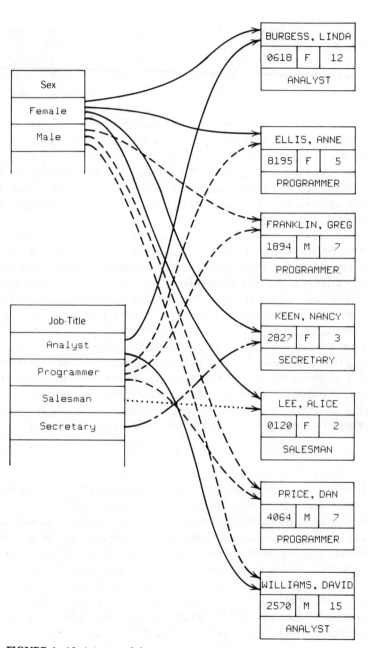

FIGURE A–10 A inverted data structure.

time-consuming update process. Inserting a new record requires not only storing the actual record, but also placing its address on all of the index lists for the relevant attribute values. Similarly, altering the contents of a record requires removing its address from the list corresponding to the old value and adding it to the list for the new one. Because insertion and modification are so complex, some systems only permit these changes to be done as batch runs during off hours. If retrievals are permitted during update, the possibility could arise of a query catching the file in an inconsistent state. This would happen, for example, if in recording the fact that an employee has married, a query arrives after that employee's record has been deleted from the list for "Single" and not yet added to the list for "Married." In practice these difficulties are avoided by not allowing queries to proceed while updating is in process. As a result, query response is degraded during update operations.

If an inversion exists for a particular attribute, then every value of that attribute that applies to any record must appear in the index. Although this requirement can make the indices quite large, it can also reduce the amount of storage required for the records themselves. For example, if an index exists for Job-Title it is not necessary actually to store values of this attribute in the personnel records. Instead, each record can simply contain a pointer to the appropriate job-title in the index. Because a pointer will often require less space than the actual value, an overall savings can be achieved. In addition, this ensures that all records having the same value for an attribute will actually have *exactly* the same representation of the attribute. In this case, the index is performing a function similar to that discussed earlier for abstract data types. It does mean, however, that retrieving an employee's job-title will require not only locating his or her record, but then making an additional access to the Job-Title index.

HASH FILES

If sequential access is not required at all, there are a number of techniques that can be used to get the fastest possible direct access to individual records in a file. *Hashing* refers to a family of techniques for assigning records to storage locations on the basis of their attribute values in such a way that they can be quickly found again. In general, hashing methods use the value of the key field to decide where to store each record. For example, suppose that a personnel file containing 500 records is to be stored on a device that has 1000 storage locations, each capable of holding a record. If the primary key is Employee Number, the storage location for each record could be determined by taking the last three digits of the key value. As shown in Figure A–11, the record for Greg Wild would be stored in location 442.

There is no storage required for indices or pointers. However, the space reserved for data must, in general, be significantly larger than what will actually be used in order to avoid conflicts that reduce processing efficiency.

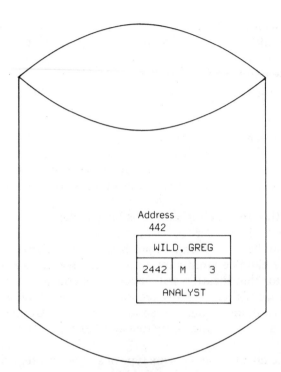

Address
442

WILD, GREG		
2442	M	3
ANALYST		

FIGURE A–11 A hashing example.

Whenever a personnel record is to be retrieved, the last three digits of the Employee Number are used to determine the address. This would appear to offer the fastest possible access because we know from the data itself exactly where to look without any indices or searching. However, this is only true as long as there are not any other employees with the same last three digits in their Employee Numbers. Because, in this case, that is probably an unreasonable assumption, this is too simple an algorithm to be useful. Other more sophisticated ways of calculating a storage address based on the value of the key can reduce the probability of trying to place multiple records in a single storage location, but unless enough space is allocated so that every conceivable key value has a unique reserved storage location, the possibility that the system will try to store two records in the same place must be allowed for. It is not difficult to handle this problem, but the more often it happens, the worse will be the overall performance of the system.

Insertion operations begin in exactly the same manner as retrievals. That is, the primary key value is used to compute the address where the new record should be placed. If that location is found to be empty, the record is stored. If the location is not empty, an overflow procedure must be invoked. This could be as simple as scanning sequentially from the calculated location until a free space is found or space might be allocated in an overflow area and the address of that space stored in an overflow pointer field at the original address.

The retrieval process must be prepared to handle this overflow situation. When a record is retrieved based on the calculated address, its actual key is compared with the one being sought. If this is not the right one, then, depending on the overflow strategy chosen, another record must be retrieved. Because it is certainly possible that we could have the bad luck of having even more than two records trying to reside at the same location, the overflow record's key would have to be checked, and it is conceivable that the process would have to be repeated.

Modifying a record in this approach is simple as long as the value of the key attribute is not being changed. The nature of hashing algorithms implies that the problem of a modified record being too large to put back in the original location can not arise. Deletions are handled simply by marking the record as invalid so that a subsequent request for that location will succeed. Of course, the deletion operation should check to see if there are any records in the overflow area that "ought" to be at this address; if one is found, it should be moved. An update that alters the value of the primary key would be treated as a deletion followed by an insertion.

It must be clear that the effectiveness of this type of storage strategy depends critically on minimizing the frequency of storage address conflicts. Basically, this depends on knowing enough about the statistical distribution of the key values to choose a hashing algorithm that maps them into the available range of addresses in as nonoverlapping a fashion as possible. Hashing techniques have been widely studied, and if the nature of the key distribution is known, a hashing algorithm that will perform well can probably be found.

This discussion began by assuming no need for sequential access. The reader is invited, as an exercise, to develop an algorithm for sequentially accessing a hashed file.

TREE STRUCTURES

A tree structure, in general, consists of nodes connected together by branches. The node at the top of a tree is called the *root* and the ones at the bottom are *leaves!* The branches are unidirectional, and each node has precisely one branch entering it, except for the root, which has none. A node may have any number of branches leaving it from zero, for a leaf node, to a maximum, which depends on the particular type of tree. A typical tree structure is illustrated in Figure A–12. Some tree structures permit data to be stored in any node, whereas in others, only the leaves hold data and the intermediate nodes are used only to establish paths. It is possible that the data for more than one record may appear in a single node.

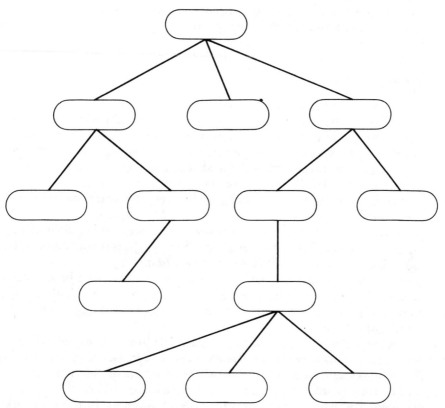

FIGURE A–12 A typical tree structure.

The main advantage of trees is that they greatly increase the efficiency of locating a record compared to most alternative structures. Such searches always begin at the root node and proceed downward. At each level, a comparison is made and a branch selected. All of the nodes connected to branches other than the selected one are automatically eliminated from further consideration. Thus, even in the simplest case where each node has only two possible branches to choose between, one half of the remaining structure is eliminated at each stage.[3] In a more elaborate structure where each node might have as many as 10 descendant branches, 90% of the remaining structure would be eliminated at each comparison. Because of this efficient searching property trees are often used to store indices even when simpler structures are used for the actual data. Numerous specific variations on the general theme of trees have been investigated that

---

[3] Whether this actually eliminates half of the remaining nodes depends on how "balanced" the tree is. The concept of balance is discussed later in this Appendix.

are especially well-suited to particular requirements. Two that are of special interest in database applications are the binary tree and the class known as B-trees.

Binary Trees

A tree in which each node has, at most, two branches leaving it is called a *binary tree*. In this type of tree, each node stores data corresponding to one record. One data item, the key, is used to determine where to place a new record in the tree. Starting with a completely empty tree, the first record to be inserted becomes the root. A location for inserting the next record is found by comparing its key value to that of the root. If the new record has a lower key, it is attached to the left branch leaving the root; if it has a higher key, it is attached to the right branch. Inserting the next, and all subsequent records is accomplished through a series of comparisons, branching left whenever the new record has a lower key and right when it is higher. Locating a record in a binary tree is handled in exactly the same way. Because binary trees have only two branching options at each stage, it is possible to represent the path from the root to any node by a sequence of bits where a 0 represents a left branch and a 1 a right branch. This sequence of bits may be used as a unique "address" relative to the root for each record in the tree (see Figure A–13).

Knowing the exact address of data is obviously useful when it must be located in a hurry. However, the use of real addresses is strongly discouraged in database systems because it violates the principle of data independence. For example, suppose that a user locates a particular record and then proceeds to store its address to save time on future accesses. Suppose in the meantime that the work of another user requires that that record be moved. Then the address remembered by the first user will be wrong, and any subsequent attempt to use it will produce erroneous and probably most confusing results.

Root-relative addresses for binary trees are free of this problem because they do not refer to particular locations in real memory. However, they still speed-up data accessing because they eliminate the need for a string of comparisons to locate a record. Of course, if a record is moved from one location to another in the tree, its root-relative address will change. Fortunately, this is not a routine occurrence in the use of binary trees, and its implications will be discussed shortly.

A binary tree always has exactly one node at the root level. There may be as many as two nodes at the next level, four at the one after that, and so on. In general, a binary tree of n levels can have up to 2^n-1 nodes. However, the actual shape of the tree will depend on the order in which the nodes have been inserted. If records with the key values 6, 3, 9, 8, 2, 4 are inserted into a binary tree in that order, the result will appear as in Figure A–14. The tree will consist of only three levels, which is obviously the shortest binary tree capable of holding six nodes. In

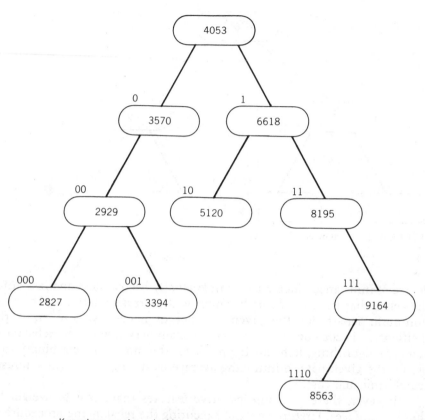

Key values are shown inside nodes.

Root-relative addresses are above nodes.

FIGURE A–13 Relative addressing in a binary tree.

addition, no path from the root to a leaf is more than one branch longer than the shortest path. This is referred to as a *balanced* binary tree, and it occurs when the data is inserted in random (unsystematic) key order. Clearly, a balanced tree results in the shortest average path length from the root to any node.

By way of contrast, consider now the tree that results when the same records are inserted in sorted key order: 2, 3, 4, 6, 8, 9. This tree is shown in Figure A–15. In this case, the binary tree degenerates to a simple list and all of the searching power of the tree structure is lost.

These two examples illustrate extremes in tree shape that can result from different record insertion orders. In actual applications, trees constructed in the natural order that the records arrived would likely exhibit some intermediate

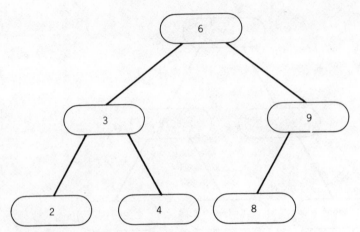

FIGURE A–14 A balanced binary tree.

degree of imbalance. Such a tree will gradually become less and less efficient, in the sense that the average path length will increase relative to the theoretical minimum length for the given number of nodes. At any point that this inefficiency is considered to be excessive, a binary tree can be rebalanced using standard algorithms. Rebalancing produces the most compact binary tree possible for the given data, minimizing average path length and, thus, (presumably) search time and cost.

However, there are some negative features that must be weighed against these advantages. First, the cost of executing the rebalancing procedure must be offset by the resulting savings in access costs. Second, the tree structure will almost certainly have to be withdrawn from use for the duration of the rebalancing. Finally, the location of any particular node in the rebalanced tree will normally be different from its location before the rebalancing; therefore, all root-relative addresses will become invalid. One could imagine replacing them by their new equivalents as part of the rebalancing procedure, but this would add enormously to the cost. A preferred alternative would involve marking a tree during rebalancing so that accessing procedures would know to go through the standard search algorithm the next time rather than to use the now outdated root-relative address.

The binary tree is an example of a so-called *static* storage structure. No attempt is made to keep static structures balanced as a part of their routine use. This makes the algorithms that manipulate these structures relatively simple and inexpensive. The price that is paid for this simplicity is the need to undertake occasional global reorganizations.

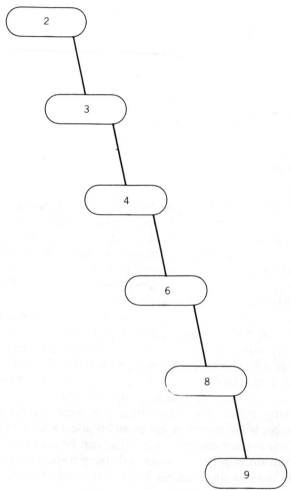

FIGURE A–15 An unbalanced binary tree.

B-TREES

The B-tree is an example of a *dynamic* data structure where the rebalancing is done incrementally as an adjunct to every insertion or deletion operation. This makes each such operation slightly more complex, but guarantees that the tree will never deviate far from its optimal shape.

Perhaps the feature of the B-tree that most clearly distinguishes it from a binary tree is that each node may contain more than one key value, hence, more

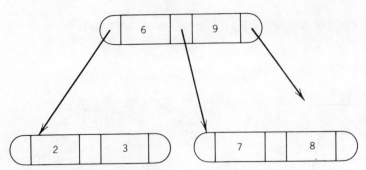

FIGURE A–16 A B-tree example.

than two branches to lower levels. Figure A–16 shows a B-tree where each node can have up to two key values, hence, three descending branches. This is known as a B-tree of order 1. In general, a B-tree of order-n may have up to $2n$ key values in each node and up to $2n + 1$ branches to nodes at the next lower level.

In the database context, it is usually assumed that large collections of records will be stored on rotating memory devices, such as magnetic disks. The time to locate a particular record on a device of this type is almost entirely determined by the number of disk accesses required. With tree structures, it is usually safe to assume that the number of disk accesses will be equal to the number of nodes that have to be visited. By storing a large number of keys in each B-tree node, the number of nodes that must be visited can be made as small as desired. Of course, if this results in nodes larger than the block size used for disk input-output, several reads would be required to read a single node. This might appear to defeat the purpose of having large nodes. This difficulty is postponed by a B-tree variation in which all data records are stored in leaves and nonleaf nodes contain only key values. This maximizes the number of keys that can be contained within a fixed-size node. A minimum number of nodes will have to be visited to locate any particular key and then one more access will be required to fetch the actual data record.

Methods have also been devised that make it possible to determine which block of a multiblock node will contain a particular key value.[4] Thus, nodes can be made larger than disk blocks without necessitating multiple reads; therefore, any number of key values can be contained within a B-tree of, say, three levels. In this case, no more than two disk accesses will ever be required to locate a record.

The price that is paid for the great searching efficiency of B-trees is that insertion and deletion are somewhat complicated. Insertion is performed by searching the tree for the node that "ought" to hold the new key. If that node is

---

[4]David B. Lomet, "Digital B-Trees," Proceedings of the Seventh International Conference on Very Large Data Bases, IEEE Computer Society Press, 1981, pp. 333–344.

less than completely filled, the new key is inserted and the operation is complete. If this node is already full, the usual algorithms specify that the node will be split into two new ones, each of which will contain half of the key values. This requires promoting one key value to the next higher level to record the fact of the split. If the node that is to receive the promoted key has room for it, the operation is finished. If not, that node must be split, in turn, and a key propagated to the next higher level, and so forth. Thus, an insertion may affect only a single node or a series of nodes beginning with that one and possibly extending all the way back to the root.

Deletion works in a similar fashion. The key to be deleted is simply removed from its node. If this reduces the number of keys in that node to less than n, the order of the B-tree, then the keys in this node and an adjacent one are redistributed to spread the resulting empty space as equally as possible. (This facilitates future insertions.) If there are not at least $2n$ keys available to be distributed, then the two nodes are merged into one. This requires removing from the parent node the key that distinguished between the two that have been merged. As with insertions, this procedure can result in propagating changes all the way back to the root.

Because the usual policy splits a full node into two new ones, the nodes in a B-tree can have as much as half the space unused. Empty space in nodes is wasteful, of course, but it increases the likelihood that a new key insertion will not require alteration to any other nodes. There is, therefore, a trade-off between storage efficiency and the processing required for insertion operations. B-trees are considered to be dynamic storage structures because of the possibility that keys may move from node to node as a byproduct of normal insertion and deletion operations. One result of this is that it is no longer possible to construct root-relative addresses like those that efficiently describe the location of each record in a binary tree. Whether the B-tree or the conventional binary tree is better for a particular application depends on the frequency of insertions and deletions relative to retrievals and the cost of inhibiting updates while a static structure is being rebalanced.

TERMS TO UNDERSTAND

bit	Free List
byte	ring
word	indexed sequential
page	dictionary lookup
field	inverted structure
record	hashing
file	tree structure

sequence   binary tree
list   B-tree
pointer   balanced binary tree

REVIEW QUESTIONS

1. What is the advantage of: (a) A list over a sequence? (b) A ring over a list? (c) Trees over other structures?

2. Explain (either in English or diagrammatically) how one would delete a record from a list.

3. Suppose that we have two pointers for each record in a list. The first pointer is called FOREW and the second BACKW. The FOREW pointer points to the following record in the list, whereas the BACKW pointer points to the preceding one. Show how deletion of a node is made much easier by the existence of the additional pointers.

4. A manufacturer sells a part P, which consists of two different types of gadgets—$G1$ and $G2$. The gadgets, in turn, consist of one or more of four available types of widgets. Specifically, $G1$ uses all of the four types of widgets, whereas $G2$ uses only types one and four. This situation can be represented using a tree structure that is called a parts explosion. Draw the tree for this particular case.

5. One possible way to hash a file of employees would be to represent the name of an employee by the sum of the corresponding positions of the alphabet for a person's name; for example, CAMMERON would be represented by:
$$3 + 1 + 13 + 13 + 5 + 18 + 15 + 14 = 82$$
Discuss the advantages and disadvantages of using such a technique. Suggest an alternative more efficient algorithm.

6. Compare indexed sequential, hashed, and inverted list data structures on the following criteria: (a) storage usage, (b) retrieval, (c) updating. When would you use each of these? (Give examples.)

7. Define and give examples of deletion, insertion, and update anomalies.

8. What is the main difference between a sequential file and an indexed sequential file? What is the significance of this difference for retrieval and update?

9. Why can a secondary key have nonunique values?

INDEX